Sample Surveys of the Victims of Crime

Sample Surveys of the Victims of Crime

edited by
Wesley G. Skogan

Ballinger Publishing Company • Cambridge, Massachusetts
A Subsidiary of J.B. Lippincott Company

This book is printed on recycled paper.

International Standard Book Number: 0-88410-221-1

Library of Congress Catalog Card Number: 76-24831

Printed in the United States of America

Library of Congress Cataloging in Publication Data

Main entry under title:
Sample surveys of the victims of crime.

1. Victims of crimes–United States–Congresses. 2. Victims of crimes–Research–United States–Congresses. I. Skogan, Wesley G.
HV6791.S27 362.8'8 76-24831
ISBN 0-88410-221-1

Contents

List of Tables

List of Figures

Acknowledgments

Many of the papers in this volume were first discussed at a conference on victimization held at the Law Enforcement Assistance Administration in 1975. I would like to thank Gerald M. Caplan, director of the National Institute of Law Enforcement and Criminal Justice, for his sponsorship of that meeting, and Winifred Reed of the Institute for her assistance in its organization. I also would like to thank Jerilynn B. Howard and Joan Lipton for their invaluable editorial assistance in the enterprise. Preparation of this manuscript was completed while the editor was a Visiting Fellow at the National Institute (Grant No. 76-NI-99-0032). Points of view or opinions stated in this volume are those of the authors and do not represent the official position or policies of the U.S. Department of Justice.

Foreword

One landmark of the past decade of criminal justice research has been the development of new survey techniques to measure the incidence of crime. Until recently, most of what we knew about crime, criminals and their victims was based upon the FBI's annual *Uniform Crime Report* and the statements of local law enforcement agencies. These reports typically recount the number of incidents that became "known to the police" in a few categories, sketch a brief portrait of persons arrested for those crimes and offer dollar estimates of the value of lost and recovered property. The information published by the FBI is collected by local police departments, who then forward the totals to Washington. Although these figures are used widely in practically every aspect of criminal justice research and planning, they are of dubious value. Fred Graham of CBS has dubbed them "easily the most suspect statistics published under the imprimatur of the United States Government."[1]

Victimization surveys were developed to provide more reliable information about the frequency of crime, and to provide new data on victims, their losses, the costs of crime and the attitudes of the general public toward crime and the legal process. The first surveys were conducted in the mid-1960s for the President's Commission on Law Enforcement and Criminal Justice, which was charged by President Johnson to seek new knowledge about crime in America. The commission sponsored three victimization surveys. The first, conducted by Albert Biderman, was aimed at developing reliable and practical survey procedures for measuring crime. Albert Reiss directed a survey of high crime areas in three cities which gathered data on victimization and citizen attitudes toward crime. The third survey was conducted by the National Opinion Research Center, under the direction of Philip Ennis. It was designed to generate estimates of victimization rates and the status of public opinion for the nation as a whole. The findings of these surveys were published in a summary report from the commission. The national survey caused a considerable stir, for it uncovered substantially more crime (three to five times more in several major categories) than local police departments had forwarded to the FBI.

Since the publication of the commission's report, victimization surveys have been conducted in many corners of the globe. Community surveys have been conducted in Portland, Cincinnati, St. Louis and other American cities. In addition, surveys have been carried out in Germany, Great Britain, Canada, Australia and all of Scandinavia. In the United States the federal government has conducted a major survey program since 1972. To date, the Census Bureau has interviewed persons in twenty-six major cities, thirteen of which have been surveyed twice. Interviews are also being conducted each month with residents of a national sample of 10,000 households. The first published reports of this work began to appear in mid-1975. A major evaluation by the National Academy of Sciences of the methodology employed in these surveys also has been completed.

This volume presents twelve especially written reports on this burgeoning activity. Many of them are the first published accounts of major research projects. The book had its genesis in a conference on victimization research which I organized for the National Institute of Law Enforcement and Criminal Justice in the summer of 1975. That meeting brought together persons who were conducting victimization survey research. Presentations were made at the conference by Anne Schneider, Richard Sparks, Michael Hindelang, Barbara Boland, Phillip Cook and Edward Jones. Those reports, along with contributions by other researchers who attended the meeting, comprise this volume. The collection speaks to most of the major issues in victimization research. A number of chapters describe patterns of victimization, the costs of crime and the relationship between victims and the police. Several chapters address methodological questions and explore the limitations of current survey techniques. Others discuss practical applications of survey technology for criminal justice evaluation and planning. The volume is addressed to researchers in both the academic community and criminal justice agencies. We hope it usefully describes our work on these topics and that it stimulates further research and the development of new applications for victimization survey techniques.

Wesley G. Skogan
Washington, D.C.
May 1976

NOTES

1. Fred Graham, *The Due Process Revolution* (New York: Macmillan, 1970), p. 75.

Sample Surveys of the Victims of Crime

Crime in the United States: A Report on the National Crime Survey*

Richard W. Dodge,
Harold R. Lentzner
and Frederick Shenk

The use of sample surveys to measure the extent of major crime by going to the victim is a development of the last decade. The original impetus for using victimization surveys was the President's Commission on Law Enforcement and Administration of Justice (The Crime Commission). In its final report, the commission stated that

> the survey technique has a great untapped potential as a method for providing additional information about the nature and extent of our crime problem and the relative effectiveness of different programs to control crime.[1]

The Crime Commission sponsored a number of studies of crime victims. These studies were significant, not only for their substantive findings, but also because they attempted to solve some of the methodological problems involved in collecting crime data by means of the sample survey.

The victimization survey has a number of advantages over traditional police statistics. Using a common set of concepts, procedures and questionnaires, and a corps of interviewers trained to use these materials, a survey can achieve a far greater degree of uniformity than is possible in a compilation of returns filed by thousands of individual police departments. It can also measure the extent and characteristics of the substantial segment of crime that is not reported to the police. When repeated over time, surveys can assess changes in levels and rates of victimization, including fluctuations in the degree to which specific crimes are

*All statements in this chapter are the responsibility of the authors, and do not necessarily represent the position of the U.S. Bureau of the Census nor the Law Enforcement Assistance Administration.

reported to the authorities. A large scale survey can provide a wealth of detail on the demographic characteristics of crime victims, including whether the offender was known to the victim.

There are also drawbacks to victimization surveys. Because crime is a low frequency event, surveys require large samples to obtain reliable results. These can be very costly. In addition, victimization surveys cannot provide the small area detail (by precinct or ward, for example) that most local planners need to make operational decisions. If a survey is restricted to city residents, crimes affecting commuters and visitors cannot be measured. Finally, some types of crime are difficult to measure through victimization surveys. These include victimless crimes, such as drug abuse, and crimes where the victim may be unaware that he is a victim (consumer fraud).

The National Crime Survey (NCS) originated late in 1969, when the Law Enforcement Assistance Administration (LEAA) of the Department of Justice and the Bureau of the Census began investigating the feasibility of using victim surveys in a large scale national study of crime. In the summer of 1972, after several years of testing questionnaires and procedures, the NCS went into the field. This chapter reports the major findings from 1973, the first complete year of the survey's operation.

DEFINITIONS

The National Crime Survey currently measures crimes that generally correspond to the Part I Index Crimes included in the FBI's Uniform Crime Reports. It excludes homicide, whose victims cannot respond for themselves (and which, in any case, is better reported than other crimes). The crimes measured by the survey are rape, robbery, assault and personal larceny (thefts which victimize individuals); burglary, household larceny and motor vehicle theft (which affect households); and two crimes against commercial and other institutions, burglary and robbery. Attempts to commit these crimes are also counted. These crimes constitute the core of what the public considers to be the "crime problem" in this country; they also appear to be amenable to the survey technique. This chapter concentrates on the findings for persons and households, making only occasional reference to the institutional survey.

The concept of larceny as used in the survey needs additional explanation. "Personal larceny" includes two crimes involving contact between victim and offender, purse snatching and pocket picking. It also includes thefts of personal belongings while victims are away from their homes. These crimes involve no *direct* contact with the offender and, in fact, generally occur out of the victim's sight (a coat is taken from a restaurant, a radio is stolen from a public park, etc.). Noncontact crimes make up the largest proportion of all personal thefts. "Household larceny" includes theft of property or cash from inside a home by persons who have a right to be there, such as household employees or acquaintances of household members (incidents involving items taken by intruders would be classified as burglaries). Household larceny also includes thefts of possessions from the immediate vicinity of the home (e.g., bicycles, lawn furniture, garden tools, etc.). The distinction between household larceny and noncontact personal larceny is based on *where* the incident occurred, with the assumption that incidents involving articles taken from inside or near the home are more usefully considered crimes against the household, while more portable items stolen away from home should be ascribed to their individual owners. This distinction provides an indication of the magnitude of larcenies occurring in the presumably more controlled home environment. Motor vehicle theft is treated separately here, as it is by the FBI.

Assault presents a different kind of problem. Research has shown that assault is more likely than other personal crimes to occur between persons who know one another. Victims of crimes where the offender is known—especially if he is a relative—are less likely to report these incidents to survey interviewers. We also suspect that the threats or violence that define assault also may be an everyday occurrence for some respondents and may be easily forgotten or not considered worth reporting. The extent of such underreporting is not precisely known, although available evidence suggests that it is concentrated in the simple assault category.

For crimes involving direct contact between victim and offender, several persons may be victimized during the same incident. One person may also be victimized more than once during a year. The NCS uses the term "victimization" to denote a specific criminal act directed against an individual victim. The number of victimizations is usually greater than the number of incidents or the number of individual victims of crime. For noncontact crimes, victimizations and incidents are usually equivalent, but a person or household could be a victim more than once.

Finally, a system was established to classify events reported in the household survey that involved elements of more than one crime. Following the convention established by the FBI, such crimes will be classified according to the following list of priorities: rape, robbery, assault, personal contact larceny, burglary, motor vehicle theft and all other larceny.[2] Thus, any combination of a personal contact crime and a noncontact crime will be classified as the former (e.g., an assault on an individual during a burglary). The details of the noncontact crime are preserved in the original data, however. Robberies involving assault can be isolated from robberies in which there were no injuries.

CHARACTERISTICS OF VICTIMS: GENERAL FINDINGS

NCS uncovered nearly thirty-seven million victimizations that reportedly occurred in 1973.[3] The distribution of these victimizations is shown below in

Table 1-1. Thefts or attempted thefts of property or cash involving no confrontation between victim and offender accounted for about 84 percent of all of them. Personal larceny without contact was the most common crime, making up 39 percent of the total. The three crimes of most concern to the public–rape, personal robbery and burglary of private homes–constituted about 21 percent of the reported victimizations, or about 7.7 million criminal acts. Generally speaking, the less serious form of each personal crime was the more prevalent. About 71 percent of all rapes were classified as "attempted," nearly two-thirds of all robberies involved no injury to the victim, and 60 percent of the assaults were "simple" rather than "aggravated." (For the reasons mentioned earlier, the "true" proportion of simple assaults is probably substantially higher.)

For crimes involving no personal contact, completed acts were considerably more common than attempts, especially for personal and household larceny. This, undoubtedly, is due to the fact that attempted crimes are easily forgotten and to the difficulty in determining whether any attempts were made, unless unmistakable evidence exists. (Such "evidence" may be clear to the potential victim, but may, in reality, have been an act of vandalism by the offender. A survey must accept the respondent's judgment in these instances.) For personal larcenies, incidents in which the stolen items were valued at under $50 were

Table 1-1. Percent Distribution of Victimizations and Victimization Rates by Type of Crime, 1973

Type of Crime[a]	*Percent*	*Rate Per 1,000*[b]
Personal Crimes		
Rape	0.4	1.8
Robbery	2.9	6.7
Assault	10.8	24.7
Larceny with contact	1.3	3.1
Larceny without contact	38.6	88.0
Household Crimes		
Burglary	17.4	91.5
Larceny	20.3	106.8
Motor vehicle theft	3.6	19.0
Institutional Crimes		
Burglary	3.8	203.7
Robbery	0.7	38.8

[a]Includes attempts.

[b]Rates per 1,000 persons twelve and over (females for rape), 1,000 households or 1,000 institutions.

Source: Unpublished data from the Bureau of the Census.

three times more common than those in which the loss was estimated at $50 or more. Higher losses were two and one-half times more frequent in household larcenies. In the two crimes against commercial establishments measured in the survey, successes were much more frequent than attempts (about 74 percent each for burglary and robbery).

Reporting the volume of crime and its distribution among the major types of crime under examination provides a useful context within which to discuss the next topic—the general risk of being victimized by each of these crimes. This risk is represented as a rate whose denominator is the total number of units in the particular group under study. For personal crimes, this unit is all persons age twelve and over (or females, in the case of rape); for household crimes, it is an estimate of the number of households; and for businesses, an estimate of the number of eligible organizations.

Converting the number of victimizations into rates per 1,000 gives us more meaningful information on the "amount" of crime in society (see Table 1-1). We find, for example, that institutions had the highest burglary victimization rate in 1973—204 per 1,000 institutions, more than twice that of private homes. The risk of robbery for commercial establishments was more than five times greater than for persons. Personal crimes involving direct contact between victim and offender comprised four of the five crimes with the lowest rates; assault at twenty-five per 1,000 was higher than motor vehicle theft at nineteen per 1,000. The lowest rate was for rape, with about two victimizations for every 1,000 women age twelve and older.

CRIMES AGAINST PERSONS

Rather than discuss each type of crime sequentially in terms of the characteristics of the victims, the procedure will be to compare specific characteristics across the range of crimes. However, personal crimes will be treated separately from household crimes because such characteristics are not always precisely comparable—e.g., age of the victim in personal crimes as contrasted with the age of the head of a victimized household.

The small number of rape victimizations uncovered in the 1973 survey makes in-depth analysis of that crime impossible, except to note that the characteristics most frequently associated with victims of rape were being black, young (sixteen to twenty-four) and separated or divorced, and having a low family income (below $3,000).

Males were more likely than females to be victimized by robbery, aggravated assault and personal larceny without direct contact, although the margin of difference for the latter crime was considerably less than for either robbery or aggravated assault. Females had *higher* rates than males for personal larceny involving direct contact.

Those under the age of twenty-five had higher victimization rates than older persons for all four crimes. Aggravated assault was more frequent than robbery among those under twenty-five, but the difference diminished with age. By age fifty, although the risk of victimization from both robbery and assault had dropped sharply, robbery was the more common crime. Despite the higher victimization rates among the young (those under twenty) for personal larceny without contact, their losses were almost always valued at under $50. With the exception of direct contact larceny, where women had higher rates than men at age twenty-five and above, women had generally lower victimization rates than men. The gap between the sexes narrowed with advancing age and was very slight among those sixty-five and over.

Blacks had higher victimization rates than whites for the three contact crimes, but whites were victimized to a greater degree by noncontact theft. Higher rates for males than females prevailed for both blacks and whites, again with the exception of personal contact larceny. The decline in victimization rates with increasing age was characteristic of both races, especially if age twenty-five is taken as the line dividing youths from adults. An exception to this trend were black robbery victims—rates among the elderly (sixty-five and over) in this group were not notably different from those under twenty-five.

Within four marital status categories—never married, married, separated or divorced, and widowed—the risks of victimization from robbery, aggravated assault and personal contact larceny were highest for separated and divorced persons. This was particularly evident among women, even though their victimization rates for robbery and aggravated assault were lower than those for males. By contrast, those who were never married suffered the highest rates from personal larceny without contact. The widowed as a group, despite low victimization rates, were more vulnerable than married persons to robbery and contact larceny. They also had apparently higher rates than all persons sixty-five and over for the three contact crimes, widowers being especially at risk in this regard.

Family income is more difficult to associate with victimization. For one thing, it dilutes the relationship between age and victimization, for youths living on their own typically have low incomes. It also masks the total number of family members and those who contribute significantly to the total income. Two families with identical incomes may have very different lifestyles and, therefore, differential exposure to victimization, depending upon whether one person provides most of the income or four persons contribute in more or less equal amounts. The main conclusion that emerges from an examination of victimization rates by family income is that persons in low income families (in this case, below $5,000) were more likely to be victimized by all three direct contact crimes. In contrast, as family income increased, so did the rate of loss from personal theft without contact. The trend was not a constant progression, but persons earning $15,000 or more a year experienced higher rates than those with lower incomes. Analysis of blacks by income is hampered by the paucity of cases in higher income categories. Nevertheless, the same pattern of declining victimization with rising income was evident for aggravated assault and contact larceny, although blacks had higher rates than whites in each instance. Robbery among blacks, on the other hand, showed no pattern or trend in terms of income. For personal larceny without contact, blacks and whites both experienced more victimizations at the higher income levels.

Another variable that sheds some light on the nature of victimization is the place of an individual in the family structure. Males living alone and nonrelated people living in households had the highest victimization rates for robbery, and these groups, along with children living in female-headed households, had the highest rates for aggravated assault. Numerically, they account for only 9 percent of the total population age twelve and older. The rates for the two groups that together comprise almost 60 percent of the population—males heading households (including wives, children, other relatives or nonrelatives) and the wives of male heads—were among the lowest observed. Females living by themselves also had low rates. Children living in households headed by females had noticeably higher victimization rates for robbery and aggravated assault than did the larger group of young people living in households with male heads. The high rate for males living alone and the low rate for females in similar circumstances apparently reflects the fact that, in addition to the usually high rates for males, most females living alone are elderly, while proportionally more males living alone are younger, including single males in the armed forces.[4] With the exception of females living alone, one thus observes a strong tendency for those outside the traditional family setting—living alone, nonrelatives of the primary family or children in households headed by females—to be disproportionately victimized by robbery and aggravated assault.

The relationship between victim and offender in crimes involving direct contact is an important element in understanding the nature of those crimes and in reducing their number or containing their effects. The NCS enables us to examine this relationship for specific crime categories and population groups. The basic distinction is between crimes involving persons unknown to the victim—"strangers"—and those in which the victim was either acquainted with or related to the offender—"nonstrangers." The percentage of stranger-to-stranger confrontations for the four direct contact crimes ranged from 96 percent for personal larceny to 62 percent for aggravated assault. Robbery was second highest, with 86 percent of victimizations involving strangers; for rape the comparable figure was 79 percent.

Our detailed examination of this relationship is confined to robbery and aggravated assault. Males, both black and white, experienced a greater proportion of robberies at the hands of strangers than did either black or white females. There was no difference within each sex category by race. There were more dramatic differences for aggravated assault. White males had the highest percentage of victimizations by strangers (71 percent), followed by black males (57 percent), white females (48 percent) and black females (27 percent).

The younger the robbery victim, the more likely he or she was to have been victimized by a nonstranger, although even among twelve to nineteen year olds, strangers carried out 79 percent of victimizations. This figure rose to 93 percent for persons age fifty and above. The same trend was observed for males and females, except that the range was much greater for women. At the lower end of the age scale, males under twenty experienced 82 percent of robbery victimizations at the hands of strangers, while the comparable figure for women was 66 percent.

There was no distinctive trend by age for aggravated assault. Women had substantially lower proportions of victimizations by strangers than did men, except among those sixty-five and over. In fact, in most cases, women were more likely to have been assaulted by persons they knew than by strangers.

Turning to marital status, married and widowed persons were more likely to have been victimized by strangers during robberies than those in other marital categories. In all categories except the widowed, women experienced a lower percentage of victimizations by strangers than men. Aggravated assault presents a somewhat different picture. Here the married and never married experienced the highest proportion of stranger-to-stranger victimization, while the widowed, separated and divorced experienced substantially fewer. Males were more likely to have been victimized by strangers, except there was no difference among the widowed. Widowers were about equally divided as to whether they were victimized by strangers or nonstrangers; the other three categories for males were dominated by strangers and did not essentially differ. Separated and divorced women had the lowest percentage of stranger victimizations for aggravated assault, about 22 percent; for men in the same situation the figure was 63 percent.

CRIMES AGAINST HOUSEHOLDS

Two of the three household crimes measured by NCS occurred either exclusively or primarily in the home or in its immediate vicinity. Ninety-six percent of all household burglaries took place in the principal residence of the household members, with the remainder occurring at other homes owned by them or in places where they were temporarily staying, including hotels or motels. Motor vehicle theft is considered a household crime because automobiles are often used as family vehicles. (Motor vehicle theft includes the loss of automobiles and other motorized vehicles, such as trucks and motorcycles. These "other" vehicles accounted for about 10 percent of all motor vehicle thefts in 1973.)

The chance of being a victim of any household crime declined as the age of the head of the household increased. Teenage household heads had the highest rates for all three crimes, with a sharp decrease among the next oldest group (twenty to thirty-four). Thereafter, the declines were less precipitous. The overall larceny rate was slightly higher than that for burglary (107 to ninety-two), although this situation reversed itself for the youngest and oldest household heads (sixty-five and over). Motor vehicle theft was less common than either burglary or larceny among all demographic groups.

Households headed by blacks had higher rates of victimization for burglary and motor vehicle theft, while larceny rates were about the same as for whites. When we eliminate households headed by teenagers (because there are relatively few blacks in this category), the disproportionate victimization of blacks becomes evident. Disparities between the two races for burglary were especially wide when household heads were twenty to thirty-four years old, and for motor vehicle theft for households headed by persons over fifty. Although the overall larceny rate was about the same for whites and blacks, whites had higher rates in the twenty to forty-nine age group and blacks had a rate about twice that of whites in elderly households.

Perhaps a better way to gauge the size of the population likely to be victimized by motor vehicle theft is to base the rate on the number of vehicles owned, rather than on the number of households. Since the number of motor vehicles exceeds the number of households (103,000,000 and 70,000,000 were the respective survey estimates), the effect of this procedure is to reduce the overall rate. In 1973 the decline was from 19 to 13 per 1,000. The risk to blacks and individuals in households headed by teenagers was accentuated when the rates were computed on this basis, for motor vehicle ownership is more common in white households and where the head is twenty to sixty-four years old.

The household's composition made a considerable difference in the risk of victimization from the three household crimes. Since husband-wife families comprised about two-thirds of all households, their victimization rates approximated those for the nation as a whole (except for a slightly lower rate for burglary). Within this family category, households consisting of only husband and wife enjoyed reported rates well below average for all three crimes, while households with children under eighteen suffered the highest rates—100 for burglary and 165 for household larceny. Families headed by women experienced above average rates for burglary and larceny, especially when the only other household members were children under eighteen. Households consisting either of persons living alone or of unrelated persons living together (about 23 percent of the total) had above average rates for burglary and below average rates for larceny. However, households consisting of one person always had lower rates than those composed of unrelated persons. For both groups, households headed by males had higher rates than those with female heads. Households consisting of unrelated persons and headed by males had the highest rates of all groups for burglary (260) and motor vehicle theft (64) and one of the highest rates for larceny. Women living alone had the lowest rates for larceny and among the lowest for burglary and motor vehicle theft.

Family income was not related to victimization in the way one might expect, perhaps due to the reasons cited earlier with regard to personal crimes. One clear statement can be made: low income families (under $3,000) had the lowest rates for larceny and motor vehicle theft. Burglary rates exhibited a curvilinear relationship to income: middle income groups ($10,000-$15,000) had the lowest burglary rates, while the lowest (under $3,000) and highest income ($20,000 and over) households shared the greatest vulnerability to burglary. There was a slight upward trend in larceny as income increased–the highest rates were in households where income exceeded $15,000. No distinctive patterns could be pinpointed for motor vehicle theft. Black households showed a moderate trend toward high rates for victimization from larceny with rising income; a clearer trend was evident in the case of motor vehicle theft.

CIRCUMSTANCES OF CRIMINAL INCIDENTS

Although crimes occur under every conceivable circumstance, the NCS data indicate situational and weapon preferences by offenders. Also apparent is differential exposure to risk of victimization based on the victim's area of residence. Such information should be useful for law enforcement and other agencies involved in aiding victims of crime, particularly in regard to resource allocation. And while many of the results substantiate other sources of operating canons, some raise questions about the validity of our prior assumptions about these matters and should spur further investigation.

Residential Patterns of Victimization

NCS generally substantiated the widely held notion that urban living carries greater risk of victimization than suburban, small town or rural lifestyles. The following descriptive analysis compares three residential areas–central cities, suburbs and nonmetropolitan (rural)–for victimization risk. The central city and suburban areas constitute Standard Metropolitan Statistical Areas (SMSAs); nonmetropolitan residences were those outside of the SMSAs. In addition to comparing overall rates, we analyzed selected socioeconomic variables for residents of the three areas and compared rates based on classes of cities grouped by size.[5]

Victimization generally decreased the further victims' residences were from central cities. In each of four city groups categorized by size, the victimization rate for crimes of violence was higher in the central city than in the surrounding suburban area. Residents of suburban areas of the smallest cities and those in the rural areas had lower victimization rates, and rural residents had the lowest ones of all. The one violent crime that did not follow this trend was assault. The largest cities (those with populations of one million or more) had the lowest rate among four size groups; the city rate was as low as three of the four suburban areas and as low as that for rural residences. A possible explanation for the relatively low assault rates in the largest cities might be socioenvironmental factors that encouraged the acceptance of assaultive violence as a routine part of

personal larcenies without contact. In 1973, 367,200 incidents—or 27 percent of all such larcenies—occurred in schools. Roughly nine-tenths resulted in losses of less than $50—petty offenses by most standards—but, then, few students carry personal items or equipment valued at more than that amount.

Turning to household crimes, it will be recalled that burglary and household larceny are defined in such a way that they primarily occur at or in the vicinity of the victim's home. Most household larcenies occurred outside of or near the home as opposed to in the home. Assumed absence of the owner appeared to have been a major prerequisite for motor vehicle theft, which most often occurred when the vehicle was parked on the street or in another outdoor location, such as a parking lot; yet about one-third took place near the owner's home, including the owner's driveway, carport and yard.

CIRCUMSTANCES AND OUTCOMES OF WEAPONS USE

In 1973 there were an estimated 1,703,600 incidents of personal violence in which weapons were used to intimidate or injure victims. Those made up about 38 percent of all violent incidents measured by NCS. Of the three types of violent crimes surveyed, personal robbery was most likely to have been committed by offenders using weapons, while rape was least likely (see Table 1-2).

Variables affecting the offender's choice of weapon probably included his or her purpose and the context in which the incident occurred. Outside factors such as legal policy and cost, which limit access to weapons, might have affected weapon choice as well. While NCS was not designed to study the offender, except in his or her relationship to the victim, or to measure the impact of legal policy or economic cost on weapon use, the data do provide some insight into the circumstances and outcomes related to the selection process. (For a detailed analysis of this issue, see Chapter Ten.) For personal crimes of violence, the survey recorded the type of weapons observed by victims during each incident. Those other than knives or firearms were categorized as "other weapons" and included such items as bottles, wrenches and baseball bats. Bare hands, or physical force, were not tabulated as weapons. Furthermore, the survey obtained no information about the victim's use of a weapon. Data gathered about incidents in which weapons were used also included the type of crime, outcome with regard to injury, victim-offender relationship, race and age of offender, and age of victim. (Data about many weapon crimes and the most serious injuries are affected by exclusion of homicides from the survey.)

If use of a weapon is premeditated, then it is not difficult to understand why, as NCS indicates, weapons were present in nearly 50 percent of all robbery incidents, but in only about 36 percent of assaults. The same reasoning may apply to rapes, which may have been initially unplanned, for weapons were used in only 25 percent of these incidents. For the vast majority of violent criminal incidents, availability of physical force evidently was support enough for

Table 1-2. Percent of Incidents in Which One or More Weapons Were Used by Type of Weapon, Injury to Victim and Victim-Offender Relationship, 1973

Type of Crime	*Incidents in which one or more weapons were used*	*Incidents in which one or more firearms were used*	*Incidents in which one or more knives were used*	*Incidents in which one or more other weapons were used*	*Incidents in which types of weapons used were not known*
Crimes of Violence	38	13	12	13	2
Victim injured	38	7	10	20	3
Victim not injured	38	15	13	10	2
Victim stranger	41	15	12	13	2
Victim nonstranger	33	9	11	13	2
Rape[a]	25	12	7	7	1[b]
Victim stranger	26	12	7	6	1
Victim nonstranger	22[b]	14[b]	4[b]	8[b]	0
Robbery	49	17	19	13	3
Victim injured	48	10	18	19	6
Victim not injured	49	22	20	9	1[b]
Victim stranger	52	18	21	13	3
Victim nonstranger	32	10	8	11	3[b]
Assault	36	11	10	14	2
Victim injured	37	6	7	23	3
Victim not injured	34	13	11	10	2
Victim stranger	38	13	9	14	2
Victim nonstranger	33	8	11	13	2

[a]Victim injury is not shown as all rape victims are considered to have suffered injury.

[b]Estimate based on ten or fewer sample cases is statistically unreliable.

Source: Unpublished data from the Bureau of the Census.

offenders to have attempted victimization. This particularly was true of male rapes of females. Of violent incidents in which a weapon was used, firearms were present in 32 percent, or in only 13 percent of the total violent personal incidents.

The victim-offender relationship clarifies another aspect of the weapon use phenomenon. Stranger-to-stranger violent incidents involved offender use of one or more weapons relatively more often than nonstranger conflicts. This pattern was particularly strong for personal robbery, and held to a lesser degree for assaults. Estimates of weapon use by nonstranger offenders for rape were unreliable due to the small number of these rapes reported. For all incidents of personal crimes of violence between strangers, including rape, knives and other weapons were used in a lower proportion of incidents than firearms. When the victims were acquainted with the offender, firearms were used in a lower proportion of incidents than knives or other weapons.

Looking at specific types of crimes and weapons, offenders who robbed strangers used firearms and knives in a larger proportion of incidents than other weapons; however, for robberies of nonstrangers, other weapons were borne by the offenders in approximately the same number of incidents as knives or firearms. Other weapons and firearms were most prevalent in stranger-to-stranger assaults, but for nonstranger assaults knives and other weapons were the more popular choices. In summary, it appears that firearms were generally used when a planned victimization of a stranger occurred, usually for economic gain. Other weapons predominated when the victimization was essentially the result of an emotional outburst or the seizing of a fortuitous opportunity to rob. Knives were popular in both circumstances.

Injury to the victim may occur whether or not the offender wields a weapon. NCS data indicate that weapon use was unrelated to injurious outcome. (This is similar to the findings of Gottfredson and Hindelang, see Chapter Four.) Weapons were used in 38 percent of violent incidents in which a victim was injured and in about the same proportion of incidents not ending in injury. For specific crimes, robberies resulting in injury were more frequently committed with knives and other weapons than firearms. Firearms and knives were more often present when injury did not occur. For assaults resulting in victim injury, about three-fifths involved weapons of other types; for those that did not end in injury (attempts) firearms were more likely to have been used.[7]

Although the data indicated no apparent relationship between race and type of weapon used, black single offenders and black gangs used weapons in proportionally more incidents than lone white offenders or white gangs. Also, there was a correlation between the age of the offender and the type of weapon used. Persons under age twenty-one resorted to knives and other weapons much more frequently than firearms. According to victims, offenders twenty-one and over selected guns relatively more often than knives or other weapons. The less frequent use of firearms by young persons may have been a consequence of their difficulty in obtaining a weapon. Legal age restrictions for firearm ownership may have limited possession, young offenders may have had less access to sources of illegal weapons, and they may have been less able to afford them, legal or illegal. Since young victims were attacked by young offenders more often than by any age group, victims twelve to nineteen years old were victimized by offenders armed with guns much less than they were attacked with knives or other weapons. Conversely, victims twenty years and over were most often attacked at gunpoint, with little difference between the number of incidents in which knives and other weapons were used. Youthful offenders operating in gangs used weapons in half of all incidents, significantly more than gangs composed of offenders over age twenty or single offenders of either age range.

CHARACTERISTICS OF OFFENDERS

No treatment of the basic components of crime would be complete without examining the characteristics of offenders. To obtain offender data for the NCS, victims of personal crimes who were able to determine whether an attack was precipitated by one or more than one offender were questioned about the sex, age and race of their assailants. Persons who could not provide information on the number of offenders were not questioned further, but only 3 percent of all victims fell into this category.

Of course, offender data, like all survey data, are based upon the victim's recollection of the incident at the time of the interview and, consequently, are subject to the effects of memory loss. In addition, one must exercise caution when using victim-derived offender data for stranger-stranger victimizations because they are subject to misperception and bias. Discretion is particularly recommended where data on race are concerned, for victim bias is unquestionably a factor, and the social consequences of using inaccurate measures are great. Nonetheless, when properly used, this information does help increase our understanding of the victimization experience.

Results from the 1973 NCS are, generally, consistent with findings from other offender studies.[8] Single offender victimizations accounted for most crimes of violence; only in the case of robbery did the number of multiple offender victimizations exceed that of single offender victimizations. Regarding the sex of offenders, victims of crimes of violence said their attackers were male in some 88 percent of all single offender crimes and 81 percent of all multiple offender crimes (mixed groups accounted for 9 percent of the total). Women were more apt to have participated in assault than any other crime but, even here, their contribution amounted to less than one-fifth of the total.

Examining the data on age, adults twenty-one years and older were considered by victims to have been responsible for nearly two-thirds of all single offender crimes of violence. Young persons between the ages of twelve to twenty committed approximately one-third of these crimes, a proportion exceeding their representation in the total population, while youngsters under age twelve were only infrequently mentioned. For victimizations involving two or more offenders, the modal age category dropped to twelve to twenty, lending support to the contention that group violence is largely a juvenile problem. Persons twenty-one and older had more multiple offender victimizations attributed to them than to groups composed of both older and younger persons; again, victims rarely perceived their assailants as younger than twelve.

Racial patterns varied by type of crime; however, for all violent attacks considered as a group, offenders were most often perceived as white. This is not surprising, since whites in 1973 constituted approximately 88 percent of the US population twelve years and older. Blacks appeared to have been overrepresented in the ranks of offenders, with 30 percent of all single and 40 percent of all multiple offender victimizations attributed to them. For both single and multiple offender robbery, blacks were more often suspected than whites, but whites were most frequently identified as the perpetrators of single and multiple offender assault.

To obtain a more accurate measure of victim risk, we must analyze the characteristics of victims as well as those of offenders. Tables 1-3 and 1-4, based upon the 1973 survey data, juxtapose the age and race of victim and offender for both single and multiple offender crimes. For purposes of this report, the distribution of offender variables has been limited to the most important and useful categories. Offenders perceived as members of "other" races, persons under the age of twelve and those of unknown race or age were excluded; their impact, in any case, would have been minor.

It has been suggested that, regarding age, a rough correspondence exists between the victim and the offender. NCS data for single offender crimes tend to confirm this. Taken as a group, two-thirds of all crimes of violence against individuals age twelve to nineteen were committed by offenders of approximately the same age and four-fifths of these crimes carried out against persons over nineteen years of age were perpetrated by adult offenders. (Unfortunately, the age categories of victims and offenders were not equivalent.)

For multiple offender crimes of violence, the relationships, as shown in Table 1-3, were more complex. Younger victims attributed close to three-fourths of their victimizations to persons age twelve to twenty, one-fifth to mixed groups and the rest to adults age twenty-one and over. However, older victims of multiple offender crimes were more likely than older persons victimized by single offenders to have perceived their attackers as youthful, even though persons age twenty to thirty-four and thirty-five to forty-nine did not consider them responsible for most of the crimes. In addition, the proportion attributed by adults to offenders age twelve to twenty did increase significantly with the victim's age, reaching a high of nearly 50 percent for the oldest group. This pattern was also evident for robbery and assault, although robbery victims age

Table 1-3. Percent Distribution of Crimes of Violence by Age of Victim and Offender, 1973

	Age of Offender						
	Single			*Multiple*			
Age of Victim	*12-20*	*21 and older*	*Total*	*All 12 to 20*	*All 21 and older*	*Mixed*	*Total*
12-19	67	33	100	73	9	18	100
20-34	15	85	100	28	45	27	100
35-49	18	82	100	35	42	23	100
50 and Older	19	81	100	49	32	19	100

Source: Unpublished data from the Bureau of the Census.

Table 1-4. Percent Distribution of Crimes of Violence by Race of Victim and Offender, 1973

	Race of Offender					
	Single			*Multiple*		
Race of Victim	*White*	*Black*	*Total*	*All White*	*All Black*	*Total*
White	79	21	100	61	39	100
Black	8	92	100	7	93	100

Source: Unpublished data from the Bureau of the Census.

twenty to thirty-four and thirty-five to forty-nine attributed approximately equal proportions of multiple offender crimes to these youthful offenders.

Contrary to certain popular beliefs, victims of violent crimes as a whole were most apt to have identified their assailants as members of their own race. Table 1-4 shows that for single offender crimes, four out of five victimizations of whites and nine out of ten victimizations of blacks were intraracial. Violent attacks on blacks by gangs were characterized by a similarly high level of racial homogeneity, but intraracial victimizations of whites dropped to roughly 60 percent. In this regard, the survey shows that, regardless of the number of offenders, whites were more likely to have been victimized by blacks than blacks by whites. The disparity between races proved to be most pronounced in the case of robbery. Some 45 percent of single offender robberies and 67 percent of multiple offender robberies of whites were said to have been committed by blacks, whereas robberies of blacks were seldom, if ever, attributed to whites. Assaults were primarily intraracial but, here again, interracial conflicts were more likely to have been reported by whites than by blacks.

CONSEQUENCES OF VICTIMIZATION AND UNREPORTED CRIMES

The National Crime Survey furnishes not only information on victim and crime characteristics but also data relating to the impact of crime on the victim—physical injuries suffered and medical expenses incurred; economic losses, including property damage; and time missed from work. Knowledge gained in this area is especially timely in light of current interest in victim compensation programs. (This issue is examined in detail in Chapter Eleven.) This section briefly examines the overall consequences of personal and household crimes and points out the differential effect of various types of crimes.

Personal Injury

Most people regard personal injury as the gravest consequence of a criminal attack. The 1973 survey shows that approximately 31 percent of all violent victimizations resulted in physical injury to the victim. (In Chapter Four, Gottfredson and Hindelang examine NCS city data on victim injury.) Robbery and attempted robbery tended to be more harmful than assault and attempted assault (both simple and aggravated), while rape, attempted or completed, was considered to be physically damaging. Regarding vulnerability to crimes of violence, women were more likely than men to have been injured and blacks suffered physical harm slightly more often than whites.

Although close to one-third of the victimizations produced injury, only 7 percent required hospital treatment, a proportion generally reflected in both robbery and assault. Black victims had a higher level of hospitalization than whites, requiring institutional care in 12 percent of all violent victimizations as compared with 6 percent for whites. Men and women, however, showed no significant differences. The survey questionnaire, as presently constituted, does not obtain information on other types of medical assistance–private or public, professional or paraprofessional.

Medical expenses are a costly accompaniment to crime-related injuries. Survey data show that victims incurred medical expenses in 6 percent of all violent victimizations, and roughly similar proportions were evident for robbery and assault. There was some evidence that victimizations of blacks, characterized by higher injury and hospitalization levels, were also more likely than victimizations of whites to have resulted in medical expenses. The distribution of expenses for blacks, however, did not differ significantly from those for whites. Some 46 percent of all medical bills that resulted from violent victimizations, irrespective of the victim's race, were estimated at $50 or less, 35 percent at $50-249 and 20 percent at $250 or more.

About two-thirds of those injured to the extent that they needed attention were enrolled in medical insurance programs that defrayed at least some medical costs, or were eligible for public medical services. Blacks were less likely than whites to have been covered, with about one-half of the injured blacks reporting eligibility, compared with 65 percent for whites.

Economic Loss

Economic loss–through theft of cash or property, property damage, or both–was a frequent companion of crime, as determined by the NCS. Approximately 80 percent of the personal victimizations and 90 percent of the household victimizations occurring in 1973 resulted in theft and/or property damage.

In the case of crimes against the person, economic losses were sustained in approximately 25 percent of all violent victimizations and 96 percent of all personal larcenies. The high success rate for noncontact crimes, such as personal larceny without contact, was largely due to the difficulty in ascertaining whether an attempt had ever been made, a problem less likely to have been encountered for violent victimizations. In fact, the small proportion of economically damaging violent victimizations reflected the importance of assaults, where economic loss by definition was confined to property damage. Only 13 percent of all assaults resulted in economic loss; one-fourth of all rapes and two-thirds of all robberies were accompanied by theft or property damage.

Survey results revealed that despite the magnitude of crimes characterized by loss, the dollar value of most losses was not great. Losses of under $50 were suffered in 70 percent of the personal victimizations involving theft or damage, while only 4 percent amounted to $250 or more. Of the violent crimes, robbery was costlier to the victim than assault; personal larceny with contact had a higher proportion of losses valued at $50 or more than personal larceny without contact. Blacks registered a slightly higher proportion of victimizations in the $50 and over category than did whites.

The NCS data show that restoration or compensation for property taken during personal victimization was infrequent. In more than 80 percent of the personal crimes accompanied by theft, the victim never recovered any of the loss. Partial restitution occurred in 10 percent of the victimizations, while complete restoration occurred only 8 percent of the time. Race did not appear to be related to the chance of recovery.

Most household victimizations resulted in economic loss, although larceny had a greater probability than burglary or motor vehicle theft. Household victimizations, on the whole, were costlier than personal victimizations; more than one-third of all incidents produced losses of more than $50, and 14 percent resulted in setbacks of $250 or more. When the distribution of losses for the three household crimes were compared, different patterns were evident. Larcenies were, in general, petty crimes involving losses of less than $50; but motor vehicle thefts, not surprisingly, resulted in major economic reversals of $250 or more. Burglaries were more evenly distributed, with roughly equal proportions in the less than $50 and $50 or more categories.

As with personal crimes, most property lost in household crimes was never recovered. However, although only one-fourth of all incidents had full or partial recovery, proportions for individual crimes ranged from 17 percent for larceny to 80 percent for motor vehicle theft.

Although not as noticeable as theft of property, loss of productivity through job absenteeism may impose financial hardship on victims of crime. The NCS measured the number of days of work lost by all household members as a consequence of personal or household crime. In 1973, work losses were registered in 5 percent of both personal and household victimizations. Overall, the more serious crimes had a higher proportion of work loss, and black victims suffered from crime-related absenteeism relatively more frequently than white victims. Violent personal victimizations tended to result in lost workdays more often than did personal larcenies; within violent crimes, rape and robbery were more disruptive than assault. Of all household crimes, motor vehicle theft was most likely to have caused work losses, while household larceny was the least likely. In any event, few crimes produced extended absences. Only 15 percent of the personal crimes and 5 percent of the household crimes resulted in losses of more than five days; most crimes were divided between less than one day and one to five days.

Unreported Crimes

Among criminologists, it has been recognized for years that "hidden criminality"—those criminal acts that never reach the attention of public authorities—constitutes a sizeable proportion, if not a majority, of all crime in the United States. However, not until recently, with the development of sample surveys, was it possible to accurately estimate the volume and composition of unreported crime. The NCS, in addition to these more basic measures, provides information on nonreporting by victim characteristics and crime consequences and also records reasons given by victims for not contacting the police.

In 1973, roughly 14 million personal victimizations, or about 70 percent of these crimes measured by the NCS, and 9 million household victimizations, or 60 percent, were never reported to law enforcement authorities.[9] In contrast, commercial firms failed to report only 20 percent of the burglaries and robberies. Regarding the relative seriousness of these crimes, a number of indicators—such as completions and attempts, economic loss, and personal injury—show that trivial acts were more likely to have escaped the attention of the police than the more serious onces. (Chapter Eight on the Portland victimization survey also examines this relationship.) Nonetheless, it is apparent that even for serious offenses, such as robbery with serious injury, aggravated assault or burglary with forced entry, a sizeable number of victimizations go unreported.

Looking at personal crimes (Table 1-5), 53 percent of all crimes of violence remained unreported, as compared with 76 percent of all crimes of theft, the less harmful of the two. Furthermore, relative to their total, violent attacks resulting in victim injury produced a higher level of reporting than noninjurious acts. Of the major crimes, assault was more likely to go unreported than robbery, but there were no signficant differences between the proportion for rape and that for each of the other two violent crimes. Personal larceny without contact had a higher proportion of unrecorded victimizations than personal larceny with contact, or, for that matter, any other personal crime. Rankings for those five types of personal crimes displayed little variation, regardless of the additional variables being analyzed.

The victim-offender relationship appeared to have had an impact on whether the police learned of a crime. Violent victimizations committed by relatives, friends or acquaintances went unreported more frequently than those perpetrated by strangers. Rape, robbery and assault, considered separately, displayed a pattern similar to that for all violent victimizations. A large number of nonstranger violent victimizations were domestic disturbances or disputes among

Table 1-5. Percent of Personal and Household Victimizations Not Reported to the Police by Selected Victim Characteristics, 1973

	Personal Crimes			*Household Crimes*		
Victim Characteristics	*Violence*	*Theft*	*Household Characteristics*	*Burglary*	*Larceny*	*Motor Vehicle Theft*
All Persons	53	76	All Households	53	75	31
Victim-Offender Relationship			Race of Household Head			
Stranger	51	76	White	53	74	32
Nonstranger	58	–	Black	50	81	24
Sex			Tenure			
Male	56	77	Owned	50	74	32
Female	49	76	Rented	55	76	31
Race			Income			
White	54	76	Under $3,000	57	82	29
Black	50	79	$3,000-7,499	54	77	34
Age			$7,500-9,999	54	74	29
12-19	66	87	$10,000-14,999	54	72	31
20-34	49	73	$15,000-24,999	46	71	35
35-49	42	67	$25,000 or more	44	72	33
50-64	45	69				
65 and older	39	69				

Source: Unpublished data from the Bureau of the Census.

friends, and as such were apt to have been regarded as private matters that did not call for police intervention. On the other hand, the fearful nature of stranger-to-stranger confrontations, no doubt, prompted many people to contact the police.

The data showed that reporting varied to some degree with the sex, age and race of the victim. Men had a higher proportion of unreported violent crimes than women, a relationship applying to robbery and assault as well; but, for personal larceny there was no significant difference between the sexes. Data revealed that nonreporting was more characteristic of youngsters age twelve to nineteen than of any other age group for all personal crimes except rape. A possible explanation for this is that, as indicated by the data, many crimes against juveniles are relatively minor incidents–schoolyard squabbles or petty thefts–and, thus, are less apt to be reported. Negative attitudes toward public authorities and toward reporting might be additional factors.

Reporting of violent crimes appeared to have been slightly more common for black than for white victims; however, reporting of crimes of theft was less prevalent for blacks than for whites. Additionally, violent victimizations of whites committed by nonstrangers were reported less frequently than those committed against blacks. But, significant differences were not encountered for violent attacks precipitated by strangers.

Turning to household crimes, 75 percent of all larcenies went unreported, compared with 53 percent for burglaries and only 31 percent for motor vehicle thefts. The fact that relatively few vehicle thefts were unreported was due probably, in large measure, to the value of the loss and the requirements set forth on claims by automobile insurers.

Burglaries and motor vehicle thefts carried out against white households were more likely to have gone unreported than those against blacks. In contrast, blacks tended to be poorer reporters than whites when household larcenies occurred.

Additional factors, specifically household tenure, family income and economic loss, were examined with respect to the reporting of household victimizations. For all household crimes, nonreporting was somewhat more characteristic of renters than homeowners, a relationship that also held for burglary and larceny but not for auto theft. Regarding income, there was some evidence, though not conclusive, that nonreporting was related to total family earnings. Households with incomes under $3,000 carried the greatest proportion of unreported victimizations, whereas those making $15,000 or more had the lowest proportion. The intervening income groups exhibited a downward trend, but the differences were not statistically significant.

The most striking relationship, and perhaps the easiest to understand, was between reporting and the extent of economic loss, excluding property damage. For all crimes except motor vehicle theft–which suffered from a loss of cases in the lower value categories–nonreporting was inversely related to property loss;

that is, as the value of loss increased, the proportion of victimizations that went unreported decreased, from a high of 89 percent in the less than $10 category to a low of 14 percent in the $250 and over range. On balance, victimized householders seemed to weigh the seriousness of the crime, as determined by the value of the loss, against whatever reasons they might have against contacting the authorities. The greater the loss, the less persuasive the arguments against reporting and the greater the chance that the crime would be reported to the police.

Roughly 56 percent of all reasons given for not reporting personal victimizations to the police and 66 percent of the reasons given for household victimizations were attributed to the belief that nothing could have been done about the crime or that the crime was not important enough to report.[10] For both personal and household crimes, "nothing could be done" was a more common response than "not important enough." In addition, the belief that the incident was a private matter was frequently cited in crimes of violence—particularly nonstranger victimizations—and completed motor vehicle thefts; while for all types of crimes the residual category "other responses" accounted for a number of specific, but unclassified responses. Most notable in their absence from the list of frequently given reasons were fear of reprisal, belief that the police would not want to be bothered and the desire not to get involved or become inconvenienced. Variations from this response pattern were not frequently encountered.

TECHNICAL NOTE

The National Crime Survey data are derived from a stratified multistage cluster sample of 75,000 housing units located in all fifty states and the District of Columbia. Each household is interviewed initially for bounding purposes (i.e., to establish a time frame to control telescoping of events into the reference period), and is then reinterviewed every six months over a three year period. The data from the first interview are not used to produce the estimates of the crime rate. The sample also incorporates a rotation feature so that additional housing units enter the sample on a regular basis to replace those which are phased out after seven interviews. Only about 4 percent of all eligible and occupied households were not interviewed in 1973.

The procedure for producing population estimates from this sample involves adjusting basic sample weights for the noninterview of both households and persons, plus two stages of ratio adjustment (three in the case of household crimes) that bring the sample up to current independent estimates of the number of persons and households. A large sample is required because crime is an uncommon event; sampling errors are still substantial for such crimes as rape and robbery, however. The one standard error level of confidence has been adopted as the minimum standard for relationships discussed in this report.[11]

NOTES

1. The President's Commission on Law Enforcement and Administration of Justice, *The Challenge of Crime in a Free Society* (Washington, D.C.: U.S. Government Printing Office, 1967), p. 22.

2. When incidents involved both commercial robbery and personal victimization, the characteristics of the latter were obtained and a personal *victimization* was counted. However, the *incident* was considered as basically a commercial incident and, therefore, was represented in that portion of the survey and should not also be counted as an incident in the household survey.

3. There is also a special category of victimizations–known as series victimizations–that has been excluded from these results. These are situations where a respondent is unable to provide details of three or more victimizations of a similar nature. In 1973 these victimizations were disproportionately concentrated in the crimes of simple assault and larcenies under $50. Series victimizations amounted to 5 percent of all victimizations when a series victimization is counted as one. However, this practice substantially understates the impact of these crimes. More research is needed to determine the relative contribution to series crimes of lack of interviewer probing, inarticulate or lazy respondents and genuine cases where being victimized is a condition of existence.

4. Members of the armed forces were included in the survey if they lived off post; nearly 1,000,000 military were tabulated in the 1973 data.

5. The residence of the victim is not necessarily the same as where the crime occurred, especially for personal crimes, but it is suspected that they coincide in most cases.

6. Persons the victim knew by sight only or was unable to identify as stranger or nonstranger were counted by NCS as strangers.

7. All rape victims, whether the incident was attempted or completed, were considered to have been injured.

8. See, for example, Albert J. Reiss, Jr., *Studies in Crime and Law Enforcement in Major Metropolitan Areas, Field Surveys III, vol. 1* (Washington, D.C.: U.S. Government Printing Office, 1967), pp. 22-67; Stephen Schafer, *The Victim and His Criminal: A Study in Functional Responsibility* (New York: Random House, 1968), pp. 63-71; and Donald Mulvihill and Melvin Tumin with Lynn Curtis, *Crimes of Violence*, National Commission on the Causes and Prevention of Violence (Washington, D.C.: U.S. Government Printing Office, 1969), vol. 11.

9. The survey considered crimes as having been reported if the victim *or any other person* informed the police, or if the police were on the scene at the time.

10. The measuring instrument recorded all reasons given by the respondent for not reporting to the police, but no effort was made to identify the most important reason.

11. For a more complete discussion of the sample design, estimation procedure and sources of error in the NCS, see U.S. Department of Justice, Law Enforcement Assistance Administration, *Criminal Victimization in the United States: 1973 Final Report* (Washington, D.C.: U.S. Government Printing Office, 1976), p. 241 ff.

Chapter 2

Patterns of Urban Crime

Barbara Boland

Each year during the late 1960s and early 1970s the *Uniform Crime Reports* recorded a substantial increase in the level of serious crime that citizens reported to the police. Over the same period, public opinion surveys were measuring a significant increase in the proportion of the population that was afraid to go out alone at night. Reacting to these two phenomena were many who questioned the validity of the apparent increase in reported crime and the reasonableness of that widespread concern, casting doubt on the extent to which crime truly was a growing or widespread problem. A great deal of crime is never reported to police, it was argued, so that measured crime could be rising not because citizens were actually experiencing more crime than before but simply because—due to heightened concern—they now reported more of what did occur. Furthermore, even if crime had risen, such widespread concern seemed unwarranted, since serious violent personal crimes are statistically relatively rare occurrences and are much more likely to represent altercations between friends and relatives than unprovoked attacks by strangers on the street and a threat to the general level of public safety.

Nonetheless, the public at large has seemed impervious to these technical arguments. Their mood has continued to be one of heightened concern about the problem of crime, especially the problem of crime on the streets in large central cities. Additionally, that concern, whether warranted or not, has had an effect on the behavior of those who live both in and around the central city. Surveys performed for the President's Crime Commission found that many city residents did not go out at night in order to avoid crime, a substantial fraction wanted to move and 9 percent of those who lived in one high crime area said that they carried weapons to protect themselves.[1] Suburbanites, it is assumed, avoid the central city and the cultural and commercial activities located there in the belief that they risk a greater chance of being victimized downtown than in most suburban locations.

There are now few who deny that a "real" increase in crime has occurred, and better data are available for assessing both the amount and impact of crime in our largest and generally highest crime cities. Survey victimization data not only avoid the problem of nonreporting to the police, that is inherent in the *Uniform Crime Reports*, but they also provide much more detailed information about crimes and victims than is available from crime reports collected by the police. Victimization data are obtained from surveys that directly ask individuals if they have been the victims of crime and inquire about the specifics of each reported criminal event. The data thus permit comparison of how public safety varies among our largest cities, and, within cities, among various social and demographic groups. The results of these surveys, along with past studies on urban crime patterns, are reviewed in this chapter in order to assess the way in which crime is most likely to affect urban residents and what is known about the factors that account for differences in public safety among our largest cities.

TWENTY-SIX CITIES VICTIMIZATION DATA

Since 1972, interviews with the victims of crime have been carried out by the Census Bureau in twenty-six of the nation's largest central cities. In each city, residents of 10,000 households–about 22,000 persons–were asked if they had been the victim of certain types of crime during the preceding twelve months. Each person twelve years or over was questioned about crimes against the person (rape, robbery, aggravated and simple assault, and personal larceny); one adult household member was interviewed to determine the extent of crimes against the household (burglary, auto theft and household theft). In addition to information about the types of crimes committed and the circumstances surrounding the event (time and place of occurrence, extent of personal injury, property damage, etc.) data on the demographic characteristics of victims, such as their race, sex, age and family income, was collected. Also, for those crimes involving direct contact with the offender, each victim was asked to report whether the offender was a person known to them or a stranger, the number of offenders involved in the incident and the victim's perception of the characteristics of the offender(s), including race, sex and age.

To facilitate comparisons with past studies, the survey crime data have been regrouped here to correspond with FBI Index Crime definitions (excluding murder). Crime rates have been computed for each city based on population. The results are presented in Table 2-1. Consistent with past observations based on FBI data, the rate of property crime (burglary, auto theft and larceny) is four to six times as great as the rate of violent personal crime (rape, robbery and aggravated assault). In each city, the least frequent crime was rape, with rates ranging from one to four rapes or attempted rapes per 1,000 residents. The most

Table 2-1. Twenty-six Cities Index Crime Rates (per 1,000 population age twelve and over)

City	*Rape*	*Robbery*	*Aggravated Assault*	*Burglary*	*Larceny*	*Auto Theft*	*Total*
Atlanta	2	23	15	119	147	13	319
Baltimore	1	30	13	81	122	15	262
Boston	2	34	17	109	159	41	362
Buffalo	2	17	14	64	115	14	226
Chicago	3	26	12	68	120	16	245
Cincinnati	2	19	22	118	161	12	334
Cleveland	2	25	15	78	106	34	260
Dallas	2	13	14	94	163	11	297
Denver	3	18	20	104	214	21	380
Detroit	3	35	18	106	141	22	325
Houston	3	20	17	96	198	15	349
Los Angeles	2	17	15	94	168	20	316
Miami	1	19	7	68	74	8	177
Milwaukee	2	17	17	83	161	13	293
Minneapolis	4	23	18	112	202	21	380
New Orleans	3	23	13	72	146	15	272
New York	1	34	4	71	67	12	189
Newark	1	34	6	107	69	17	234
Oakland	3	31	16	142	158	19	369
Philadelphia	1	32	17	73	133	18	274
Pittsburgh	2	17	13	57	124	20	233
Portland	3	18	16	100	195	17	349
San Diego	2	12	16	79	231	12	349
San Francisco	3	33	14	84	172	20	326
St. Louis	1	19	13	87	110	22	252
Washington, D.C.	1	20	6	55	91	8	181

Source: U.S. Department of Justice, Law Enforcement Assistance Administration, *Crime in Eight American Cities* (Washington, D.C.: U.S. Government Printing Office, July, 1974); U.S. Department of Justice, Law Enforcement Assistance Administration, *Crime in the Nation's Five Largest Cities* (Washington, D.C.: U.S. Government Printing Office, April, 1975); U.S. Department of Justice, Law Enforcement Assistance Administration, *Criminal Victimization Surveys in 13 American Cities* (Washington, D.C.: U.S. Government Printing Office, June, 1975).

Note: Burglary and larceny rates here are computed per 1,000 population age 12 and over and not per 1,000 households as in LEAA publications.

frequent crime in all but three cities was household larceny, which ranged from a high of 230 larcenies per 1,000 population in San Diego to a low of 60 per 1,000 population in New York. In New York, Newark and Oakland, the most frequent crime was burglary. On average, the residents of these twenty-six cities reported being the victim of 250 index crimes per 1,000 residents during the year preceding the survey.

Residents of Denver and Minneapolis reported the highest number of index crimes–about 380 per 1,000 residents–and the residents of Miami and Washington, D.C., the lowest number–about 180 per 1,000 residents. Ranking of these twenty-six cities as "safe" or "unsafe" cities on the basis of all of these crimes is likely to be misleading because of the predominance of the less serious property crimes in the total index and because variations in crime rates across these cities differ by type. In nineteen of the twenty-six cities, 40 percent or more of the incidents recorded were larcenies, which citizens say they do not report to the police about 70 percent of the time–usually because they do not consider the event important enough to warrant the effort. Consequently, New York, which reports a relatively low larceny rate but a relatively high robbery rate, appears to be among the safest of the twenty-six cities if one looks only at the total crime rate, but it ranks among the more risky if one looks only at the rates for robbery.

Of all the crimes measured by the Census Bureau's victimization survey, robbery–defined as theft or attempted theft by force or threat of force–is perhaps the one crime that best fits the public's notion of the "crime problem." Typically, robberies are perpetrated by persons who are strangers to their victims–about 90 percent of those reported in the survey are said to have been committed by strangers. About 68 percent of all robberies of individuals occur on the street; most of the remainder occur either in or near the home or in closed public places, such as hallways or stairwells. About 95 percent involve only one victim, but nearly two-thirds involve more than one offender. Over half involve the use of a weapon, the type varying considerably from city to city. In New York, for example, 40 percent of all robberies involved a knife and 12 percent a gun; in Detroit 20 percent involved a knife and 26 percent a gun. Of all the personal violent crimes, robbery poses the greatest threat to the average citizen. In part this is because of its frequency–in general robbery is much more frequent than either murder or rape–but also because other violent crimes, especially murder and aggravated assault, are more likely to involve victims and offenders who have had some previous relationship. A Violence Commission survey in 1967 of police records in seventeen cities found that 85 percent of murders and 80 percent of aggravated assaults take place over private matters between persons who were either intimates or well known to each other.[2]

Interestingly, victimization survey estimates of the stranger-nonstranger ratio for assaults are quite different from those based on police data. In the twenty-six cities, the victims of assault report, on average, that about 70 percent were perpetrated by strangers. Studies of the survey methodology, however, indicate that a substantial proportion of assaults that are reported to the police are not then reported to the survey—undoubtedly because many do not wish to discuss such private matters with interviewers.[3]

Focusing specifically on robbery presents a picture of safe and unsafe cities that, in general, accords with popular perception. Those with robbery rates above the mean (twenty-five per 1,000 residents for this sample of twenty-six cities) are predominantly older northeastern or northcentral cities, including New York, Boston, Detroit and Newark. Southern and western cities, with the exception of San Franciso and Oakland, typically enjoy robbery rates which are below the sample average.

VICTIMS AND OFFENDERS

Within cities, crime rates vary considerably across neighborhoods and demographic groups. City level victimization surveys do not provide information on the spatial distribution of crime within cities, but they do provide a detailed account of the demographic patterns of victimization in each city surveyed (see Table 2-2).

The demographic characteristics of robbery victims exhibit a substantial amount of similarity in the twenty-six cities. In general, men are more likely to be victimized than women, blacks are more likely to be victimized than whites and victimization typically declines with increasing age and income. There are, however, some exceptions. The patterns by age in Pittsburgh, Miami and Atlanta, for example, suggest little or no differences in victimization rates between the young and the old, and patterns by income in Miami and Dallas show little tendency to decline among the higher income groups. A great deal of diversity among cities is apparent in the victimization patterns by race. In thirteen of the twenty-six cities, nonwhites are considerably more likely to be robbed than whites; in ten cities the frequency of robberies against blacks and whites are about equal, or only marginally different. In two cities, Oakland and San Francisco, whites were considerably more likely to be victimized than blacks. In all cities, victims overwhelmingly identified their offenders as male (overall 96 percent were committed by males) and judged that about 55 percent were twenty years of age or under. The majority of offenders were identified as nonwhite, but the exact proportion varied considerably by city, ranging from about 55 percent in Portland, Minneapolis and San Diego, where the average population percent nonwhite is about 9 percent, to about 90 percent in Detroit, Philadelphia, Newark, Baltimore, New Orleans and Washington, D.C., where the average population percent nonwhite is about 50 percent.

The frequency with which members of each racial group are victimized by members of the same or opposite group is shown in Table 2-3. The figures show, for example, that nonwhites living in New York are victimized by whites at the

Table 2-2. Personal Robbery Victimization Rates by Characteristics of Victims

City	Total	*Sex*		*Age*					*Race*		*Income*				
		Male	*Female*	*12-19*	*20-24*	*25-34*	*35-49*	*50+*	*White*	*Nonwhite*	*$3,000*	*$3,000-7,499*	*$7,500-9,999*	*$10,000 14,999*	*$15,000+*
Atlanta	16	24	9	33	15	15	18	12	17	15	21	19	19	12	5
Baltimore	26	42	14	34	20	20	26	26	23	30	37	29	23	26	20
Boston	31	45	20	42	40	28	25	24	31	32	42	37	32	25	23
Buffalo	16	23	11	29	18	16	13	10	14	22	23	19	16	13	12
Chicago	27	36	17	30	37	31	24	19	20	38	38	29	18	24	21
Cincinnati	15	23	8	29	16	12	11	9	13	17	23	14	14	13	9
Cleveland	24	31	17	32	35	26	22	15	17	34	33	28	22	17	15
Dallas	10	17	4	20	11	4	8	2	10	10	7	10	9	10	11
Denver	18	27	9	40	20	15	11	9	18	16	29	18	14	16	14
Detroit	32	44	22	54	37	34	23	22	25	40	47	39	32	24	23
Houston	17	24	11	25	27	20	11	9	15	25	22	29	17	13	10
Los Angeles	17	24	9	29	17	13	13	11	9	17	19	13	8	10	7
Miami	10	15	6	9	12	9	11	9	8	16	12	10	7	9	10
Milwaukee	18	23	13	33	19	14	12	14	17	25	34	26	13	16	12
Minneapolis	21	28	15	42	24	16	19	12	21	19	33	28	17	13	16
New Orleans	18	28	10	25	18	19	18	13	19	16	22	21	16	15	11
New York	24	32	18	30	28	27	22	20	23	30	20	28	27	22	20
Newark	29	39	21	32	25	27	28	30	20	34	47	33	26	17	14
Oakland	22	30	15	30	22	19	19	21	28	14	36	25	16	20	19
Philadelphia	28	45	14	14	27	29	22	23	20	44	38	36	31	23	17
Pittsburgh	15	22	9	21	16	16	11	13	14	20	25	16	16	12	9
Portland	17	24	10	34	19	17	12	10	17	12	21	15	6	9	9
San Diego	11	17	7	25	17	10	4	6	11	10	29	16	9	8	8
San Francisco	29	38	20	53	30	31	25	20	33	17	56	35	24	27	22
St. Louis	17	25	9	24	24	15	14	11	14	18	19	18	8	12	10
Washington, D.C.	17	26	10	20	19	19	15	14	21	16	27	19	15	13	15

Source: U.S. Department of Justice, Law Enforcement Assistance Administration, *Crime in Eight American Cities* (Washington, D.C.: U.S. Government Printing Office, July, 1974); U.S. Department of Justice, Law Enforcement Assistance Administration, *Crime in the Nation's Five Largest Cities* (Washington, D.C.: U.S. Government Printing Office, April, 1975); U.S. Department of Justice, Law Enforcement Assistance Administration, *Criminal Victimization Surveys in 13 American Cities* (Washington, D.C.: U.S. Government Printing Office, June, 1975).

Note: Burglary and Larceny rates here are computed per 1,000 population age 12 and over and not per 1,000 households as in LEAA publications.

rate of two robberies per 1,000 nonwhite population and by nonwhites at the rate of twenty-six robberies per 1,000 nonwhite population. In general, nonwhites are always more frequently victimized by other nonwhites than whites, but the magnitude of the differential varies considerably across cities. In Chicago, robberies by whites against nonwhites are so rare as to preclude the calculation of a rate per 1,000 population; in Minneapolis the white-nonwhite victimization rate is only 50 percent lower than the nonwhite-nonwhite rate. Similarly, the victimization experience of whites varies by city. In Denver, Portland, Minneapolis and San Diego, whites are equally likely to be victimized by whites or nonwhites; in Detroit, Newark and New Orleans, nonwhite-white victimization rates are seven times greater than the white-white rate. In most cities, whites are more likely to be victimized by nonwhites than whites.

Victimization data reveal which social and demographic groups are most frequently victimized and some of the personal characteristics of the most likely offenders but they do not provide a measure of the true risk various individuals face in particular situations. Most persons assess the risk of crime, given their personal characteristics, in terms of their chances of being victimized if they frequent a particular place at a particular time. Victimization rates do not measure risk in this way for two reasons. First, rates calculated from the surveys reflect the behavior not only of offenders but also of potential victims. The reason, for example, that the elderly appear to enjoy a greater degree of personal security than the young is very likely due to the fact that they go out much less frequently because they are afraid of crime and not because they are less vulnerable when they do appear in public places unescorted. Thus, victimization rates measure only a part of the impact of crime: they tell us which persons end up being victims, but nothing about changes in the behavior of potential victims that are motivated by a desire to avoid vulnerable situations or locations. Second, the victimization surveys collect no information on the most likely location of crime within cities. Most persons are aware that some neighborhoods within cities are safer than others, and it is undoubtedly locational differences in crime rates that underlie some of the demographic patterns observed both within and among cities. Persons who live in the same areas or frequent the same places as offenders are more likely to be victimized than persons who are able to avoid contact with high offender populations. The spatial distribution of crime, while not measured by the city surveys, is suggested by several previous studies.

A study by Lynn Curtis using 1967 data for the cities of Boston, Philadelphia, Chicago, Atlanta and San Francisco analyzed spatial patterns of personal violent crimes (assault, murder, rape and robbery) that had been solved by the police. A consistent pattern emerged in these five cities. Murder and assault exhibited a high degree of localization in the poverty-slum areas of each city; the greatest amount of geographical dispersion was exhibited by robbery, with rape falling somewhere in between. Most robberies took place in the same poverty-slum areas as the assaultive crimes, but, in addition, a number occurred in areas

Table 2-3. Robbery Victimization Rates by Race of Offender(s) and Race of Victim(s)* (rates per 1,000 population)

Race of Victim	*Race of Offender*	*W*	*NW*	*T*	*Race of Victim*	*Race of Offender*	*W*	*NW*	*T*
Atlanta					Milwaukee				
W		4.6	10.5	15.0	W		4.6	9.9	14.6
NW		0.3	13.7	14.0	NW		0.2	22.5	22.7
Baltimore					Minneapolis				
W		4.1	17.1	21.2	W		7.5	8.4	15.9
NW		0.6	29.0	29.6	NW		4.7	9.5	14.2
Boston					New Orleans				
W		8.4	19.7	28.1	W		2.3	15.0	17.3
NW		4.2	22.8	27.0	NW		0.7	14.7	15.4
Buffalo					New York				
W		3.9	8.8	12.7	W		3.5	14.3	19.7
NW		1.4	19.6	21.0	NW		2.2	26.1	28.2
Chicago					Newark				
W		5.0	11.3	16.6	W		2.3	15.3	17.6
NW		0.0	37.0	38.0	NW		1.0	31.3	32.5
Cincinnati					Oakland				
W		5.3	7.2	12.5	W		4.5	19.5	24.0
NW		2.0	14.4	16.6	NW		1.3	11.3	12.6
Cleveland					Philadelphia				
W		5.6	9.4	15.0	W		2.7	16.3	19.0
NW		2.2	30.2	32.4	NW		0.5	38.1	38.7
Dallas					Pittsburgh				
W		3.6	5.5	9.1	W		3.6	9.4	13.0
NW		0.2	9.6	9.8	NW		1.8	16.7	18.5
Denver					Portland				
W		7.3	7.7	15.0	W		6.5	7.7	14.2
NW		2.4	10.0	12.7	NW		1.2	13.0	14.2
Detroit					San Diego				
W		3.1	21.2	24.3	W		4.4	5.2	9.6
NW		1.1	37.4	38.5	NW		1.3	7.3	8.6
Houston					San Francisco				
W		5.6	8.3	13.8	W		7.8	20.2	28.0
NW		0.9	21.5	22.4	NW		1.8	12.8	19.6
Los Angeles					St. Louis				
W		4.6	7.0	11.6	W		4.2	9.4	13.6
NW		1.6	25.6	27.0	NW		0.2	16.0	16.3

Table 2-3 continued

Race of Victim	*Race of Offender*	*W*	*NW*	*T*	*Race of Victim*	*Race of Offender*	*W*	*NW*	*T*
Miami					Washington, D.C.				
W		1.9	5.5	7.4	W		1.5	16.6	18.1
NW		0.4	13.5	13.9	NW		0.2	14.3	14.5

*Figures in this table, derived from unpublished census tabulations, refer to individual robberies only, i.e., commercial robberies have been excluded. Also excluded are a small number of individual robberies, usually less than 3 percent, where the victim was not able to identify the characteristics of the offender(s).

contiguous to the residential areas of offenders or in downtown and neighborhood commercial areas. Only in San Francisco did offenders invade higher income areas in order to victimize residents. Robberies in poverty-slum areas typically involved a black offender and a black victim. Those in adjacent neighborhoods and business areas involved black offenders and both black and white victims. The San Francisco "invasion" robberies typically involved black offenders and white victims.[4]

One of the most intensive studies of the spatial distribution of robbery (including purse snatchings) was carried out in Oakland, California, between 1966 and 1968 by Susan Wilcox. The relative frequency of individual and commercial robberies in various locations were analyzed to uncover the relationship between robbery patterns and types of land use. Fifty-six percent of individual robberies involving female victims and 70 percent of those involving male victims occurred within one-half block of a major street. The modal robbery of a male occurred in or within a few blocks of a low income neighborhood commercial area containing bars, taverns and other types of skid row activity. Females were rarely victimized in these areas, perhaps because most women do not frequent such places unescorted. Rather, crimes against women were concentrated on the fringes of the downtown shopping area or neighborhood commercial centers, suggesting that women are highly vulnerable while moving between active shopping areas and parked cars or nearby residences.[5]

The picture of crime that emerges from these studies bears a considerable similarity to popular perceptions of crime. While only a small proportion of nonwhites commit violent crimes and violent crime is only a small proportion of all crime, it is also true that most of the violent street crime that does occur is committed by nonwhites. It is also apparent, from both these spatial and demographic patterns, that a substantial amount of violent urban street crime is confined to poverty areas within large cities where offenders reside. A sizeable proportion, however, also occurs in areas of cities that provide services to all residents, i.e., major commercial and retail centers.

CRIME PATTERNS

Although it is generally true that rates for many crimes increase with city size both in the U.S. and most Western nations, it is also apparent from both official crime reports and victimization surveys that there is considerable variation in public safety even among large central cities. Some of the differences between cities doubtless are due to variations in their demographic composition, but it is not clear that this can account for all of them. In the twenty-six cities surveyed by the Census Bureau, for example, the correspondence between race or income distributions and the robbery rate is not clear-cut. On the whole, southern cities enjoy the lowest robbery rates, but they also have the lowest average incomes and the greatest inequality in its distribution. Several cities experiencing high robbery rates have relatively small nonwhite populations, e.g., New York, San Francisco and Boston.

Numerous studies, employing a variety of different types of geographic units, have described the spatial distribution of crime and identified some characteristics of their populations that are correlated with rates of crime and delinquency. The general findings of these studies as well as a review of their theoretical underpinnings can be found in summaries by Sutherland and Cressy, and by Wilks.[6] Some of the findings are consistent with general patterns observed in the city victimization data, and they provide an indication of the nature of the forces that underlie the level and patterns of crime.

One of the consistent statistical regularities reported by prior studies is that variations in crime rates and their association with population characteristics are crime-specific—i.e., patterns of variation are different for different types of crime. For a number of years official statistics have indicated that murder rates are about twice as high in the South as in other regions of the country; robbery traditionally has been highest in the Northeast; aggravated assault is higher in the South and West than in the North Central states and the Northeast; and burglary and larceny rates generally are highest in the West.[7] Some of these regional patterns can be observed in the city survey data. As previously mentioned, robbery rates are typically highest in the old Northeast and North Central cities. Of the six cities with the highest robbery rates (Detroit, Boston, Newark, New York, San Francisco and Philadelphia) four are located in the Northeast. Similarly, with respect to larceny, all of the western cities have above average larceny rates and four of the six highest larceny rate cities (San Diego, Minneapolis, Denver, Portland, Houston and San Francisco) are located in the West. The city pattern for burglary is less clear, with the four highest cities each from a different region. Most of the western cities, however, have burglary rates above the sample average of eighty-nine burglaries per 1,000 population over twelve. Denver, Los Angeles, Oakland and Portland have above average rates, and San Diego and San Francisco below average rates. (Murder rates are, of course, not measured by the survey and the aggravated assault rates, as previously mentioned, are not likely to be accurately measured by survey methodology.)

Unfortunately, few studies have focused specifically on the problem of variations in crime rates among large cities, but those that have confirm the notion that geographic patterns vary by type of crime. A study of cities with over 100,000 population by Karl Schuessler and Gerald Slatin, using factor analysis and data on seven major offenses in 1950 and 1960, identified two factors that were strongly associated with crime rates. These two factors, which they designated "minority relations" and "anomie" were, however, differentially related to personal and property offenses. The minority factor score, which was loaded heavily on percent nonwhite, was consistently associated with murder and aggravated assault; the anomie factor score, which represented such variables as percent divorced and the suicide rate, was consistently related to robbery, burglary, auto theft and larceny. They concluded that no single factor could be identified that would account for all of the variation in offense rates among cities and that their evidence indicated that the social processes underlying crimes against the person differed from those underlying crimes against property.[8]

A study by Richard Quinney examined correlations between specific crimes and population characteristics using 1960 data for three different types of geographic areas—rural, urban and Standard Metropolitan Statistical Areas. Like Schuessler and Slatin, he found that some population measures were differentially correlated with specific crimes. In all three geographic samples, socioeconomic variables (median years of schooling, median family income, percent of males in white collar jobs) typically were negatively correlated with murder and aggravated assault but positively correlated with burglary, larceny and auto theft.[9]

Likewise, in the city victimization data, specific crimes are differentially related to various population characteristics. The crimes of household burglary and personal robbery provide a particularly clear-cut case. The simple correlations presented in Table 2-4 suggest a different relationship on almost all of the nine variables considered. Household burglary, for example, is negatively correlated with population size and density, proportion nonwhite, and percent foreign born, and positively correlated with measures of the proportion of high and low income families. Personal robbery, on the other hand, is positively correlated with population size and density, proportion nonwhite, and percent foreign born, and not at all correlated with the measures of dispersion in the income distribution.

This brief review of the ecology of crime is not meant to be definitive or specifically to identify *the* empirical correlates of particular types of crimes but to illustrate the crime-specific nature of the empirical patterns that have been observed in the past, which, in general, are consistent with patterns observed in the twenty-six cities data. These patterns suggest that the general phenomenon of crime encompasses a wide diversity of behaviors and that at least some of the underlying causal processes may vary by type of crime. Understanding what underlies the level and pattern of crime in a given area thus requires consider-

Table 2-4. Correlations of Twenty-six Cities' Household Burglary and Personal Robbery Rates with Various Population Characteristics

	Household Burglary	*Personal Robbery*
1970 Population	–0.361	0.221
Population Density	–0.589	0.616
Percent Nonwhite	–0.261	0.393
South	–0.210	–0.399
Percent Families with Income over $15,000	–0.258	0.045
Percent Families in Poverty	0.334	0.045
Percent Foreign Born	–0.330	0.243
Percent Under Eighteen Years	0.163	0.001
Population Change 1960-1970	0.169	–0.459

Source: Computed from data presented in references cited for Table 2-1.

ation of a number of different causal phenomena and their differential relationship to specific crimes. This is not to deny that there may be some general causal processes that are significantly related to all serious crimes in all areas. Yet some variables that are associated with robbery rates, for example, may have little association with larceny rates. Likewise, policies that contribute to the control of larceny may contribute nothing to the control of robbery. Making this distinction is important since most persons consider robbery to be a much more serious crime than larceny and therefore deserving of greater efforts at control.

The trend in criminological research in recent years has been away from a search for a single causal theory of all crime and toward the study of particular types of crime and the development of specific rather than general causal theories.[10] Recent studies in the ecology of crime that attempt to devise theoretical explanations for their observations reflect this orientation and many of the specific explanations are quite varied. Almost all, however, reflect the sociological approach to the study of human behavior. The empirical correlates of crime are not considered to directly represent causal factors–e.g., race or low income are not considered to directly cause crime, but rather they are thought to be indicators of the underlying social structure of particular areas.

The sociological approach tends to view objective opportunities as given, and then to look for the influence that such factors as culture, tradition or family play in determining the life experiences and associations of individuals. Those in turn determine the development of predispositions toward engaging in criminal behavior. Theoretical explanations thus focus on understanding the "historical life experiences" that teach an individual to recognize a situation as constituting a criminal opportunity and lead him to take advantage of it. These influences increasingly are thought to determine not only the general prevalence of crime among various population groups but also the specific type of criminal behavior that will be preferred. This point of view does not deny that immediate objective circumstances may be important, and their role is often noted. But the level of analysis at which sociological inquiry is focused considers such conditions to be secondary, and their independent contribution to the level of crime has not systematically been investigated. Consequently, very little in the ecology of crime literature tells us what objective conditions contribute to which crimes, and how much. It is possible that some of the differences in crime rates that we observe among cities are due, in addition to differences in culture and social structure, to differences in law enforcement strategies or to differences in physical and environmental conditions that facilitate specific crimes.

Recently, economists, whose profession does focus specifically on the effect of objective circumstances in influencing human behavior, have begun to inquire into the problem of what factors contribute to the level of crime. The economic framework specifically recognizes that individuals vary in cultural background and therefore also in attitudes toward engaging in particular types of behavior. However, given cultural influences, most persons do respond to changes in objective circumstances. Specifically, the economic framework suggests that in some crude way the costs and benefits of various behavioral alternatives are taken into account, and that when changes in objective circumstances either lower benefits or raise costs, some individuals (not necessarily all) will find that the benefits no longer outweigh the costs. These individuals then cease to engage in that activity. This is the notion, in simplified terms, that lies behind the econometric work on the question of deterrence. The economic view of deterrence is that both the probability and severity of punishment are costs associated with the commission of crime and that therefore, when either the severity or probability of punishment increases, criminal activity will decrease.

Since the late 1960s, a number of research studies have been done that attempt to test empirically the deterrence hypothesis. Most have employed regression analysis and official data on crime to estimate the impact of the probability and severity of punishment upon crime rates in various jurisdictions. Data are available at the state level to measure the effect of the probability of imprisonment and time served in state prisons on the level of crime; at the city level, data are available to measure the effect only of the probability of arrest on the level of crime. Estimates have been made for both specific crime types and all serious crimes taken together. At least with respect to the probability measures, the results of those studies have been remarkably consistent. Almost all suggest that higher probabilities of imprisonment and arrest are associated with lower levels of crime.[11]

SUMMARY AND CONCLUSIONS

This chapter has utilized both new and past data to review what is known about how crime affects the residents of large cities and what factors seem to account for observed differences in crime rates among cities. While a great deal of urban crime occurs in the poverty-slum areas of central cities and primarily affects the residents of them, not all crime—and particularly street crime—is confined to those areas or to the low income and minority groups that live there. The problem of street crime appears likely to affect anyone who risks exposure to high offender populations. This is obvious to many citizens, and they have adjusted their behavior when they can to avoid contact with these populations. What has not been obvious is how to provide greater safety to those who cannot or do not wish to relocate their residences and other activities to safer areas.

Geographic patterns of crime in general suggest that a variety of causal phenomena must be considered to understand what contributes to the level and pattern of crime for a particular area. Sociologists have generally focused on discovering those causes that are associated with differences in the social structure and culture of particular areas. Such factors are crucially important for understanding why crime exists and why, among individuals faced with the same opportunities, some commit crimes and others do not. Most persons, after all, do not act on the opportunity to commit a mugging when they meet a weaker and richer stranger on a dark street with no available witnesses, even though it is highly likely that they could get away with it. Such factors certainly are significant, and it is therefore important to try to identify the differences in culture, given demographic compositions, that appear to be associated with varying levels of crime. The disadvantage of this approach from the point of view of crime control, however, is that the role of variables like "culture" and "social structure" are very difficult to understand in any kind of a rigorous or precise fashion and, therefore, also are difficult to manipulate by conscious design. The economic approach to crime begins where the sociological approach leaves off and asks: After the effect of "social structure" has been taken into account, what effect might the cost and benefits of immediate circumstances contribute to the level of crime? This view of criminal behavior is not necessarily incompatible with the sociological model described above; each can advance our understanding of what contributes to the level of public safety. From the point of view of crime control, however, it is especially important to consider the findings of an analytic approach that focuses on the role of conditions or circumstances that can be altered by governmental or private action.

NOTES

1. Jennie McIntyre, "Public Attitudes Toward Crime and Law Enforcement," *The Annals* 374 (November 1967): 34-46.

2. Lynn A. Curtis, *Criminal Violence: National Patterns and Behavior* (Lexington, Massachusetts: Lexington Books, 1974), pp. 46-47.

3. Albert D. Biderman, "When Does Interpersonal Violence Become Crime?—Theory and Methods for Statistical Surveys" (paper prepared for a meeting on Access to Law, Research Committee on the Sociology of Law, International Sociological Association, Girton College, Cambridge, England, September 1973), pp. 15-19.

4. Curtis, pp. 119-47.

5. Susan Wilcox, *The Prevention and Control of Robbery, Volume III, The Geography of Robbery* (Davis: University of California, The Center of Administration of Criminal Justice, April 1973).

6. E.H. Sutherland and D.R. Cressy, *Criminology* (Philadelphia: J.B. Lippincott Co., 1974), pp. 172-201; and J.A. Wilks, "Ecological Correlates of Crime and Delinquency," in President's Commission on Law Enforcement and Administration of Justice, *Task Force Report: Crime and its Impact—An Assessment* (Washington, D.C.: U.S. Government Printing Office, 1967), pp. 138-56.

7. Federal Bureau of Investigation, *Uniform Crime Reports, 1974* (Washington, D.C.: U.S. Government Printing Office, 1975).

8. Karl Schuessler and Gerald Slatin, "Sources of Variation in U.S. City Crime, 1950 and 1960," *Journal of Research in Crime and Delinquency* 1, no. 2 (July 1964): 127-48.

9. Richard Quinney, "Structural Characteristics, Population Areas, and Crime Rates in the United States," *Journal of Criminal Law, Criminology and Police Science* 57, no. 1 (March-December 1966): 45-52.

10. Marshall B. Clinard and Richard Quinney, *Criminal Behavior Systems* (New York: Holt, Rinehart and Winston, Inc., 1967), pp. 3-4.

11. The results of some of these studies are reviewed in Gordon Tullock, "Does Punishment Deter Crime?" *The Public Interest* 36 (Summer 1974), pp. 103-111. The most sophisticated analysis of deterrence to date is that of Issac Ehrlich, "Participation in Illegitimate Activities: A Theoretical and Empirical Investigation," *Journal of Political Economy* 81, no. 3 (May-June 1973): 521-65.

Chapter 3

Crimes and Victims in London

Richard F. Sparks

In the decade since the first victimization surveys were carried out for the President's Commission on Law Enforcement and Administration of Justice,[1] the use of social survey methods to study crime has become the basis of a growth industry of substantial proportions. As is the case with many other industries based on a new and expensive technology, the biggest investment in victimization surveying has been made in the United States—in particular, through the ambitious program of surveys (the National Crime Panel) currently being carried out by the Census Bureau on behalf of the Law Enforcement Assistance Administration, discussed in other chapters in this book. But—as is also the case with many such industries—victimization surveying rapidly acquired a multinational character. By the end of 1975, victimization surveys had been carried out, either by academic researchers or by government or private research organizations, in Canada, Australia, Sweden, Norway, Denmark, Finland, Switzerland, England, Holland, West Germany and Belgium.[2] For a variety of reasons, it is too early to attempt to make cross-national comparisons of crime or victimization rates on the basis of these survey data; indeed, it may never be realistic to undertake such comparisons, any more than it is now realistic to compare rates of police-recorded crime in different countries. Taken together, however, the findings of these surveys are of considerable interest, not merely for the similar patterns of crime, victimization and societal reaction that several of them reveal, but for the light that they shed on problems inherent in the victimization survey method itself.

In view of the size of the investment to date in the victimization survey technique, it is perhaps surprising that very little research has so far been done on a simple but crucial question, to wit: Does the technique actually work? More specifically, to what extent can survey respondents remember incidents—

even fairly recent ones—in which crimes were committed against them? If they do remember such incidents, how accurately and precisely will they remember *when* the incidents took place? Will they tell a survey interviewer about them? Will they describe the incidents accurately—and will their descriptions generally be the same as (or at least be compatible or reconcilable with) those that would be given by the police and/or the courts? To what extent will respondents report spurious incidents of victimization—through fantasy, or through misinterpretation of the situation or misunderstanding of the criminal law?

It was primarily to investigate these and other methodological questions that I and my colleagues Hazel Genn and David Dodd carried out a victimization survey in London in 1973.[3] When our research was first planned, at the beginning of 1971, we knew of only one small study[4] that had been done on the crucial question of respondents' recall of offenses. One part of our project, therefore, involved a "reverse record check." We selected (from metropolitan police records) a sample of persons in three Inner London areas who had reported to the police an incident involving an alleged offense occurring within the fifteen months preceding our survey. We then interviewed those persons, in order to see how many of them would mention the incidents in question to our interviewers, and how accurately the incidents themselves would be described. This research strategy can admittedly achieve only a partial validation of the victimization survey method; it deals only with incidents that were reported to the police, and that (in part for that reason) may be more readily recalled and disclosed to an interviewer than incidents of which the police were not notified. But as a practical matter it would have been difficult, if not impossible, for us to have selected a sample of victims of unreported incidents; and in view of the limited information available even about reported ones, we felt that a study of them would be worthwhile.

After we began our research, results from pilot studies[5] carried out in connection with the Census Bureau project mentioned earlier became available to us. These pilot studies, which also involved reverse record checks, provided a valuable comparison with our own work. But it was unclear how far the results of these studies would be valid in the rather different conditions applying to surveys on crime in England; and in any case, as we shall see, their findings on certain crucial issues differed markedly from our own.

The first objective of our research, then, was methodological: we were concerned to investigate the feasibility of using social survey methods to measure crime. But the victimization survey need not be—and in our view should not be—thought of merely as a measuring instrument. In addition, such surveys can be used to obtain a wide range of information relating crime and societal reaction to it, and to develop and test a variety of criminological theories. In addition to a sample of known victims, therefore, we interviewed random samples of adults living in our three London areas and collected data on their perceptions and definitions of crime and their attitudes to the criminal justice system, as well as information on their experiences as victims. Finally, we attempted a comparison between survey-estimated rates of crime in the three areas and rates computed from police statistics of recorded crime in those areas. Criminologists in England have relied to an even greater degree than their colleagues in the United States on the picture of crime and criminals that emerges from official statistics compiled by the police and other agencies of the criminal justice system. So far as offenders are concerned, this "official" picture has to some extent been supplemented, if not displaced, by the self-report studies carried out in recent years by Belson, West and others.[6] But the description of offenses in England has been (and still is) largely based entirely on the statistics of "indictable offenses known to the police" compiled from police returns and published by the Home Office in the annual *Criminal Statistics for England and Wales.*[7] It was thus important, in our view, to try to discover something about the accuracy or inaccuracy of those statistics and to consider the implications of the "dark figure" of unrecorded crime for the understanding of crime and societal reaction to crime in England.

Even here, however, much of our work was methodological and exploratory in character: in particular, we found ourselves having to grapple with a number of problems of estimation and adjustment (discussed more fully below) in our attempts to calculate crime and victimization rates for our three survey areas. It is important to note, moreover, that those three areas were deliberately chosen so as to provide contrasts in certain respects; they were not selected at random. *The reader is warned, therefore, against any attempt to make inferences, from our data, about the prevalence of crime in London as a whole.* We think that, taken together, our three areas are probably not untypical of Inner London. But we have no way, at present, of proving this; and, in any case, our main concern was with differences between our survey areas and not with those areas' typicality or representativeness of London as a whole. As we shall see, our findings are not dissimilar in certain respects from those of victimization surveys in the United States and in other countries; at a minimum, we feel that we managed to identify a number of common problems to be resolved by researchers using this technique in the future.

SURVEY AREAS AND SAMPLES

The choice of London as a survey site presents any researcher with a staggering selection of contrasting areas from which to choose his subject population. The criteria on which our own final choice was based were as follows. First, since part of our sample was to be drawn from police records of known victims, it was necessary to use police subdivisions as sampling areas, rather than, for example, local authority ward boundaries (which do not, in general, coincide with police areas). This was also necessary if police-recorded crime rates were to be compared with estimates based on our survey (given that a sample of the whole of the Metropolitan Police District, i.e., Greater London, was not feasible). Second, we thought that in order to insure that a random sample of the population of each area would yield a reasonable number of victims, we should choose police subdivisions in which relatively high rates of victimization might be expected–i.e., those with relatively high recorded crime rates.[8] Finally, in order to get an idea of factors associated with victimization, and to study differences in attitudes and in definitions and perceptions of crime, we were anxious to find areas that differed markedly from each other, especially in respect of social status and ethnicity. On the basis of these criteria, we selected one police subdivision from each of the three London boroughs of Lambeth, Hackney and Kensington. For the benefit of readers unfamiliar with London, a brief description of each area follows.

Brixton

The area to which we refer as "Brixton" is located in what is now known as the London Borough of Lambeth, in South London. Though I shall for convenience use the name "Brixton" to refer to the whole of this police subdivisional area, that name is popularly reserved, by residents of the area, for the central commercial district surrounding the Brixton railway station. This central district (and its neighboring residential area) has, since the 1950s, increasingly become one of West Indian settlement; it now constitutes one of the oldest and most stable West Indian communities in Britain. The majority of these black[9] immigrant families live in crowded multioccupation dwellings, some of which were at one time the large and fashionable residences of a bygone wealthier white population. Although the area can in no way be called a ghetto in the American sense of that term, the cultural influence of the West Indians (most of whom are of Jamaican origin) can readily be observed; in all, black immigrants account for about 15 percent of the resident population, or for about 13,000 of the 85,000 persons living there according to the 1971 census. Around the central area of Brixton, there are areas of better housing, inhabitated by middle class whites and some more well-to-do West Indians. The area as a whole, therefore, is relatively heterogeneous as London districts go, in both ethnic and social class terms.

Hackney

Our second area, in the London Borough of Hackney, was chosen because, despite recent population change, it still retains many of the cultural and social characteristics traditionally associated with London's East End.[10] It is primarily a working class residential district, with a high percentage of public housing; though there are a number of relatively new high rise housing developments, there are also several prewar estates, typically in poor physical condition, in which the poorest families (including some regarded as "problem" families by the local welfare authorities) are kept. Though the area contains a relatively stable core of white working class residents, it has recently had an influx of West Indian and African immigrants, who in 1971 constituted about 8 percent of the area's 62,000 population.

Kensington

Our third survey area is located in the fashionable and expensive borough of Kensington, which lies to the west and southwest of Hyde Park. The area's restaurants and shops attract large numbers of tourists and other visitors; the bulk of its permanent residents constitute a stable and relatively homogeneous upper middle and middle class community whose lifestyles and experiences would, we assumed, contrast strongly with those of residents in our other two areas. The area presents problems for survey research, however, since it also contains the Earl's Court "bed-sitter belt" in which the large Victorian houses have been subdivided to provide accommodation for a mixture of students, short-term foreign visitors and other transients. Perhaps the most striking fact about the demography of the area is that (according to the 1971 census) no less than 40 percent of the 52,000 residents were single, widowed or divorced females.

In each of these three areas, we selected three independent samples. The first—which will be referred to as the main victim (MV) sample—consisted of persons who had reported to the police an incident involving an assault, burglary or theft (including car theft) during the first ten months of 1972.[11] Our fieldwork was conducted at the beginning of 1973; respondents were asked about incidents that might have happened to them during the preceding twelve months. The objective of our reverse record check was thus to see how many of the "target" incidents on which we had information would be mentioned by the MV sample. The second sample—designated the telescope (T) sample—consisted of a small number of persons who had reported incidents to the police in the months October-December 1971. These cases were included in order to see what proportion incorrectly reported that their incidents had occurred during the year 1972—that is, to investigate the phenomenon known as "time telescoping." The third and largest sample consisted of persons chosen at random from the electoral registers in our three survey areas; I shall refer to it as the register (R) sample.

This sampling plan raised several methodological problems, not the least of which was the unsatisfactory nature of the electoral register as a sampling frame. The register of course excludes those who, by reason of nationality or length of residence, are not qualified to vote; though updated annually, it also includes the names of those who have since moved from their registered addresses. In Britain as a whole this last group is about 15 percent of the registered population;[12] in relatively small urban areas like the ones where we conducted our survey, the figure is undoubtedly higher. It was necessary for us to use the electoral register, however, since it was the only practicable sampling frame from which we could obtain names and addresses of individuals; we needed this information since we had the names and addresses of our known victims (i.e., the MV and T samples), and we did not want our interviewers to be able to distinguish the latter group of cases from the rest of the sample. It is important to note that, in fact, the interviewers did not know that any of their cases had been victims of crime; they were told that all of their cases had been selected from the electoral register, in order to avoid possible biasses in the reverse record check.[13]

The overall response rate for the survey was just under 41 percent, being 45 percent for the R sample and 35 percent for the MV and T samples combined. The main reason for nonresponse in all three survey areas was that respondents were either known to have moved away or could not be contacted by interviewers (after five callbacks) at the designated address; the refusal rate was less than 9 percent. In common with other researchers,[14] we had especially great difficulty in locating persons originally identified from police records as being victims of assault or personal theft; whether this is because such persons are extremely mobile, or because of inaccuracies in the records, we do not know. So far as we could judge, nonresponse did not appear to produce any gross bias in terms of age, sex or area of residence. There is some evidence that in our sample length of residence was negatively associated with victimization; thus, the data on our R sample probably understate victimization rates, especially in Kensington.

RESULTS OF THE REVERSE RECORD CHECK

Our final MV sample included 241 persons who had reported offenses committed against them to the metropolitan police in the period January 1 to October 31, 1972. Overall results for the reporting by this sample of the "target" incidents on which we had information are summarized in Table 3-1. It will be seen from this table that over 90 percent of the sample definitely mentioned the target incident during their interviews. Since we had information from police records not only on the date and type of the offense, but also (in

Table 3-1. Recall and Reporting of Target Incidents in the MV Sample*

Recall Accuracy	*Number*	*Percent*
Reported Accurately (within month of actual occurrence)	123	51.9
Telescoped Forward	51	21.5
Telescoped Backward	45	19.0
Not Reported	18	7.6
Total	237	100.0

*Excludes four cases which could not be classified.

Source: Computed from the London survey data collected by the author in 1973.

most cases) on the time and place at which the incident took place and was reported, the offender (where apprehended), and a description and value of any property involved, the matching of respondents' accounts and police records was seldom a problem. There were only four cases in which the respondent mentioned an incident of the type that we knew he had reported to the police, but was too vague about either the date of the incident or its nature to enable us to make a definite identification; these cases have been excluded from Table 3-1, though in fact we felt that in three of the four the "target" incident had probably been recalled.

If the recall and reporting to interviewers of "target" incidents are considered on an "all or nothing" basis—that is, without regard to the accuracy with which respondents placed the events in time—our Hackney residents did significantly worse than those in the other two areas, mentioning only 84 percent of their target incidents, against 96 percent for the other two areas. There were also some differences among types of offense. Burglaries were the most consistently reported, with over 97 percent being mentioned to interviewers; this is consistent with the findings of the Census Bureau's pretests in Washington, Baltimore and San Jose,[15] and suggests clearly that this type of crime is highly salient in the minds of most respondents.[16] In contrast to the Census Bureau's three studies, however, we did *not* find much lower rates for assaults: in fact, the proportions of assault and theft (other than burglary) reported to our interviewers was about the same, at about 89 percent.[17]

Table 3-2 shows that there was a slight decline in the percentage of "target" incidents reported to interviewers as the length of time between the incident and the interview increased; 12 percent of the incidents occurring in the first half of the reference period were not mentioned, compared with about 4 percent in the second half.[18]

We were unable to find more than a few attributes that seemed to

Table 3-2. Recall and Reporting of Target Incidents by Time Period in the MV Sample

Time Period	*Reported*	*Not Reported*	*Total*	*Percent Reported*
January 1 - February 20	29	4	33	87.5
February 21 - April 11	29	4	33	87.9
April 12 - June 1	37	5	42	88.1
June 2 - July 22	45	2	47	95.7
July 23 - September 11	42	1	43	97.7
September 12 - October 31	37	2	39	94.9
Total	219	18	237	92.4

Source: Computed from the London survey data collected by the author in 1973.

discriminate in any meaningful way between those respondents who did recall and report to interviewers their "target" incidents and those who did not. Thus there was no evidence of a consistent association between nonreporting and race, sex, marital status or length of residence; nor was there any consistent relationship with age, though the proportion not reporting among those aged sixty-one and over was twice as high as in the sample as a whole. Nor were there any consistent or significant relations between reporting of "target" incidents and any of the attitudinal or perceptual questions that we asked concerning the respondent's local neighborhood, the prevalence of crime in that area, safety of the streets, etc. Bearing in mind the significantly lower reporting rate in Hackney, and the social class composition of that area's residents, it might be expected that social class by itself would be associated with nonreporting, but in fact our data provide scant support for that conclusion. There are suggestions in the data that reporting of "target" incidents is associated with level of educational attainment; those who finished their education before or at the secondary school-leaving age were twice as likely not to mention "target" incidents as those who left after the school-leaving (minimum) age.[19] This association (which did not, in our sample, attain statistical significance) is consistent with the hypothesis that recall and reporting of incidents is in part a function of the verbal fluency needed to complete a fairly long and complicated interview that sometimes required a fair amount of relatively abstract conceptualization on the part of respondents.[20] But if there is such an effect it cannot—in our data—be a very strong one; it appears to be very heavily overlaid by the results of simple memory failure, operating in a more or less random fashion among different types of respondent.

This conclusion is supported by a comparison of those incidents that were not reported with those that were: on the information available to us from police records, there was little to distinguish the two groups. (For example, those who did had mentioned their "target" incidents were just as likely to mention *other* incidents that had happened to them during the preceding year—in one case, no fewer than nine—as the rest of the sample.) In only one case did it seem clear, on the facts available to us, that the nonreporting of an incident was due to inhibition on the part of the respondent rather than to forgetting. In this case, the respondent was an elderly woman; her daughter had been accused of attempting to murder her, though the charge was later reduced to one of assault. We discovered later that (contrary to our instructions to interviewers) the daughter had been present during the interview with her mother.

ACCURACY OF TIME PLACEMENT OF INCIDENTS

Given that most of our MV sample remembered, and reported to our interviewers, the fact that their "target" incident had occurred, how accurately were they able to say *when* that incident had happened? Before considering this question, it is well to note that the precision of our MV sample's responses here was not very great. In fact, about 60 percent of the sample could apparently give only the month in which the incident had occurred, and could not or did not venture to give a date within that month (often, when they did, it turned out to be wrong). The proportion of the sample recalling "target" incidents as occurring in the correct month was slightly higher in the second half of the reference period than in the first; the difference was not significant, however. On balance, there were a few more incidents "telescoped" forward (that is, reported as having occurred later than in fact they did) than backward; the difference was slight, however.

For each target incident reported to our interviewers, we calculated the number of days between the date of the incident according to police records and the date given by the respondent in the interview (using the middle of the month when no more precise date was mentioned); this variable was signed positive for forward-telescoped cases. Over the sample as a whole, the mean value of this algebraic difference variable was +15.75 days, indicating a moderate amount of net forward telescoping. It would be natural to expect that the (absolute) value of this variable would increase as the time between the "target" incident and the interview increased; in fact, however, the association between the two time periods was only moderate ($r = +0.138$, just significant at the 5 percent level). Further analysis suggested, however, that this was due to the existence of two groups of repondents: first, a group of "rememberers" whose recollections were generally accurate no matter how much earlier the incident had occurred, and, second, a group of "not-so-good rememberers" for whom accuracy of time placement was more strongly dependent on the time elapsed since the incident took place (for the latter group, $r = +0.308$ correlating days' worth of inaccuracy with days between incident and interview).

Very few attributes, either of the target incidents or of the respondents, were significantly associated with accuracy or inaccuracy of time placement. The dating of incidents was most accurate for burglaries and assaults, least accurate for thefts; beyond that, no significant associations emerged. It would thus appear that inaccuracy of recall and reporting, like complete failure of recall or reporting, can be regarded as a more or less random phenomenon, which is unlikely by itself to introduce any serious biasses into between-group estimates from victimization survey data.

This is not to say, of course, that telescoping is not a phenomenon to be contended with when making population estimates from sample survey data. I have already noted that the net effect of telescoping in our sample was in a forward direction (i.e., incidents were reported as having happened later than in fact they did). Such a net effect will obviously tend to inflate survey estimates of victimization rates at the beginning of the reference period (unless bounding or some other technique is used to prevent this). The relative error introduced into estimates for this reason will depend on many things (in particular, the length of the reference period[21]); such error may well be more than offset by nonreporting of incidents that did happen within the reference period—e.g., through forgetting or backward telescoping out of the reference period. (This appears to be the case, even with the relatively high proportion of reported target incidents mentioned by our sample; it would almost certainly be true if nonreporting were as high as that suggested by the Census Bureau's pilot studies.[22]) Even if the two types of response errors did effectively cancel each other out so far as aggregate rates of victimization are concerned, they are likely to lead to some distortion of the pattern of victimization reported. More salient incidents (e.g., burglary, serious assault) are apparently more likely to be recalled and mentioned to interviewers than petty incidents of theft or damage.

Two other pieces of evidence from our survey on the issue of telescoping may be mentioned. The first relates to the T sample of cases (N = 55) who were known to have reported incidents to the police in the period October-December 1971—that is, in the three months preceding the beginning of our reference period. One of these cases had to be excluded, since we could not be sure whether or not the target incident had been reported;[23] of the remaining fifty-four cases, thirty, or about 56 percent, recalled the target incidents and reported them correctly (as not having occurred within the reference period). Ten, or 19 percent, recalled them as having occurred some time in 1972; these cases thus represent forward external telescoping. One respondent mentioned the incident, but placed it earlier than in fact it happened; the remaining thirteen (or 24 percent) did not mention their incidents at all. In all, therefore, about one in five of this group incorrectly reported their incidents as having happened within the survey reference period.

Finally, a comparison of the monthly distribution of the R sample's incidents with that of all indictable offenses recorded by the metropolitan police showed that survey-reported incidents tended to cluster in the second half of the year—57 percent against 49 percent. No such clustering appeared, however, with respect to the extra offenses (i.e., other than the target offenses) reported by the MV and T samples. It seems likely, therefore, that the apparent forward shift in the R sample's incidents is mainly due to a higher degree of nonreporting of incidents in the earlier months of the reference period.

VICTIMIZATION IN THE R SAMPLE

Our final R sample contained 545 respondents; subject to the point made earlier about in- and outmobility, comparison of the sample with census data suggested that the sample was broadly representative, in terms of basic demographic characteristics, of the resident populations aged eighteen and over in our three areas.

Of these 545 persons, no less than 244, or just under 45 percent, reported (in answer to the series of screening questions on our questionnaire) that they had personally experienced, within the preceding twelve months, one or more incidents that appeared to them to fit the descriptions of crimes mentioned in the screening questions.[24] The total number of incidents mentioned was approximately 582. This total is necessarily somewhat inexact, since a small number of respondents claimed to have been victims of a particular type of crime—usually relatively minor theft or damage to property—on many different occasions during the preceding year, but could give no closer estimate of the number than "every week" or "at least once a month." In such cases the maximum number of incidents recorded was nine;[25] the total of 582 incidents is thus almost certainly an underestimate.

Table 3-3, which is based on responses to the screening questions, gives the total numbers of incidents of different types reported by respondents in the three areas. It will be seen from this table that about one-quarter of the things mentioned in all three areas fell within a category which could be classified as "personal violence": that is, they involved either actual assaults, attempted assaults or threats of violence, or theft from the person (which in some cases would have amounted to robbery[26]). By way of comparison, such crimes accounted for less than 5 percent of all of the indictable offenses recorded by the metropolitan police in 1972.

An examination of the details of these "violent" offenses (as recorded in the crime incident forms completed by interviewers) shows, however, that many of them were very trivial by any reasonable standard and that the amount of serious violence experienced by our sample was extremely small. Of the eighty-three incidents classified (by us) as involving offenses of assault or robbery, no less than forty-eight—or 58 percent—involved only attempted or threatened violence, rather than the actual use of it. None of the eleven robberies involved anything described by the respondents as actual physical injury; the same was true for the twenty-five incidents of theft from the person, most of which were purse snatchings. Of the thirty-five actual assaults—as distinct from the merely attempted or threatened ones—eleven cases were said to involve physical injury; but in only two of these cases was the injury more serious than bruises, abrasions or cuts. Only four cases involved the use of a weapon other than the offender's fists or feet; only seven persons said they required medical attention as a result of violent crime, and of these only three were required to stay in hospitals over one day. The offenses against property reported by our respondents diverge less sharply from the pattern that one might expect from police statistics: even so, very many involved only small amounts of loss.[27] About one-sixth of the total involved attempted theft only; of those incidents in which there was said to be some property taken or damaged, only about 11 percent were said to involve property worth more than £50.

Many problems of analysis and interpretation are raised by our data. Of these problems I shall mention three that seem to me to have special methodological

Table 3-3. Incidents Reported as Having Occurred Within the Preceding Year in Three Survey Areas (based on R sample responses to screening questions)

Type of Crime	*Area of London*							
	Brixton		*Hackney*		*Kensington*		*Total*	
	Number	*Percent*	*Number*	*Percent*	*Number*	*Percent*	*Number*	*Percent*
Assaults	15	7.3	13	8.5	7	3.1	35	6.0
Attempted and Threatened Assault	25	21.1	16	10.5	30	13.5	71	12.2
Theft from Person	16	7.8	13	8.5	15	6.7	44	7.6
Burglary and Attempts	11	5.3	20	13.1	29	13.0	60	10.3
Thefts in Dwelling	13	6.3	7	4.6	12	5.4	32	5.5
Thefts of, or from, Motor Vehicles	39	18.9	23	15.0	36	16.1	98	16.8
Other Thefts	64	31.1	33	21.6	85	38.1	182	31.3
Damage to Property	23	11.2	28	18.5	9	4.0	60	10.3
TOTAL	206	100.0	153	100.0	223	100.0	582	100.0

Source: Computed from the London survey data collected by the author in 1973.

importance; each has been encountered in other victimization surveys, including the National Crime Panel.

The first of these concerns the so-called "series" offenses mentioned above: i.e., cases in which the respondent stated that he had experienced a number of incidents of a particular type, but could not (or would not) give details of particular instances–often because they were simply too numerous for him to remember. Cases of this kind lead to obvious difficulties in calculating victimization rates or measuring the incidence of crime. The solution to this problem adopted in the National Crime Panel's reports to date[28]–simply to exclude series incidents from published victimization rates–seems to me to be no solution at all: the fact that a respondent cannot give sufficiently precise details (especially details of time and place) concerning a number of incidents does not show that the incidents in question did not happen. But it is also true that *some* cases of this kind may be best understood, not as involving a large number of discrete incidents, but as indicating a more or less persistent or chronic condition of intimidation, harassment or what have you: the wife constantly terrorized by a drunken husband, the tenant at the mercy of an unscrupulous landlord, or the child regularly bullied into giving up his lunch money would be examples. In such cases, the significant element is surely not this or that particular incident–or even an aggregate of incidents–but the continuing state that periodically gives rise to those incidents: the appropriate measure is one of prevalence, not of incidence.[29]

It must be pointed out that this is not always the case when series of incidents are reported. The series may go on only for a relatively short period of time, as happened with a man in our sample whose car, left parked in the street outside his home in Brixton, was regularly damaged by neighborhood vandals over a period of three months or so. Moreover, situations of chronic intimidation may exist without any incidents involving actual victimization–e.g., a bullying husband may not need to inflict actual violence on his hapless wife. The borderline is not, in any case, a clear one. In our sample, one West Indian woman living in Hackney reported nine separate incidents involving theft, damage to her apartment, assault (including attempted poisoning), indecent assault and threats. She was able to attach at least approximate dates to most of these incidents. Yet–as further interviews made clear–they were merely small threads in the tumultuous fabric of her daily life in the slum in which she and her family were housed by the local authority. Were the separate incidents she mentioned (almost certainly, by the way, an underestimate of her actual victimization) the most important thing about her life in the preceding year, from a criminological point of view? Or should we rather, in such cases, seek to describe and explain the social state or condition giving rise to those incidents? As it happened, none of this repondent's incidents fell into the series category; but they would have done so if she had been a less articulate respondent, and perhaps they *should* have done so.

A second, and related, problem concerns the distribution of incidents in our sample. Over the sample as a whole, the mean number of victimizations of all kinds was 1.07; but, as I have mentioned, about 55 percent of the sample reported no incidents (of the kinds about which we asked) in the preceding twelve months. The distributions of numbers of incidents mentioned, of all types combined, is summarized in Table 3-4; this table, like the preceding one, is based on responses to the screening questions. Analysis of these data showed clearly that there were more "multiple victims" (and also more nonvictims) than would be expected by chance, given the mean rates of victimization in the sample; that is, there were significant differences between observed distributions, for both violent and property offenses, in all three areas, and expected numbers predicted by a mathematical Poisson distribution. A similar finding was reported by Reynolds, in his surveys in Minneapolis,[30] and in surveys of violent victimization conducted by Aromaa in Finland[31] and Wolf in Denmark;[32] it also appears to have emerged in a number of other victimization surveys in the United States, including the National Crime Panel (NCP) surveys.[33]

We experimented with several modifications of the Poisson model, in an attempt to generate theoretical distributions that would more closely match those observed in our sample. Thus, we attempted to fit the Greenwood-Yule model involving the assumption of differing degrees of "proneness";[34] in a sample like ours, this model yields expected values identical to those derived from the model proposed by Coleman and others,[35] which assumes "contagion" in the sense that each successive incident (e.g., of victimization) increases the probability of subsequent incidents for the same individual.[36] While these models gave a much better approximation to the distribution of incidents actually observed in our sample, the fit was still far from perfect; the same was true for a model assuming the existence of an "immune" group who—because of precaution taking, or whatever—had a zero probability of victimization.[37]

Finally, following an approach suggested by Coleman,[38] we attempted to pin down the concept of differential "proneness" to victimization empirically, by examining the distributions of incidents for subgroups of our sample defined by different combinations of demographic and attitudinal variables. Briefly, this approach involves trying to identify subgroups with different mean rates of victimization, such that within each subgroup the distribution of 0, 1, 2 . . . *n* incidents conforms to the simple Poisson model; if the latter condition is met, the mean and variance for each subgroup will of course be approximately identical.[39] Here too we were not particularly successful; in each case, no matter how the sample was split up, there remained one or more subgroups for which the simple Poisson model clearly would not fit.

In retrospect, I think it would be surprising if we had been able, by using any simple combination of attributes, to partition our sample into subgroups fulfilling the conditions just mentioned. Nonetheless, we were clearly able to make some progress in this direction. For example, when we split the sample

Table 3-4. Distribution of R Sample Victimization Incidents by Sample Area (based on responses to screening questions)

	Area of London							
	Brixton		*Hackney*		*Kensington*		*All Areas*	
Number of Incidents	*Number*	*Percent*	*Number*	*Percent*	*Number*	*Percent*	*Number*	*Percent*
None	101	55.5	104	58.1	93	50.5	298	54.7
1	40	22.0	40	22.3	40	21.7	120	22.0
2	13	7.1	11	6.1	32	17.4	56	10.3
3	14	7.7	18	10.1	8	4.3	40	7.3
4	6	3.3	2	1.1	3	1.6	11	2.0
5	2	1.1	3	1.7	1	0.5	6	1.1
6 or more	6	3.3	1	0.6	7	3.8	14	2.6
Total	182	100.0	179	100.0	184	100.0	545	100.0
Total Number of Incidents	208	–	151	–	223	–	582	–

Source: Computed from the London survey data collected by the author in 1973.

according to age (which in our survey, like most others, was strongly associated negatively with victimization, especially of violent offenses), we found excessive "multiple victimization" appeared to exist only among those aged twenty-six to thirty-five; for the rest of the sample, the number of "multiple victims" was no greater than would have been expected purely by chance from a Poisson process. Further analysis showed that among the twenty-six to thirty-five age groups, it was the female respondents who accounted for most of the excess of victimization; moreover, this was almost entirely due to the extremely high numbers of incidents (in one case, no less than eighteen) reported by a few West Indian females (cf. the case briefly discussed above). If those cases were excluded, the amount of "multiple victimization" in different categories of age and sex was not much greater than would have been expected by chance.

The results of this kind of analysis must obviously be treated with great caution. Nonetheless, the issue is one that clearly deserves much further study. Why do some people become victims of crime on one or more occasions, whereas others do not? To what extent is the "precipitation" of crime (e.g., through provocation) important? What are the determinants of the risk of becoming a victim, or of different types of crime? To what extent does victimization depend on the victim's having placed himself in a position of special risk (e.g., by failing to lock his house or car), and to what extent is it a function of particular locales (e.g., particular streets, housing developments, taverns) or particular jobs (e.g., policeman, nightclub bouncer)? These questions are plainly important, not only for sociological theory but for public policy.

It should also be clear that the highly skewed distribution of victimization found in our survey and others has some methodological implications for the use of survey methods in this area. For one thing, it means that much of the data collected on incidents of victimization will in fact come from a relatively small proportion of one's sample; reference to Table 3-4 will show that in our survey about 60 percent of the 582 incidents mentioned came from about 13 percent of the sample. For another, it means that the victimization rate—e.g., the mean number of victimizations per 10,000 persons—is utterly misleading as an indicator of the risk of becoming a victim; it will be far too high for the great majority, and much too low for the unfortunate minority of "multiple victims." Finally, the extreme variability of the distribution of victimization means that sampling errors will necessarily tend to be relatively large. All of these problems are illustrated, with a vengeance, by the current National Crime Panel surveys.

One possible explanation of the generally observed distributions of multiple victimization is, of course, response bias: it may simply be that there are some respondents who remember (or invent) and report large numbers of incidents, which are forgotten (or repressed) by others. We found no evidence of this in our own sample;[40] nonetheless, it cannot be ruled out as constituting at least a part of the explanation. It brings me, moreover, to the third major methodological issue illustrated by our survey (and several others): this concerns the problem of differential *definition* of situations by particular groups of respondents.

The problem can be illustrated by the data in Table 3-3 above. It will be seen from that table that over 80 percent of the assaults reported by the (largely middle class) respondents in Kensington were in fact merely threats or attempts; in contrast, attempted and threatened assaults constitute only 55 percent of all assaults in the (almost entirely working class) area of Hackney, and only 62 percent in the more mixed area (in both racial and social class terms) of Brixton. The overall *rates* of reported assault are broadly similar in the three survey areas; but the *proportions* of actual as opposed to attempted or threatened assault are quite different. Very similar relationships are evident in the National Crime Panel data published to date, across categories of race and family income.[41] The same pattern has also been observed in surveys of violent victimization in the Nordic countries.[42]

There are at least two possible explanations for this finding.[43] On the one hand, the data may reflect real differences in different groups' experiences and in their ways of coping with potentially violent situations. It may, for example, be that our Kensington respondents were better at ignoring such situations, or at talking their way out of them, or at walking (or running) away from them; or that those who threatened them were less determined to turn their threats into action. Though our data on this point are scanty, they do suggest this possibility: there were several cases of attempted assault in Kensington in which the respondent stated that he or she avoided trouble by physically removing himself or herself from the situation. No such account was mentioned in Brixton or Hackney. In those two areas, a much more common response to the threat of violence was by some form of self-help, as the following quotation indicates: "Three of those black guys came up to me in the street [in Brixton] one night. They tried to attack me but I hit them and they ran off." Similarly, in the National Crime Panel data there are marked differences between blacks and whites, and across income levels, in the proportions of assaults that are aggravated rather than simple, or actual rather than merely attempted:[44] these may reflect subcultural norms relating to the use of violence in response to provocation or to a tendency to carry weapons.

It seems probable, however, that these patterns of reported victimization are in part the result of response bias: that is, they are partly due to the fact that certain groups (e.g., middle class persons, whites) define as "assault" certain actions or situations that are not defined as "assault" by other groups (e.g., lower class persons, blacks). Thus, when asked: In the past year, did anyone threaten you in any way with violence of any kind?, our Brixton and Hackney respondents might often have failed to recall such incidents; even if they did recall them, they might not have regarded them as coming within the scope of the concept of "being threatened with violence." Consider the situation in which an argument between acquaintances has led to threats of fisticuffs (or even an exchange of blows); even if asked at the time, the participants might sincerely deny that anything akin to an "assault" or "violence" had taken place, simply because they regarded what happened as having been within culturally permissible limits—e.g., because it did not involve unprovoked aggression (in their terms) or because no stranger was involved.[45] Even if one participant did at the time regard the other's actions as constituting an "assault" or a "threat," he might retrospectively redefine the incident in the light of later events—e.g., if he won the fight; in either case he would be unlikely to mention it later, in response to an interviewer's question about "threats of violence."

In our survey we attempted to investigate variations in the definition of "violence" by asking our respondents' views about a set of hypothetical situations involving violent behavior. These hypothetical incidents all involved some element of provocation (e.g., an argument in a cafe, an intruder in the home, one person's spreading malicious rumors about another); the violent responses described varied from blows with fists to serious injury caused by use of a blunt instrument. In each case, respondents were asked to say whether they approved or disapproved of the hypothetical violent actor's behavior. They were also asked what they thought the actor was feeling (admittedly a bad term); responses were classified according to whether they mentioned fear, anger or some other emotional state, or whether they regarded the violence as justified in the situation (e.g., "He had a right to").

We found generally consistent differences between respondents in different social classes (and thus between survey areas) on both of these measures. Middle and upper class persons were more likely to disapprove of the violent behavior, and less likely to regard it as justified, than were working class persons. These differences are consistent with the view that our middle class respondents had a lower "threshold" in relation to the definition of impermissible violence; this in turn suggests that they would be more likely to see certain situations as "assaults" or "threats" than working class persons in the same situation.

If such definitional bias does indeed exist, and if it is systematically related to social class, race, age, sex or any other important attribute of the population, it clearly poses a serious problem for victimization researchers. In principle, if the direction and magnitude of such biases were known, it would be possible to ratio-adjust survey estimates to compensate for them, just as one now adjusts to compensate for nonresponse. But it is plain that we now know far too little about subcultural or other nonidiosyncratic variation in the definition of situations involving criminal behavior (and in related matters such as the differential salience of those situations) to undertake to make adjustments of that kind. Albert Biderman has suggested an approach that may help to overcome this problem: briefly, this involves asking respondents about injury that they might have sustained, rather than about norm-defined things like assault.[46] Even this approach can only be of limited use, however, since the great majority of incidents involving actual assault, and, of course, all of those involving merely threats or attempts, do not result in any kind of injury.

COMPARING POLICE AND SURVEY STATISTICS

Making comparisons between estimates of crime from victimization surveys and police statistics raises a whole host of further problems. These problems are especially acute when (as in our London survey) the comparisons relate to relatively small urban areas, since many adjustments must be made to both survey data and police statistics in order to render the comparison meaningful.

Thus, it was necessary for us to remove from the police statistics "victimless" crimes (such as receiving stolen property) and crimes committed against businesses; this was easy to do for most types of crime, but had to be estimated for some categories of theft. Moreover, we had to make allowance for crimes included in the police statistics for our areas that had been committed against nonresidents of the area; such incidents accounted for about 17 percent of all of the recorded crime in Kensington in 1972. It was also necessary to make some allowance for recorded crimes against persons under eighteen and for crimes against persons not on the electoral register, since neither of these groups would have been included in our sample.

On the other hand, we had to deflate our survey estimates to remove incidents reported by residents of our three areas that had occurred elsewhere and those incidents that would probably have been regarded by the police as nonindictable (and would thus not have been included in the statistics of known crimes); this last adjustment meant removing from our survey data the great bulk of offenses of damage to property and almost all of the attempted and threatened assaults. Finally, we had to make an adjustment for "household" offenses like burglary and car theft, to take account of the numbers of adult members of the victimized households. In theory, we should have made further adjustments to take into account nonrecall of incidents and "telescoping" and to allow for inmigration and outmigration during the reference period; in practice, we were forced to assume that these two pairs of factors simply canceled out. Taken together, these adjustments to our survey data reduced the number of incidents used to calculate crime rates (for the resident adult populations of the three areas) by approximately one-third.[47]

These adjustments leave us with an estimate of the numbers of assaults, robberies, thefts from the person, burglaries and thefts in dwellings, thefts of and from motor vehicles, other personal thefts, and serious offenses of damage to property committed in our three survey areas against adult residents of those areas in 1972, and with police statistics relating to that same universe of crime. The comparison of these two estimates is made in Table 3-5, which also gives ratios of survey-estimated crime to police-recorded crime in the three areas.

It will be seen that in all areas, for all types of crime, the numbers estimated on the basis of our survey data are greatly in excess of the numbers recorded: for

Table 3-5. Comparison of Survey-estimated Crimes in 1972 and Adjusted Numbers of Crimes Recorded by Police in Three Areas (based on R sample adjusted data)

	Brixton			Hackney			Kensington		
Crime	*Survey*	*Police*	*Ratio*	*Survey*	*Police*	*Ratio*	*Survey*	*Police*	*Ratio*
Assaults, Robbery and Theft from Person	8,700	509	17.2	5,900	188	31.3	4,900	164	29.9
Burglary, Theft in Dwellings	6,000	1,224	4.9	6,100	611	10.1	7,215	2,800	2.6
Thefts of and from Motor Vehicles	9,400	1,222	7.7	4,600	720	6.4	5,400	964	5.6
Other Thefts	18,800	468	40.2	7,200	135	53.1	19,800	347	57.2
Other Crimes (including damage of 20 and over)	1,700	164	10.3	1,300	63	20.3	1,300	177	7.3
Totals	44,700	3,589	12.5	25,100	1,717	14.6	38,700	4,469	8.6
Estimated Population aged 18+		61,176			45,848			47,415	

Source: Computed from London survey data collected by the author in 1973.

all three areas combined, the overall ratio is about eleven to one. It is less in the case of burglaries (about 4.2 to 1); but in the case of offenses against the person, and other thefts, the disparity between the two sets of figures is enormous by any criterion. Given the magnitude of these differences, it should be clear that only the most drastic of adjustments—for which we had absolutely no justification—would be needed to bring the two estimates even approximately into line; even if we assume that because of sampling fluctuations our survey estimates are at the lower limit of the 95 percent confidence interval, the overall ratio between survey and police figures would still be in excess of eight to one.[48]

Respondents who had mentioned incidents to our interviewers were asked if they had reported those incidents to the police.[49] On the basis of replies to this question, we estimated that the police had probably been notified (not always by the respondent himself) of about 35 percent of the incidents on which Table 3-5 is based; the percentage was slightly higher in Kensington and somewhat lower in Brixton and Hackney. There were also variations by type of offense: over half of the burglaries were said to have been reported to the police, compared with about 30 percent of the assaults and 20 percent of thefts and other offenses.

Nonreporting to the police is, of course, a part of the explanation of the differences between survey and police figures shown in Table 3-5. But, in common with other researchers,[50] we found that nonreporting by victims could not explain the whole of the difference. The rest must thus be due to the joint effects of (1) redefinition by the police of reported incidents as not involving a (recordable) crime, and (2) the nonrecording, for whatever reason, of those incidents that were defined by the police as (recordable) crimes. Indeed, it appeared from our data that of all of the incidents of which the police might have been notified in 1972, only about a third appear to have wound up in the police statistics.

It is important to emphasize, I think, that there are many good reasons why this should be the case. As mentioned earlier, British police statistics are relatively free of the kind of "readjustment" notoriously common in the United States. But they are governed by an organizational imperative that is central to the role of any police agency—namely, the need to define incidents in relation to evidence that would support a criminal prosecution. Very often this evidence is minimal or nonexistent, even in an incident that seems (to the victim, and even to the police) to involve a crime; burglaries without physical "breaking" into the premises would be an example.[51] Or again, it may be that the investigating officer does not believe the complainant's story, or that he uncovers other evidence that would support quite a different view of the facts. Even more importantly, it may be that the incident is satisfactorily resolved by the officer answering the call, and that prosecution (and thus recording of the incident for statistical purposes) would be pointless; many family disputes fall into this category. Finally, even if the incident is provisionally accepted, and recorded, as one involving a crime, it may subsequently be written off as "no crime" for statistical purposes if the injured party asks to have the charge dropped or simply refuses to give evidence. Again, many assaults—especially between acquaintances and family members—fall into this category. We were in fact informed by the metropolitan police that, in 1972, no less than 28 percent of the crimes initially recorded by the stations in Brixton and Hackney, and 18 percent of those recorded in Kensington, were subsequently written off in this way.[52]

Further research on these matters is badly needed in England, not merely for the light that it would throw on police recordkeeping practices, but also for the understanding of the decisionmaking processes involved in the handling of crime incidents by both police and public.[53] Meanwhile, it is important to emphasize the consequences of the very large "dark figure" of unrecorded crime that our findings indicate. If those findings are correct—and I think that, if anything, they are conservative on this point—then only a very small fraction of all of the crime that occurs in any year, and that *could* be recorded in the official statistics, will eventually wind up there. Most of the nonrecorded crime will of course be of a very trivial kind. Nonetheless, a lot of recorded crime in England is also comparatively unserious.[54] It follows that the official statistics of crime are extremely susceptible even to very small changes in the proportions of incidents that are perceived, defined as crime, reported to the police, defined by them as crimes and written down in the appropriate place. Even in the case of burglaries and thefts from dwellings, where the ratio of survey to police estimates suggests that the "dark figure" of unrecorded crime is relatively low, it still appears that only about one offense in five is recorded. If this is so, then a 5 percent increase in the *proportion* of incidents recorded would by itself lead to an increase of over 20 percent in the *numbers* recorded, which is more than enough to give the impression of a "crime wave."

SOME CONCLUSIONS

Our London survey illustrates, I think, a number of important issues confronting victimization researchers in the second decade of this new method's use. So far as the recall and reporting to interviewers of incidents are concerned, the results of our reverse record check are encouraging. We can, of course, only speculate as to the reasons for the difference between our results and those obtained by the Census Bureau researchers in the Washington, Baltimore and San Jose pretests, but there are at least four things that may help to explain the much higher proportions of target incidents (especially of assault and theft) reported by our MV sample. First, we may well have had a much "better" sample—either of more salient incidents or of responsive respondents—than those used in the Census Bureau pretests; we have no data that would suggest that this was true, but it obviously cannot be ruled out as a possibility. Second, our interviews lasted on the average just over an hour; the screening questions, which came at the end of the interview, followed a variety of other questions about various aspects of crime, which may have made respondents more likely to remember things that had happened to them. By contrast, in most of the Census Bureau pretest interviews, the screening questions must have been asked after about ten minutes. Third, it seems to me that the method that we used to introduce our screening questions–which involved getting respondents to "bracket" the reference period in their minds and to recall other salient dates (e.g., birthdays, job changes, vacations) within that period–helped them to remember more, and more accurately, than they would have done otherwise. Finally, it may be–since crime is rarer even in Inner London than in much of the United States–that incidents involving criminal victimization stood out more clearly in our respondents' minds than in the minds of their American counterparts. Whatever the explanation may be, it needs to be remembered that our MV and T samples were all known to have reported at least one incident to the police within the reference period; recall and reporting rates would undoubtedly have been lower for offenses that had not been reported to the police. Those incidents are thus perhaps even more common than their numbers (in our R sample data) suggest.

The other three issues discussed in this chapter–concerning series offenses, the distribution of multiple victimization and the differential definition of incidents–are in my view of an entirely different order. They are not merely methodological problems of this kind of survey research, to be overcome in the interests of perfecting a more accurate measuring instrument. On the contrary, in different ways they go directly to the question of the social *meaning* of the phenomenon of victimization, and thus to the issue of the meaning of crime. Future research should thus deal with them as substantive issues, and not merely as technical irritations.

For example, what proportion of series incidents is best understood not as a plague of discrete incidents–rather like the boils of Job–but as an indication of chronic or persistent *states* of victimization, of which the majority of the population is fortunately free? Much one-time victimization can probably be regarded, from both the victim's point of view and society's, as an isolated (and virtually random) incident with few if any persistent consequences; there may be as little profit in trying to explain why certain persons are victimized once as there is (in my opinion) in trying to explain why most persons commit some form of crime on this or that isolated occasion. But the minority of apparently "victimization-prone" persons may present a different problem. To what extent can repeated victimization be explained by the actions, or the attributes, of the victim–and to what extent does it inhere in particular identifiable social situations or places?

To what extent are estimates of victimization–including our own–distorted by systematic differences in the definition of situations–especially those situations involving relatively complicated interpersonal transactions, dependent on intent and consent, such as assault? An incident recalled as an "argument," a "quarrel" or a "fight" has a different *meaning* for a respondent from one recalled as an "assault" or a "threat," even if the observable physical facts are the same. This domain of meaning needs to be much more fully explored by victimization researchers in the future.

Until it is, the measures of crime obtained from victimization surveys run the risk of being extremely misleading. For example, I have noted that our survey estimates of the types of crime that we studied were about eleven times as great as the numbers of crimes in the police statistics of our three London areas. This means: we found about eleven times as many incidents that *could* correctly have been recorded—according to the rules of English criminal law—in police statistics. It would be absurd to assert that we found eleven times as many incidents *of the kind typically recorded in the police statistics* as were actually found there. The sifting of incidents, by the public and by the police, is far from being a random process. In my opinion, it would be misleading to reserve the word "crime" for just those incidents that were sufficiently serious (in some sense) to survive the social and organizational processes of perception, definition and reporting to the police. But it would be equally misleading not to recognize that police statistics are the outcome of that series of social processes, and to ignore the extreme dangers of uncritically assuming that those statistics automatically reflect—even approximately—the amounts and types of criminal behavior that do in fact take place. If victimization surveys can help to make that point clear, they will be well worth their cost, no matter how imperfect their own estimates of the volume of crime in society may be.

NOTES

1. Albert D. Biderman et al., *Report on a Pilot Study in the District of Columbia on Victimization and Attitudes to Law Enforcement, Field Surveys I*; Philip H. Ennis, *Criminal Victimization in the United States: A Report of a National Survey, Field Surveys II*; Albert J. Reiss, Jr., *Studies in Crime and Law Enforcement in Major Metropolitan Areas, Field Surveys III*, vol. 1; all published by the President's Commission on Law Enforcement and Administration of Justice (Washington, D.C.: U.S. Government Printing Office, 1967). (These reports will hereinafter be cited as *Field Surveys I, II* and *III* respectively.)

2. See, for example, A.A. Congalton and J.M. Najman, "Unreported Crime," *Statistical Report No. 12*, New South Wales Bureau of Crime Statistics and Research, 1974 (also reports 13 and 14 in the same series); P.R. Wilson and J.W. Brown, *Crime and the Community* (St. Lucia: University of Queensland Press, 1973); Irvin Waller and Norm Okihiro, "Burglary and the Public," (Toronto: University of Toronto Centre of Criminology, August 1974, mimeo.); Kauko Aromaa, *Arkipäivan Vakivaltaa Suomessa* (Everyday Violence in Finland), Kriminologinen Tutkimuslaitos, Sarja M: 11 (Helsinki: Kriminologinen Tutkimuslaitos, 1971); Preben Wolf, "Vold I Danmark og Finland 1970/1971. En

sammen ligning af voldsofre," Project Noxa. Forskningsrapport nr. 1, Nordisk Samarbejdsrad for Kriminologi 1971/72 (Copenhagen, mimeo, n.d.). Surveys in all four Nordic countries are described in a paper by Preben Wolf and Ragnar Hauge, "Criminal Violence in three Scandinavian Countries," in *Scandinavian Studies in Criminology*, vol. 5 (London: Tavistock, 1975). For England see Mary Durant, Margaret Thomas and H.D. Willcock, *Crime, Criminals and the Law* (London: Her Majesty's Stationery Office, 1972), esp. pp. 232-53. To my knowledge, reports on the surveys conducted in other countries mentioned in the text have not yet been published.

3. Full results of this survey are reported in R.F. Sparks, H.G. Genn and D.J. Dodd, *Surveying Victims: A Study of the Measurement of Criminal Victimization, Perceptions of Crime and Attitudes to Criminal Justice* (London: John Wiley and Sons Ltd., 1977). At the time of this study the present author was assistant director of research at the Institute of Criminology, University of Cambridge; support for the research was provided by a grant from the British Home Office. Neither the Cambridge institute nor the Home Office is responsible for any of the views expressed in this chapter.

4. See A.J. Reiss, Jr., "Systematic Observation of Natural Social Phenomena," in H.L. Costner, ed., *Sociological Methodology 1971* (San Francisco: Jossey-Bass, 1971), p. 3.

5. U.S. Bureau of the Census, "Victim recall pretest (Washington, D.C.): Household survey of victims of crimes" (Unpublished report, June 10, 1970); Linda R. Yost and Richard W. Dodge, "Household surveys of victims of crime, second pretest (Baltimore, Maryland)" (Unpublished report, November 30, 1970); Anthony Turner, "San Jose Methods Test of Known Crime Victims," *Statistics Technical Report No. 1* (Washington, D.C., Law Enforcement Assistance Administration, June, 1972).

6. W.A. Belson, "The extent of stealing by London boys and some of its origins," reprint series of the Survey Research Centre, London School of Economics, No. 39 (1969); H.B. Gibson, S. Morrison and D.J. West, "The confession of known offenses in response to a self-reported delinquency schedule," *British Journal of Criminology* 10 (1970): 277; see also Lynn MacDonald, *Delinquency and Social Class* (London: Faber and Faber, 1971).

7. These volumes are "command" papers published annually by Her Majesty's Stationery Office in London. Typical of descriptive research based on these statistics and other police-compiled data on "crimes known to the police" is F.H. McClintock and N.H. Avison, *Crime in England and Wales* (London: Heinemann, 1968).

8. In fact, it was necessary to use statistics relating to divisional (not subdivisional) areas, since population data for the smaller areas were not available at the outset of our London research. The statistics we used were unpublished; we are grateful to Deputy Assistant Commissioner H.D. Walton for making them available to us.

9. In this paper I shall use the term "black" to refer to West Indians and Africans only, excluding from comparisons based on our sample data the small number of culturally quite different Indians and Pakistanis whom we interviewed.

10. See, for example, Michael Young and Peter Willmott, *Family and Kinship in East London* (London: Routledge and Kegan Paul, 1957); Peter Townsend, *The Family Life of Old People* (London: Routledge and Kegan Paul, 1957).

11. Cases selected for the initial pool for the MV sample were drawn from files of crime reports at Scotland Yard; they were drawn at random, though different sampling fractions were used owing to the small numbers of violent offenses recorded in two areas. From this initial pool, a subset was then selected in accordance with experimental designs (four independent Latin squares in Brixton, randomized blocks in Kensington and Hackney). In the event these designs proved to be too ambitious, owing mainly to the difficulty of locating victims. See Sparks, Genn and Dodd, Ch. II, for a more detailed discussion.

12. See P.G. Gray and F.A. Gee, *Electoral registration for Parliamentary elections; an inquiry made for the Home Office*, Government Social Survey, SS391 (London: Her Majesty's Stationery Office, 1967).

13. In this respect our practice differed from that followed in the Washington and Baltimore pretests, see note 5, above.

14. Cf. the studies referred to in notes 1 and 5, above.

15. See note 5, above.

16. In their Toronto study of burglary, Waller and Okihiro found that incidents of burglary were often recalled after five or six years, though exact dates were often foggy; the main part of this survey used a reference period of sixteen to seventeen months.

17. In fact, our category of "assault" includes some cases of theft from the person (purse snatching) where the violence used or threatened did not amount to robbery. It also included a number of incidents initially recorded as assault that were subsequently written off by the police as "no crime" because the victim (usually female) had refused to give evidence; in all of these cases the description of the incident on the crime report made it clear that an assault had, in fact, occurred.

18. Thus the exponential model of memory decay suggested by Sudman and Bradburn does not give a very good fit to our sample data, at least as they are arranged in Table 3-2. But it is apparent that for our data the value of the nontime-related parameter a in their model is very close to 1.0, whereas the time-related parameter b_1 must be very small (close to 0.01). For a discussion of this model see Seymour Sudman and Norman F. Bradburn, *Response Effects in Surveys*, National Opinion Research Monographs in Social Research No. 16 (Chicago: Aldine, 1974), pp. 66-80.

19. For most of our sample this minimum age would have been fourteen; it was raised to fifteen in the early 1960s.

20. This suggestion is reinforced by the fact that respondents who were rated by interviewers as "not cooperative" or "somewhat cooperative" were significantly more likely not to mention target incidents than were those rated "very cooperative"; there was a similar though not significant association with interviewers' ratings of the respondents' understanding of the questions.

21. The relative error introduced into estimates by forward external telescoping will be greater if a six month reference period is used than if a twelve month one is used, because in the former case the total number of incidents

involved (the denominator used in calculating relative error) is only half as great. Making allowance not only for nonrecall but for backward telescoping out of the reference period, our data show a "success" rate (i.e., of incidents correctly reported as having occurred within the reference period) of 89 percent over twelve months and 88 percent over the last six months.

22. See note 5, above.

23. When correctly reported, these incidents would have been mentioned in response to a general "catch-all" question at the end of the specific screening questions, viz., Have you, or any member of your household, *ever* been the victim of a crime?

24. Details of the incidents were recorded on crime incident forms for about three-fourths of the incidents mentioned (the bulk of those for which this was not done were "series" incidents for which the respondent could not remember dates or details). Classifications based on the content of screening questions and on crime incident form descriptions were generally though not invariably concordant. About 11 percent of cases with incident forms were judged to have involved no crime at all; these cases were removed from the screening totals.

25. Lower estimates were offered and accepted in some cases, e.g., "three or four" (coded as 3); the maximum of nine was coded only when it appeared that the respondent's estimate was nine or more.

26. Cf. note 17 above; the distinction between the legal categories of robbery and theft from the person, in purse-snatching cases, proved as difficult with survey respondents' descriptions as it had with police crime reports.

27. For burglaries and car thefts the amounts of property were naturally higher: e.g., 27.6 percent of the burglaries were alleged to have involved property worth more than £50. However, it is important to note that in our MV and T samples' cases there was often disagreement between the respondent's statement of the amount of property involved and the amount recorded in crime reports.

28. See, for example, U.S. Department of Justice, Law Enforcement Assistance Administration, *Criminal Victimization in the United States, 1973 Advance Report* (Washington, D.C.: U.S. Government Printing Office, May, 1975), pp. 29-30.

29. I am indebted, on this point and many others, to Albert D. Biderman.

30. Paul Reynolds et. al., "Victimization in a Metropolitan Region: Comparison of a Central City Area and a Suburban Community" (Minneapolis: Minnesota Center for Sociological Research, October 1973, mimeo).

31. Aromaa, *Arkipäivan Vakivaltaa Suomessa.*

32. Appendix by Karin Zedeler, in Wolf, *Vold I Danmark og Finland.*

33. Unpublished tabulations relating to commercial victimization in the city surveys (table 2A); to my knowledge this is the only instance in which the distribution of incidents is computed in the current NCP program.

34. M. Greenwood and G. Udny Yule, "An inquiry into the nature of frequency distributions representative of multiple happenings with particular reference to the occurrence of multiple attacks of disease or repeated accidents," *Journal of the Royal Statistical Society* 83 (1920): 255-79.

35. James S. Coleman, *Introduction to Mathematical Sociology* (New York: Free Press, 1964), pp. 299-307.

36. Intuitively, this model does not in fact seem particularly likely, of course. We did encounter some respondents who professed a belief that their having been burgled once made it more likely that they would be burgled again; so far as we could judge, however, they had no evidence for this view.

37. Since such a model has two parameters—the size of the hypothesized "immune" group and the transition rate for the "nonimmune" group—we could not fit it to our data without making some further assumptions. Experimentation showed, however, that in order to get even an approximately good fit the "immune" group would have to have been implausibly large—about two-thirds of the sample. (Or *is* that implausibly large? It might not be, at least over the short term, if people *became* "immune" as a result of taking precautions after an earlier victimization.)

38. Coleman, p. 379.

39. Though the group means will of course differ. For a test of significance of the difference between variance and mean in a Poisson population, see E.S. Keeping, *Introduction to Statistical Inference* (Princeton: Van Nostrand, 1962), p. 254.

40. In fact, since on this assumption both the expected and the observed numbers of multiple victims would be increased by unbiased responses, the goodness of fit of models such as the simple Poisson one would generally not be much affected. For a further discussion see Sparks, Genn and Dodd, ch. IV.

41. See, for example, U.S. Department of Justice, Law Enforcement Assistance Administration, *Criminal Victimization in the United States, 1973 Advance Report*, tables 3, 6; and U.S. Department of Justice, Law Enforcement Assistance Administration, *Criminal Victimization Surveys in 13 American Cities* (Washington, D.C.: U.S. Government Printing Office, 1975).

42. Wolf and Hauge.

43. Which are not, of course, mutually exclusive. In addition, events such as minor assaults may have different salience for different groups, and may thus be differentially remembered.

44. Cf. note 41, above.

45. It is possible that this explains the finding in the San Jose Methods Test that crimes in which the offender and victim were related or acquainted were much less frequently mentioned. See "The San Jose Methods Test," p. 9.

46. See Albert D. Biderman, "When Does Interpersonal Violence Become Crime?" (Paper presented at a meeting of the International Sociological Association, Cambridge, England, 1973).

47. Originally, we had thought that it would be necessary to make another adjustment, in order to remove thefts of property worth £5 or less: such crimes are not, since 1972, included in the Home Office published statistics of "indictable offenses known to the police." Since these low-value thefts accounted to about 20 percent of *all* recorded "known offenses" in England and Wales, their exclusion involved a good deal of phony decriminalization, at least on paper. However, we discovered that such thefts had not been removed from the (unpublished) statistics provided for us by the metropolitan police; we have therefore not excluded them from our data.

48. Unadjusted mean rates of victimization for the broad categories used in

Table 3-5 are well in excess of twice their associated standard errors. However, for a variety of reasons, we were not able to calculate standard error estimates for the adjusted data; it seems likely that they are larger than the unadjusted ones, and the results of our analysis must thus be treated with caution.

49. Space does not permit a detailed discussion of our sample's reporting behavior, but in general it can be said that—as other victimization researchers have found—reporting to the police was largely "incident-specific" and depended little on the attributes of the victims themselves, including their expressed attitudes to the police. "Seriousness" of the incident—in both objective and subjective terms—appeared to be the major determinant of reporting. See further Sparks, Genn and Dodd, ch. V.

50. See, e.g., *Field Surveys II*, pp. 7-13; *Field Surveys III*, pp. 159-71; *Field Surveys I*, 109-13; and Reynolds et al., ch. IV.

51. In fact, in about a third of the incidents that we classified as burglary, it was said that no property had been taken; the comparable proportion among offenses recorded as burglary by the metropolitan police is only about 10 percent.

52. Information provided in a personal communication from Mr. T.C. Jones, statistical advisor to the metropolitan police.

53. See, e.g., Maureen Cain, *Society and the Policeman's Role* (London: Routledge and Kegan Paul, 1973), esp. chs. 3-7; John R. Lambert, *Crime, Police and Race Relations* (London: Oxford University Press, 1970), chs. 4-5; and Michael Banton, *The Policeman in the Community* (London: Tavistock, 1964).

54. In general, the published English *Criminal Statistics* (like the *Uniform Crime Reports* in the United States) do not distinguish clearly between different degrees of harm within broad legal categories such as "violence against the person." It is known, however, that many of the recorded offenses in this category are within the legal category of "assaults occasioning actual bodily harm" (Offenses Against the Person Act 1861, §47): See McClintock and Avison, p. 38. In English law this type of harm need not be at all serious: it has been said that it includes "any hurt or injury calculated to interfere with health or comfort."

Chapter 4

Bodily Injury in Personal Crimes*

Michael R. Gottfredson and
Michael J. Hindelang

The systematic collection and analysis of crime statistics was originally designed to serve legislative ends. In 1778, Jeremy Bentham suggested that such data could serve as a "political barometer . . . indicating the moral health of the country. . . ."[1] He reasoned that by categorizing crimes and then monitoring the types evidencing fluctuations, legislative bodies could adjust penalties accordingly. For example, if a particular category of crimes was found to be increasing, then, from Bentham's utilitarian perspective, an increase in the penalties attached to those crimes would be indicated. The link between the legislative purpose and the collection and classification of crime statistics was also apparent in France, as reflected in the first annual report of criminal justice, published in 1827. In the introduction to that series, Guerry de Champneuf wrote that these statistics would "assist in determining the circumstances which cooperate in increasing or diminishing the number of crimes."[2] A century later, the International Association of Chiefs of Police devised and implemented a data collection and crime classification system that evolved into the FBI's uniform crime reporting (UCR) program. The *UCR Handbook* suggests that "the information collected under the UCR program should be a portion of the data a law enforcement agency compiles for its own effective and efficient operation."[3]

*Portions of this chapter are drawn from a final project report entitled "An Analysis and Classification of Injury and Loss in Personal Victimizations" by Michael R. Gottfredson and Michael J. Hindelang (Statistics Division, Law Enforcement Assistance Administration, Washington, D.C., 1976). The project was supported by grant 75-SS-99-6002 awarded to the Criminal Justice Research Center, Albany, New York, by the Statistics Division, National Criminal Justice Information and Statistics Service, Law Enforcement Assistance Administration, U.S. Department of Justice. Points of view or opinions stated in this chapter are those of the authors and do not necessarily represent the official position or policies of the U.S. Department of Justice.

In light of this connection between crime statistics and legislative goals and the current American practice of generating crime statistics as a by-product of law enforcement activities, it is not surprising that these statistics reflect a statutory orientation—that is, one in which the classification of criminal events is designed to comport with legal codes. Because of this classificatory approach and a lack of alternative data sources, behavioral scientists who study crime typically do so using this legal orientation. Thus, researchers have studied criminal homicide,[4] justifiable homicide,[5] rape,[6] aggravated assault,[7] robbery,[8] burglary[9] and other legally defined categories of criminal behavior. The difficulty of this approach is that behaviorally dissimilar events often fall into the same category, while events with some common elements do not. For example, as Sellin and Wolfgang have pointed out, the range of activities that can be classified as robbery is vast.[10] The standard definition of robbery includes thefts which are accompanied by the element of force or threat of force. This includes violent street robberies, bank robberies and drunk rolls, as well as schoolyard lunch money "shakedowns." Under the present system, no attempt is made to classify robberies with regard to the degree of violence involved. According to Beattie:

> There are robberies committed with an extraordinary amount of unnecessary violence. There are robberies designated as 'strong-arm' in which the victim may be brutally attacked or robbed when in a stupor or unconscious.[11]

All, unfortunately for the researcher, are placed in the same category. Although the legal categories used to classify offenses encompass a broad range of crimes, some elements of crimes do cut across legal boundaries. For example, assault, rape and robbery may all involve physical injury. For some purposes, studying particular behavioral phenomena—such as physical injury, the use of weapons or financial loss—that transcend legalistic categories may be more informative. Our aim is to explore one important element of many personal victimizations—bodily injury to the victim.

A number of studies have examined the question of the nature and extent of injury to victims of personal crime within UCR categories, primarily the index offenses. For example, several studies that rely on police offense reports for data concerning injury to victims provide valuable insights into the extent and nature of injury to robbery victims. Normandeau drew a 10 percent random sample of all robberies listed by the Philadelphia police between 1960 and 1966, which provided information on 1,785 victims.[12] The extent of injury in his sample varied dramatically: 44 percent of the victims received no injury, 26 percent received minor injuries and 30 percent received either medical or hospital treatment. Similar data are reported by Conklin, who studied all robbery incidents known to the Boston police in the first six months of 1964 and

1968.[13] For the 1964 data, 68 percent of the victims received no injury, 11 percent received minor injury and 21 percent required either medical or hospital treatment; the 1968 data showed similar percentages. Conklin also studied the nature of injuries suffered by robbery victims. In the 1964 sample, 4.5 percent of the victims were cut, stabbed or shot; 21 percent were beaten, punched or hit with a weapon; and 27 percent were shoved, pushed or knocked to the ground. These findings demonstrate that within a certain crime category (robbery) both the extent and nature of injuries suffered by victims vary substantially.[14]

Studies of victims of aggravated assault using police offense reports indicate that victim injury in assaultive crimes also varies greatly. For example, Pittman and Handy, who reviewed a 25 percent random sample of the 965 crimes classified as aggravated assault by the St. Louis police during 1961, found that while the victim was injured to some degree in all of the sampled cases, 53 percent of the victims were "seriously wounded" and 47 percent were not.[15] The President's Commission on Crime in the District of Columbia, which studied police reports in that city, found that, of the 131 aggravated assault victims studied, 84 percent were injured, 35 percent to the extent that they required hospitalization.[16]

In its study of rape in seventeen American cities, the President's Commission on the Causes and Prevention of Violence found that 21 percent of the 617 rape victims received injuries in addition to the rape.[17] Further evidence of variability in the nature of injury in rape is provided by Amir's study of 646 rape victims in Philadelphia.[18] He found that 15 percent of the rapes involved no force, 28 percent involved "roughness" (e.g., holding or pushing), 25 percent slapping and 20 percent "brutal beating."

All these descriptive studies of injury have relied upon particular legal categories of offensive behavior. A major limitation inherent in attempts to assess correlates of physical injury suffered by victims of personal crime is that the categories of crime under study may artificially limit the types of variables that may be considered. For example, theft-related variables (e.g., the amount of loss) cannot be considered in assault victimizations if the UCR offense categories are used because, if theft is part of the victimization, the offense becomes robbery. We intend to explore the phenomenon of physical injury irrespective of common legal categories. This may permit us to isolate important correlates of injury that may be obscured when a crime-specific approach is taken.

THE SAMPLE

In conjunction with its National Crime Survey Program, the Law Enforcement Assistance Administration has undertaken victimization surveys in twenty-six American cities. In each city, a probability sample of 10,000 households—or about 22,000 individuals—was drawn. In each housing unit selected, interviews were conducted with household members twelve years of age or older. Each eligible household respondent was interviewed about victimizations that he or she may have suffered during the preceding year.[19] For each victimization reported to the interviewer, a series of detailed questions was asked. These questions dealt with the amount of loss, the extent and types of injury suffered, weapon use, medical attention, reporting to the police, etc.

Data discussed in this chapter are from surveys conducted in the first eight cities to be surveyed—Atlanta, Baltimore, Cleveland, Dallas, Denver, Newark, Portland (Oregon) and St. Louis. The data discussed here are estimates of population parameters based on the sample results; hence, these estimates include some sampling error. However, because of the large numbers of sample cases, the sampling errors for most estimates presented here are small.

RESULTS

In these eight cities an estimated 208,719 victims of personal crime were identified.[20] Everyone who was personally attacked was asked: What were the injuries you suffered, if any? Anything else? Twenty-five percent of the victims of personal crime reported suffering some form of injury.[21] Of those, 78 percent reported receiving minor injuries, such as bruises, black eyes, cuts or scratches.[22] The next largest proportion of those suffering injuries reported "other" injuries (13 percent), followed by knife or gunshot wounds (8 percent), broken bones or teeth (7 percent), and internal injuries or having been knocked unconscious (7 percent). Additionally, 2 percent reported rape injuries and 1 percent "attempted rape injuries."

Before analyzing the correlates of injury, we should note the distribution of injury within the UCR offense categories. The survey was designed so that the data collected could be categorized according to UCR definitions. Preliminary methodological work indicates that the survey data may be accurately classified according to these definitions.[23] The UCR personal crime categories that are amenable to study with these data include rape, robbery, aggravated assault, simple assault and personal larceny with contact (purse snatching and pocket picking without force). Consistent with UCR procedures, attempts are included in each category.

With the exception of personal larceny with contact, in which, by UCR definition, there can be no injury to the victim, each category contained a substantial proportion of victims who suffered some injury. The greatest proportion of injured victims in any crime category was in the rape classification, in which 48 percent reported injury, followed by aggravated assault (35 percent), robbery (29 percent) and simple assault (24 percent). Thus, the victimization survey data show a great deal of variation in bodily injury both among and within the UCR categories of personal crime.

Almost two-thirds of the aggravated assaults did not involve any injury to the victim. Since an assault is classified as aggravated if it involves serious bodily injury to the victim or the presence of a deadly weapon, most assaults reported to survey interviewers were apparently classified as aggavated because of the presence of a deadly weapon rather than because of serious injury. In addition, actual injury occurred slightly more often in aggravated assault than in robbery (36 percent versus 29 percent), despite the fact that the FBI considers robbery to be more serious than aggravated assault for UCR index purposes.[24]

A more complete picture of the variability of physical injury within and among the UCR classes can be drawn by examining the nature of injuries suffered in each type of personal victimization. Most injuries in each type of crime category were relatively minor—bruises, black eyes and cuts. More than 50 percent of the injured rape victims, 80 percent of the injured robbery victims, 69 percent of the injured aggravated assault victims and 90 percent of the injured simple assault victims suffered such injuries. On the other hand, victims who were injured suffered gunshot or knife wounds in 18 percent of the aggravated assaults, 7 percent of the robberies and 2 percent of the rapes. Thus, while the extent of physical injury varies among crime categories, the nature of physical injury varies both among and within crime categories. Analyses such as this, which use the UCR classification, may provide valuable information about the heterogeneity of injury within categories. However, to examine whether similarities of victimizations can be related systematically to victim injury, the correlates of physical injury must be assessed without regard to predefined categories.

CORRELATES OF PHYSICAL INJURY

Victimization survey data make available a wide variety of details about the victimization that can be studied in relation to injuries suffered by the victim. These details include the time and place of occurrence, use of weapons by the offender, use of self-protective measures by the victim, prior relationship between the victim and the offender, demographic characteristics of the offender and the number of offenders.[25]

Personal crimes reported as having occurred between 6 A.M. and 6 P.M. were less likely to result in injury to the victim than were such crimes occurring between midnight and 6 A.M. (22 percent versus 32 percent); crimes occurring between 6 P.M. and midnight resulted in injury 28 percent of the time. The places in which victimizations occurred were categorized as "in own home," "near own home," "inside commercial buildings." "on the street" and so forth. Except for the categories "in own home," where nearly one-third of the victimizations resulted in injury, and "inside commercial buildings," where only 18 percent resulted in injury, in every place of occurrence category about 25 percent of the victimizations resulted in injury.

Table 4-1 shows the variation in injury associated with the presence and type of weapon in personal victimizations. When the offender had a weapon, 30

Table 4-1. Percent of All Victimizations Resulting In Injury by Presence Of A Weapon[a]

	Injured		
	Yes	*No*	*Total*
Weapon	30% (24,961)	70% (59,459)	47% (84,421)
No Weapon	24% (23,233)	76% (72,159)	53% (95,392)
Total	27% (48,195)	73% (131,618)	100% (179,812)
Gun	17% (6,177)	83% (30,774)	(36,952)
Knife	28% (6,688)	72% (17,081)	(23,769)
Other	52% (13,090)	48% (12,208)	(25,298)

[a]Includes only those cases where weapon use was ascertained. Also, more than one weapon could have been used.

Source: Analyses of data tapes provided by Bureau of the Census for the eight High Impact cities interviewed in 1972.

percent of the victimizations resulted in injury; when the offender did not have a weapon, 24 percent of the victimizations resulted in injury. However, more important than whether the offender had a weapon, was what type of weapon the offender had. When the offender had a gun, the rate of injury was the lowest, 17 percent; when the offender had an "other" weapon (clubs, bottles, chains, etc.), the rate of injury to the victim was three times as high, 52 percent. When the offender had a knife, the rate of injury was only slightly greater than when the offender was unarmed (28 percent versus 24 percent).

When a gun is present, both the victim and the offender probably will be cautious about risking the possibility of injury, since any injury caused by a gun is likely to be serious. On the other hand, "other" weapons may not instill a similar fear in either the victim or the offender. Further, "other" weapons may be used by offenders in impulsive acts that often result in injury to the victim.

In all personal victimizations, respondents were asked whether, during the victimization, they did anything to protect themselves or their property, and, if so, what they did. Self-protective measures may involve such behaviors as hitting or kicking the offender, using a weapon, holding onto one's property, yelling for help, reasoning with the offender and leaving the scene. Half of the victims of personal crimes took some self-protective measure. Rates of injury varied greatly, depending on the nature of self-protective measures taken. About 20 percent of those who took self-protective measures, but fully 50 percent of those who hit or kicked the offender, sustained injuries; 16 percent of those victims who left the scene, 20 percent of those who tried to reason with the offender, 22 percent of those who held onto their property and 27 percent of those who used or brandished a weapon were injured.

These results clearly show that victims who use self-protective measures that involve attacking the offender have substantially higher rates of injury than do those who use no self-protective measures or who use such measures as leaving the scene, reasoning with the offender and holding onto their property. Unfortunately, the survey instrument used in these eight cities does not provide any information about the time sequence of events. Some victims may resort to a self-protective measure only after having been attacked, while others, by using self-protective measures, may provoke the offender to attack. Until more detailed information about the dynamics of the victim-offender interaction is gathered, making causal inferences about the relationship between the use of self-protective measures and injury to the victim is not possible.

Another important question that can be addressed by victim survey data is the extent to which characteristics of the offender, such as age, race, sex and prior relationship to the victim, are associated with differential rates of injury. Of those victimizations reported by respondents in the survey, about 80 percent involved offenders who were strangers to the victim.[26] For personal victimizations in which the offender was a stranger, 23 percent of the victims were injured, while for victimizations in which the offender was not a stranger, 35 percent of the victims were injured. To some extent, this finding helps to account for the disproportionately high rate of injury for victimizations occurring in the home, since such victimizations disproportionately involve nonstrangers. The higher rate of injury in victimizations involving nonstrangers is attributable to the fact that five out of six nonstranger victimizations in the eight cities were assaultive victimizations in which theft or attempted theft was not involved. It should not be surprising that in assaultive victimizations between nonstrangers—victimizations in which theft is not a motive but rather in which arguments stemming from day-to-day frictions may escalate—rates of bodily injury are relatively high.

Although the offender's prior relationship to the victim is an important factor in accounting for variation in injury, the demographic characteristics of the offender are not. For example, 26 percent of the victims of male offenders and 30 percent of the victims of female offenders sustained bodily injury. Victimizations involving offenders who are perceived by the victim to be twenty-one years of age or older have virtually the same rate of injury to victims as victimizations involving offenders perceived to be under twenty-one years of age (27 percent versus 26 percent, respectively).[27] In addition, 30 percent of those confronted by white offenders and 25 percent of those confronted by black offenders or offenders of "other" races suffered injury.

MULTIVARIATE ANALYSIS

Our analyses thus far suggest that various elements of the victimization event are associated with differential rates of bodily injury. Obviously, considering such elements in this serial fashion fails to take into account the interdependence among the elements. For example, both the victim-offender relationship and the use of self-protective measures were shown above to be related to injury at the zero-order level. Analyses not reported here, however, indicate that self-protective measures are more likely to be taken by the victim when the offender is a nonstranger; whether these two variables are independently related to injury is not clear from the data discussed so far.

To investigate the simultaneous effects of variables associated with injury, we used the technique of predictive attribute analysis (PAA), originally developed by Macnaughton-Smith.[28] PAA is a devisive hierarchical classification technique in which subgroups are formed in a stepwise fashion according to the strength of association between the attributes and the criterion. In our analysis the criterion (injury versus no injury) and the independent variables to be used in the classification are dichotomous variables.

The clustering process works from a vector of associations. First, the correlation of each attribute with the criterion is examined and the sample is split on that attribute possessing the highest degree of association with the criterion. This split defines the first two subgroups. By employing such a clustering rule, the resulting subgroups will differ in relation to the criterion more than if any other attribute in the set had been used to divide the sample.

Each of these two subgroups is then treated as an entity and is similarly divided. Within each group a new vector of associations between the remaining independent variables and the criterion variable is formed, and the group is split on that attribute with the highest association with the criterion, forming two subgroups. By redividing each successive subgroup, the procedure will result in a hierarchical classification system in which the groups are maximally heterogeneous in relation to the criterion.

As with any classification technique, rules must be adopted to guide the formation of the subgroups. For PAA, the rules should increase the discriminatory ability of the scheme while ensuring maximum reliability of the resulting solution. These rules include the measure of association to be employed, the minimum value of the statistic for which a split will be allowed, the minimum number of cases in any subgroup for which an additional split will be allowed and the minimum number of cases permissible in the subgroups after a split has been made. Thus, if the statistic measuring the degree of association is too small, the discrimination provided by the split may not be large enough to warrant the division. If the number of cases in the subgroup is too small or the split results in subgroups with a small number of cases, the solution may not be reliable. Of central importance, then, are the rules to be adopted to guide the formation of the hierarchical classification. The following rules were adopted: (1) the value of the statistic, in this case Somers' *d*,[29] an asymmetric measure of association, had to be greater than or equal to ±0.10 for a split to be made; (2) no subgroup containing fewer than 900 weighted cases was further divided; (3) no split was made if either of the resulting subgroups contained less than 450 cases; and (4) no split proceeded if it resulted in a subgroup containing less than 5 percent of the cases in its parent group. This last rule was adopted to preclude divisions that might be based on high discriminatory ability, yet which produce fairly trivial subgroups.

Adopting PAA as a method of analysis seems appropriate based on the results thus far presented. PAA takes into consideration overlap among the attributes in their relation to the criterion—once a division has been made on a particular attribute, further divisions are made within groups. This is essentially the same as saying that the first attribute will be held constant in later constructions of the association vectors. Additionally, PAA considers the joint effects of variables, which appears to be important in these data.

As noted above, PAA operates on attributes or dichotomized variables. For the analyses reported below, elements of the victimization were used as the independent variables. These elements included the use of self-protective measures by the victim, the use of weapons by the offender, the amount of loss suffered by the victim, the time and place of occurrence, whether the offender had a right to be where the victimization occurred, the victim's prior relationship to the offender, various characteristics of the offender and the number of offenders. Although some of these variables formed natural dichotomies (such as whether or not the offender was a stranger to the victim), many of the variables were "dummy" coded. For example, each victimization was categorized as having involved or not having involved a gun. Once these dummy variables were created, a PAA was completed using the stopping rules enumerated above.

In analyses like PAA, cross-validation procedures are customarily used. Our cross-validation involved using a random half of the sample for "constructing" the PAA solution. The other half of the sample was used to "validate" these results. The data presented below reflect the construction sample results. Due to space consideration, the validation sample results are not presented here. When the construction sample solution was "forced" on the validation sample, the results were found to be strikingly similar. The terminal groups from the construction solution were ranked according to injury rates and found to have a Spearman's *Rho* of 0.94 with the injury rate ranking in the validation sample.

Figure 4-1 presents the number of victimizations falling into each classification, the percentage in each classification suffering injury, a brief description of

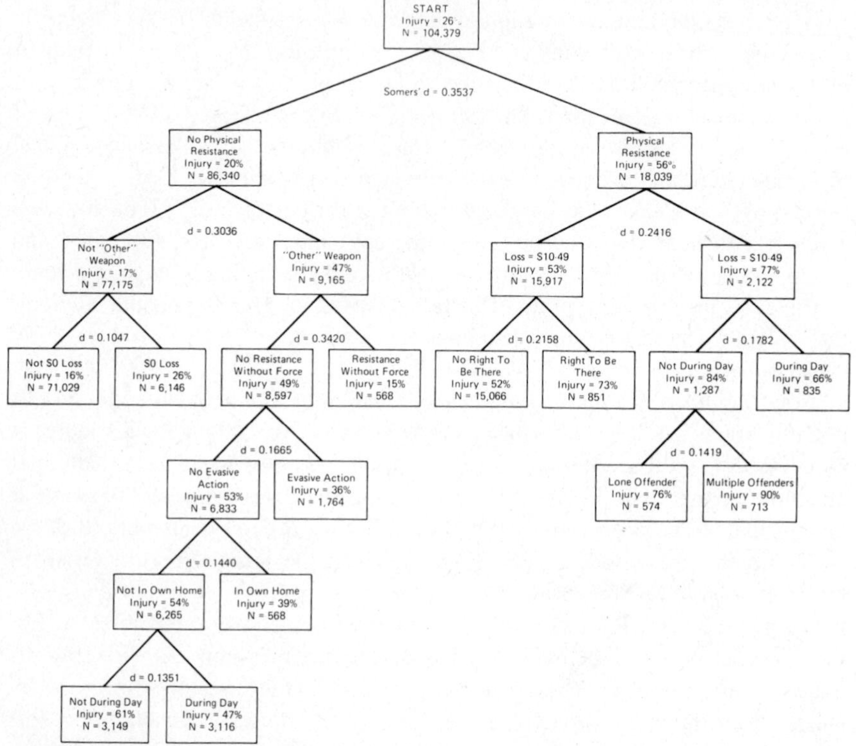

Source: Computed from a fifty-percent sample of the eight High Impact Cities survey data collected by the U.S. Bureau of the Census in 1972.

Figure 4-1. Predictive Attribute Analysis of Injury: Random Half Sample, Eight City Aggregate

the variable used to make the split resulting in classification and the value of the Somers' d statistic that indicated that the division should be made on that attribute.

As foreshadowed by earlier analysis, the attribute most highly associated with injury (Somers' $d = 0.354$) was whether or not the victim resisted the offender with physical force.[30] Therefore, two groups were formed, one consisting of all victimizations in which the victim did not use physical force (of which 20 percent of victimizations resulted in injury), the other consisting of all victimizations in which the victim did use physical force (of which 56 percent resulted in injury).

Within the subgroup not using physical force in resistance, the attribute most highly associated with injury was whether the offender used an "other" weapon (e.g., a rock, club or a bottle). Where *both* an "other" weapon was not used *and* the victim did not use physical force, 17 percent of the victims were injured—a rate somewhat below the overall injury rate for the sample. However, when both an "other" weapon was used and the victim did not use physical force, the percentage of injured victims (47 percent) was considerably greater than that for the sample as a whole (26 percent).

An advantage of using predictive attribute analysis as a classification tool may be seen by examining the attribute that further subdivided the part of the sample in which the victim used self-protective measures. Although within the class of victimization in which the victim did not use physical force the attribute "other" weapon was found to be the next most predictive attribute, within the class in which the victim did use physical force, the most predictive attribute turned out to be a monetary loss category. Among those victimizations in which the victim used physical resistance *and* the total loss (due to property loss or damage, and monetary loss) was not between $10 and $49, 53 percent were injured. On the other hand, among victimizations in which the victim used physical force and lost between $10 and $49, the injury rate was 77 percent. Thus, when only three attributes were considered, the percentage of injured victims falling into each class ranged from 17 to 77 percent.

Similar subdivisions of the sample continued, according to the criteria outlined above, until the stopping rules were met. The analysis resulted in twelve terminal categories, which were composed of combinations of the following variables: self-protective measures, weapon used, loss, whether the offender had a right to be in the place where the victimization occurred, time of occurrence, number of offenders and whether the victimization occurred in the home of the victim. Injury rates ranged from 15 percent (for those in which the victim did not use a physical force self-protective measure; was confronted by an "other" weapon; and used the self-protective measure of reasoning with, arguing with or threatening the offender) to 90 percent (for those in which the victim used some physical force self-protective measure, had a loss of between $10 and $49, was victimized at night and was victimized by more than one offender). As is often the case when PAA is used, these extreme groups account for relatively small proportions of the total sample. Nonetheless, PAA demonstrates that much of the variability in injury rates in personal victimizations is due to a relatively small number of attributes.

CONCLUSION

We have defined injury as a positive response to the questions: What were the injuries you suffered, if any? Anything else? Our earlier analyses show great diversity in the type of injury reported in response to this question—from minor scratches to gunshot wounds and internal injuries. Because many minor injuries fall within the above definition of injury, alternative definitions were used in separate analyses not shown here. For example, one operational definition of injury was a positive response to the question: Were you injured to the extent that medical attention was required? Another criterion of injury was whether the victim received hospital treatment for his or her injuries. For each of these alternative definitions, the relationships reported in this chapter generally hold true.

Our results suggest that the outcome of a victimization often depends upon the sequence of alternative courses of action that the participants choose to follow. For example, an offender initiating a robbery may do so either by threatening or by actually using force against the victim. A victim confronted with a threat or actual violence may choose either to submit to the offender or resist. An offender faced by a resisting victim may either desist or escalate the level of force. How this pattern of moves and countermoves evolves determines whether the victim sustains injuries.

The alternative moves available to victims and offenders when various weapons are used in the victimization may help explain the relationship between type of weapon and extent of injury. Recall, for example, the relatively low rate of injury when a gun was present, in comparison to the relatively high rate when an "other" weapon was used (17 percent versus 52 percent). An offender with a gun may rely primarily on the threat of using it rather than on an actual attack to convince the victim to cooperate. On the other hand, an offender with a club or bottle (an "other" weapon) may feel the need to establish the credibility of his weapon by actual attack. In addition, an offender may be much more reluctant to use a gun than a less lethal weapon. Furthermore, a victim may be much more likely to use a self-protective measure when faced by an "other" weapon than when faced by a gun. As Figure 4-1 shows, however, even among those not using a physical force self-protective measure, being confronted by an offender with an "other" weapon is closely related to bodily injury.

In some instances, the victim may be faced with the dilemma of risking physical injury to avoid property loss. As noted above, whether or not the victim uses a physical force self-protective measure was the variable most strongly associated with injury. Separate analyses of property loss (not discussed here) indicated that when self-protective measures are used in theft-related victimizations, the likelihood of property loss is reduced. Fourteen percent of the victimizations resulted in loss when a self-protective measure was taken, compared to 51 percent when no such measure was taken. The relation between self-protective measures and loss may be less ambiguous than that between self-protective measures and injury. While the use of a self-protective measure could stimulate an injury, it is less likely that employing such a measure would stimulate a loss of property. Thus, the victim's use of physical force self-protective measures may stimulate many injuries, but it may also thwart many thefts. Thus, some victims are apparently trading bodily injury in return for retaining possession of their property. For the victim primarily concerned with reducing his or her risk of injury in theft-related victimizations, the optimal strategy is clear: give up the property without a struggle.

Our results indicate that examining the victim-offender interchange—the participants' moves and countermoves—is fundamental to understanding the phenomenon of bodily injury in personal victimizations. Victimization survey results provide the first large scale source of systematically collected information on this topic. However, substantial refinement of the data collection instrument will be required before definitive statements can be made regarding the causal relationships among the elements of victimization we have discussed.

Despite these and other shortcomings, the National Crime Survey victimization studies provide researchers with detailed, uniform data about the nature and extent of criminal victimization. Physical injury is but one important phenomenon that can now be investigated independently of legally based data collection and classification systems. As Sellin suggested nearly four decades ago,

> the application of scientific criteria to the selection and classification of [crimes and criminals] independently of their *legal* form is essential to render them valuable to science. . . . If a science of human conduct is to develop, the investigator in this field of research must rid himself of shackles which have been forged by the criminal law.[31]

NOTES

1. Jeremy Bentham, "A Review of the Hard Labour Bill," cited by Thorsten Sellin, "The Significance of Records of Crime," *Law Quarterly Review* 67 (1951): 489.

2. Cited in *ibid.*, p. 489.

3. Clarence Kelley, *Uniform Crime Reporting Handbook* (Washington, D.C.: Federal Bureau of Investigation, 1974), p. 1.

4. Marvin Wolfgang, *Patterns in Criminal Homicide* (Philadelphia: University of Pennsylvania Press, 1958); Marvin Wolfgang and Franco Ferracuti, "Subculture of Violence: An Interpretive Analysis of Homicide," *International Annals of Criminology*, Ier Semestre (1962); Alex Pokorny, "A Comparison of Homicide in Two Cities," *Journal of Criminal Law, Criminology and Police Science* 56 (1965): 479-87; and Terrence Morris and Louis Blom-Cooper, *A Calendar of Murder: Criminal Homicide in England Since 1957* (London: Michael Joseph, Ltd., 1964).

5. Gerald Robin, "Justifiable Homicide by Police Officers," *Journal of Criminal Law, Criminology and Police Science* 53 (1963): 225-31.

6. Joseph MacDonald, *Rape Offenders and Their Victims* (New York: Charles Thomas, 1971); and Menachem Amir, *Patterns in Forcible Rape* (Chicago: University of Chicago Press, 1971).

7. David Pittman and William Handy, "Patterns in Criminal Aggravated Assault," *Journal of Criminal Law, Criminology and Police Science* 55 (1964): 462-70; and Alex Pokorny, "Human Violence: A Comparison of Homicide, Aggravated Assault, Suicide, and Attempted Suicide," *Journal of Criminal Law, Criminology and Police Science* 56 (1965): 488-97.

8. Andre Nomandeau, "Trends and Patterns in Crimes of Robbery" (Ph.D. dissertation, University of Pennsylvania, 1968), p. 116; and John Conklin, *Robbery and the Criminal Justice System* (New York: J.B. Lippincott Company, 1972).

9. Thomas Reppetto, *Residential Crime* (Cambridge, Massachusetts: Ballinger Publishing Company, 1974).

10. Thorsten Sellin and Marvin Wolfgang, *The Measurement of Delinquency* (New York: John Wiley and Sons, 1964).

11. Ronald Beattie, "Criminal Statistics in the United States," *Journal of Criminal Law, Criminology and Police Science* 51 (1960): 49-65.

12. Normandeau, p. 116.

13. Conklin, p. 119.

14. The fact that the studies cited above used official statistics for data concerning injury may indicate that the extent and nature of injuries within UCR categories is even more variable than reported in these studies. Evidence suggests that the extent of injury is correlated with the decision to report crimes to the police. That is, victims tend to filter out crimes involving less serious injuries by not reporting them to the police. See, Michael J. Hindelang and Michael R. Gottfredson, "The Victim's Decision Not to Invoke the Criminal Process," William McDonald, ed., *The Victim and the Criminal Justice System* (Beverly Hills, California: Sage Publications, Inc., 1976).

15. Seriously wounded was defined as being incapacitated to the extent that the victim required hospitalization. Pittman and Handy, Table 3.8.

16. President's Commission on Crime in the District of Columbia, *Report* (Washington, D.C.: U.S. Government Printing Office, 1966), p. 75.

17. Donald Mulvihill, Melvin Tumin and Lynn Curtis, *Crimes of Violence, Volume II: A Staff Report Submitted to the National Commission on the Causes and Prevention of Violence* (Washington, D.C.: U.S. Government Printing Office, 1969), p. 235.

18. Amir, p. 151.

19. With the exception that persons twelve and thirteen years old were interviewed by proxy.

20. The personal crimes included rape, robbery, aggravated assault and larceny from the person. Attempts were also included for all categories.

21. Interviewers were instructed to record only physical (bodily) injuries that the victim received from the attack, such as bruises, broken bones, gun wounds and so forth. Mental anguish was not considered as injury. See, U.S. Bureau of the Census, *National Crime Survey Central Cities Sample Interviewer's Manual* (Washington, D.C.: U.S. Department of Commerce, Social and Economic Statistics Administration, 1972).

22. It should be stressed that this is a multiple response question—victims may give several answers; and, thus, not all victims who received these minor injuries received *only* minor injuries.

23. For a study of this classification problem, see Anthony Turner, "San Jose Methods Test of Known Crime Victims," *Statistics Technical Report No. 1* (Washington, D.C.: Law Enforcement Assistance Administration, June 1972).

24. Research has shown that non-index offenses may also have serious

consequences to victims in terms of injury, a finding that serves to emphasize the problematic nature of injury-related research that uses the UCR classification system as a basis for analysis. Sellin and Wolfgang report that in their analysis of 145 juvenile offenses that resulted in some bodily injury to the victim, 62 percent would have been classified as non-index offenses under the UCR classification rules. In addition, 28 percent of the bodily injury cases, classified by UCR rules as simple assaults and, hence, non-index offenses, were more serious in terms of harm to the victim than were 76 percent of those cases classified as aggravated assault. Overall, offenses classified as simple assaults resulted in proportionately more serious physical harm to the victim than did robberies with personal violence. Sellin and Wolfgang, p. 192.

25. In this chapter we have not included victim characteristics among the correlates studied. Our primary focus here is on the situational aspects of the victimization that are associated with injury. For an analysis of the relationship between victim characteristics and injury, see Michael Hindelang, *Criminal Victimization in Eight American Cities* (Boston, Massachusetts: Ballinger Publishing Company, 1976).

26. Offenders were categorized as "strangers" if the victim reported that they were strangers or were known by sight only, or if the victim did not know whether they were strangers. "Nonstrangers" included relatives, persons who were well known but not related and casual acquaintances.

27. Because it was expected that victims may have difficulty in estimating the age of offenders, only the broad dichotomy "under twenty-one years old" and "twenty-one or over" was used.

28. Peter Mcnaughton-Smith, "The Classification of Individuals by the Possession of Attributes Associated with a Criterion," *Biometrics* 19 (1963): 364-66.

29. Robert Somers, "A New Asymmetric Measure of Association for Ordinal Variables," *American Sociological Review* 27 (1962): 799-811.

30. Such as hitting, kicking or slapping the offender.

31. Thorsten Sellin, *Culture, Conflict and Crime* (New York: Social Science Research Council, 1938), pp. 23-24.

Chapter 5

Police Response to Victimization: Effects on Citizen Attitudes and Perceptions*

Roger B. Parks

Several studies in recent years have examined the potential relationships between the experience of victimization and attitudes toward, or perceptions of, the police.[1] The consensus is that these relationships are weak or nonexistent. Victims, or those reporting a victimization of another household member, generally give about the same ratings of police services as do those not victimized.

There may be two explanations for these findings. One could argue that citizens do not believe police can alter the probability that they or another household member will be victimized. If this is the case, citizens would be less likely to hold police accountable when such an event occurs. Victims' ratings of police services ought to be, on the average, no lower than the ratings of nonvictims.

Alternatively, one could argue that the experience of individual or household victimization does affect citizens' ratings of police service, but that police actions taken in response suppress the relationships. Citizens receiving a satisfactory police response to a victimization may rate their police service the same or even better. On the other hand, an unsatisfactory police response may produce unfavorable ratings. Combining ratings from these two groups may mask the true relationships.[2]

This interpretation is explored in this chapter. Where evidence supports this

*The data analysis and chapter preparation was supported in part by the Advanced Productivity Research and Technology Division of the National Science Foundation through grant GI-43949, and in part by the Indiana University Research Committee. The author gratefully acknowledges this support and the very helpful comments and critiques offered by Frances P. Bish, Jnana Hodson, Elinor Ostrom, Wesley G. Skogan and Gordon P. Whitaker. Any findings, opinions or views expressed are those of the author and do not necessarily reflect those of the supporting agencies.

explanation, the types of police actions that are positively associated with citizens' perceptions of satisfactory response to reported victimization are examined.

PREVIOUS FINDINGS

McIntyre, reporting on studies conducted by the Bureau of Social Science Research (BSSR) for the President's Commission on Law Enforcement and Administration of Justice in 1966, notes that serious victimization is uncommon and that less serious victimizations seem to be quickly forgotten.[3] She reports finding little or no relationship between experiences of victimization and attitudes toward the police or crime in either the BSSR studies or those conducted by the National Opinion Research Center (NORC) for the same commission.[4] But Block, also reporting findings from the NORC survey, indicates a relationship between the experience of victimization and lesser support for increases in police power.[5]

Smith and Hawkins report no differences in their scale of police fairness between those reporting victimizations and others.[6] Ostrom et al. report weak relationships between victimization and ratings of police in a study of citizens in Indianapolis and surrounding suburbs.[7] Ostrom and Whitaker, reporting on a study of citizens in Chicago and its suburbs, find similarly weak relationships.[8]

Smith and Hawkins provide evidence that dissatisfaction with police response is related to unfavorable attitudes toward police among those reporting victimization.[9] Bordua and Tifft also find that police responses to citizen complaints are related to citizen satisfaction levels.[10] Furstenberg and Wellford present additional evidence consistent with these findings, but argue that attitude changes provoked by specific experiences are relatively rare.[11] Taken in total, these studies provide some support for the hypothesis that police actions in response to a victimization may suppress the victimization-attitude-perception relationships. This chapter will further explore this hypothesis by drawing upon data collected during 1972 in a study of law enforcement services in the St. Louis, Missouri, metropolitan area.

THE ST. LOUIS STUDY

The St. Louis study was conducted by an Indiana University team directed by Elinor Ostrom.[12] Information was collected on the levels of service provided by twenty-nine police agencies to citizens residing in forty-four neighborhoods in both the city of St. Louis and surrounding incorporated and unincorporated portions of St. Louis County. A complex "most similar systems" research design matched the forty-four residential neighborhoods using criteria of homeownership and age distribution within three restricted ranges of neighborhood wealth.[13] Attention was given to neighborhood racial composition so that racial effects could be addressed. A final stratification was made to take into account the size and type of police agencies providing primary police service to the neighborhoods.

In the St. Louis study, data were collected from a number of sources. This chapter focuses on data collected in interviews with a sample of citizens residing in each of the forty-four neighborhoods. The sampling unit for these interviews was the household. Rather than attempting to randomize household respondents through enumeration and further sampling, fieldworkers were instructed to interview the first adult member of the household with whom they established contact. The hour and day of the interviews were controlled to facilitate a distribution across household members.[14] In most instances, the demographic characteristics of the samples closely matched those of the neighborhoods as a whole.[15]

Of the nearly 4,000 respondents in the St. Louis study, 20 percent reported that they or a member of their household had been a victim of criminal activity in the past twelve months. About 6 percent reported victimizations that occurred outside their neighborhood; 14 percent reported one or more victimizations within their neighborhood. The 20 percent figure is virtually the same as that reported for the NORC national sample in 1967.[16] Studies that have found higher victimization levels tend to be those that include a higher proportion of central city or ghetto respondents.[17] In the St. Louis study, the seven neighborhoods within the city of St. Louis had above average levels of victimization, but the variation among neighborhoods within and outside the city was high.

Several respondent and household characteristics were associated with victimization, particularly victimization in one's own neighborhood. Black respondents were more likely to indicate that they or another household member had been the victim of criminal activity in their own neighborhood than were white respondents (21 percent to 13 percent). As the wealth of the neighborhood increased, respondents and members of their households were less likely to have been victimized (25 percent in the lower wealth stratum, 16 percent in the middle and 10 percent in the higher stratum).[18] Both race and neighborhood wealth were independently related to victimization. In each wealth category, black respondents were more likely to have been victimized or to have a household member who was victimized in their own neighborhoods than were white respondents (12 percent of blacks in the higher category and 10 percent of the whites, 21 percent to 16 percent in the middle and 27 percent to 19 percent in the lower range).

The respondent's age and education were also related to victimization. The education relationship virtually disappeared, however, when the wealth of the respondent's neighborhood was controlled. Better educated respondents lived in wealthier neighborhoods where fewer victimizations occurred. Similarly (with one exception), the age relationship disappears when the respondent's race was controlled. Approximately 21 percent of the black respondents in every age category reported one or more victimizations in their own neighborhood. For the white respondents, 12 percent under eighteen and between thirty-one and sixty-four and 10 percent over sixty-five were victimized or had a household member who was victimized in their own neighborhood. Curiously, white respondents between ages nineteen and thirty were almost as likely to have been victimized or to have a household member who had been victimized in their own neighborhood as were black respondents (19 percent for whites in this category to 21 percent for blacks overall). Why this occurred is presently unclear.

The more than 550 respondents who reported one or more victimizations of themselves or another household member in their own neighborhood provide a pool of responses from which to examine the relationships among police actions, respondents' satisfaction with those actions, and respondents' evaluations and perceptions of local police services. First, however, the simple relationships between victimization and respondents' evaluations and perceptions will be presented.

VICTIMIZATION, EVALUATIONS AND PERCEPTIONS

Respondents' evaluations of local police service ought to be more sensitive to local happenings than to those that occur outside their own neighborhoods. As the data in Table 5-1 show, this does seem to be the case.[19] Respondents who indicated that they or another household member were the victim of criminal activity that occurred outside their own neighborhood gave approximately the same evaluations of their local police as did their nonvictim neighbors. Victimization within one's own neighborhood was related to lower evaluations of the local police. The strength of the relationship, measured by Goodman and Kruskal's gamma, is generally low or negligible, however.[20] Each of the reported relationships is negative, indicating generally lower evaluations from those who experienced victimization. The relationships are much stronger for victimizations inside one's own neighborhood. This would be expected if there were a connection in the respondents' minds between victimization and evaluations of their local police.

Potentially confounding factors are respondent's race and the wealth of the respondent's neighborhood. Whether it is due to lower levels of police service, abrasive contacts with the police, general dissatisfaction with one's life chances, excesses of rhetoric on the part of local spokesmen or some combination of these and other factors, blacks and/or residents of less wealthy neighborhoods generally evaluate their local police less favorably than do other citizens. As noted earlier, such individuals are also more likely to indicate that they or a member of their household have been the victim of criminal activity. The percentages in each evaluation category might thus reflect racial and neighborhood wealth variations rather than victimization.

Controlling for race and neighborhood wealth provides evidence that such was not the case. For four of the five evaluation measures, the relationships between evaluation and victimization remain about the same for both blacks and whites and for each wealth category. The single exception is the overall evaluation of police service variables. Here the relationship between more local victimization and lower evaluations is stronger for blacks (gamma = –0.31) than for whites (gamma = –0.17). Similar differences are also found for neighborhood wealth (gamma = –0.28 in the lower range, –0.20 in the middle and –0.11 in the higher range), but much of this can be attributed to racial differences in the strata. The stronger relationship among blacks than among whites is reflective of generally lower levels of satisfaction with police response to reported victimizations found among black respondents. This will be addressed in the following section.

Turning to respondents' perceptions of neighborhood crime trends and of local police response rate when summoned, victimization outside of one's neighborhood does appear related to these perceptions. As shown in Table 5-2, respondents who were victimized or who had a household member who was victimized were more likely to think that crime was increasing in their neighborhood (gamma = +0.35) and less likely to respond that their local police came very rapidly when called (gamma = –0.15). There is little variation in the strength of the relationship between victimization and perception of neighborhood crime trends across racial or wealth categories, but the relationship between victimization and perception of response rate does show some sensitivity to racial differences (gamma = –0.21 among blacks and –0.12 among whites). Black respondents consistently reported longer police response times than did whites when the police were summoned following a victimization. This may explain the difference in strength of relationships found here: if black victims do receive slower service when they call the police, the more strongly negative relationships between victimization and perceptions of local police response rate among blacks may be due to this difference in police response.[21]

VICTIMS' SATISFACTION WITH POLICE RESPONSE AND THEIR EVALUATIONS AND PERCEPTIONS

If evaluations and perceptions of local police services are only weakly related to the experience of victimization, which explanation should be entertained? Is there no connection in people's minds between police activity and their experience of victimization, or does the type of police response to a victimization mask such a connection?

Tables 5-3 and 5-4 provide evidence that helps answer this question. Here, analysis focuses on respondents who (1) were victimized or who had a household member who was victimized in their own neighborhood and (2) indicated that

Table 5-1. Household Victimization and Evaluation of Local Police

	Percentage of Respondents by Evaluative Response and Victimization Category				
Respondent Rating of Local Police	*No Victimization*	*Victimization Outside Own Neighborhood*	*Victimization Once in Own Neighborhood*	*Victimization Twice in Own Neighborhood*	*Strength of Relationship (Gamma)*
Police Service					
Outstanding	29	28	21	13	–0.21
Good	49	46	43	44	
Adequate	19	17	25	23	
Inadequate	2	7	7	10	
Very Poor	2	2	5	10	
N*=	(3,079)	(230)	(464)	(88)	
Police-Community Relations					
Outstanding	19	17	11	16	–0.19
Good	55	52	51	39	
Adequate	18	22	21	27	
Inadequate	5	6	7	9	
Very Poor	3	3	10	10	
N =	(2,536)	(185)	(376)	(82)	
Police are Honest					
Strongly Agree	20	20	17	16	–0.14
Agree	74	70	71	66	
Disagree	5	8	9	13	
Strongly Disagree	1	2	3	5	
N =	(2,548)	(189)	(384)	(80)	
Police Are Courteous					
Strongly Agree	26	30	23	25	–0.07
Agree	70	61	69	63	

Disagree	4	5	5	11	
Strongly Disagree	1	2	2	1	
N =	(2,649)	(197)	(405)	(80)	
Police Treat All Equally					
Strongly Agree	14	16	14	16	−0.14
Agree	70	62	62	46	
Disagree	12	16	17	25	
Strongly Disagree	4	5	8	13	
N =	(2,499)	(184)	(372)	(76)	

*Number of respondents. See note 20.

Source: Computed from St. Louis survey data collected by the author and others in 1972.

Table 5-2. Household Victimization and Respondent Perceptions

Respondent Perception	*Percentage of Respondents by Perception Response and Victimization Category*				
	No Victimization	*Victimization Outside Own Neighborhood*	*Victimization Once in Own Neighborhood*	*Victimization Twice in Own Neighborhood*	*Strength of Relationship (Gamma)*
Neighborhood Crime Trend					
Increasing	24	34	48	62	+0.35
Staying Same	58	53	41	28	
Decreasing	9	8	7	7	
No Crime	9	6	4	3	
N =	(2,931)	(217)	(436)	(89)	
Police Response Rate in Neighborhood					
Very Rapid	52	46	49	32	–0.15
Quickly Enough	41	41	34	32	
Slowly	6	10	12	14	
Very Slowly	2	4	6	8	
N =	(2,835)	(223)	(445)	(88)	

Source: Computed from St. Louis survey data collected by the author and others in 1972.

Table 5-3. Satisfaction With Police Response and Evaluation of Local Police: Victimization in Own Neighborhood Reported to the Police

Respondent Rating of Local Police	*Percentage of Respondents by Evaluative Response and Satisfaction With Police Response*		
	Satisfied With Police Response	*Not Satisfied With Police Response*	*Strength of Relationship (Gamma)*
Police Service			
Outstanding	26	0	+0.75
Good	48	27	
Adequate	20	33	
Inadequate	4	22	
Very Poor	3	17	
N =	(329)	(99)	
Police-Community Relations			
Outstanding	16	2	+0.62
Good	55	29	
Adequate	19	29	
Inadequate	6	11	
Very Poor	4	28	
N =	(271)	(82)	
Police are Honest			
Strongly Agree	20	6	+0.66
Agree	74	62	
Disagree	5	22	
Strongly Disagree	1	9	
N =	(364)	(85)	
Police are Courteous			
Strongly Agree	30	6	+0.78
Agree	67	67	
Disagree	2	22	
Strongly Disagree	1	6	
N =	(294)	(88)	
Police Treat All Equally			
Strongly Agree	19	4	+0.67
Agree	65	42	
Disagree	12	32	
Strongly Disagree	4	23	
N =	(267)	(84)	

Source: Computed from St. Louis survey data collected by the author and others in 1972.

Table 5-4. Satisfaction With Police Response and Respondent Perceptions: Victimization in Own Neighborhood Reported to the Police

	Percentage of Respondents by Perception Response and Satisfaction With Police Response		
Respondent Perception	*Satisfied With Police Response*	*Not Satisfied With Police Response*	*Strength of Relationship (Gamma)*
Neighborhood Crime Trend			
Increasing	45	63	–0.33
Staying Same	43	31	
Decreasing	7	6	
No Crime	5	0	
N =	(312)	(94)	
Police Response Rate in Neighborhood			
Very Rapid	58	17	+0.69
Quickly Enough	32	37	
Slowly	7	29	
Very Slowly	3	17	
N =	(315)	(102)	

Source: Computed from St. Louis survey data collected by the author and others in 1972.

the victimization was reported to the police. The findings are striking. Respondents who were satisfied by the police response to a reported victimization gave virtually the same responses as did those who reported either no victimization or a victimization that occurred outside of their own neighborhood (see Tables 5-1 and 5-2 above). Only in their perceptions of neighborhood crime rate did they differ from their nonvictimized neighbors.

On the other hand, respondents who were dissatisfied with the police response after they were called were much more negative in their evaluations and perceptions. All relationships between satisfaction (or the lack thereof) and evaluations are substantial or very strong, as is the relationship between satisfaction and perceived police response time. The relationship with perception of neighborhood crime trend is only moderate. This may indicate that although the police actions *can* restore victims' confidence in the police, they cannot do as much to restore their sense of neighborhood security.

Approximately 100 respondents who were victimized or who had a household member who was victimized in their own neighborhood, but who stated that the victimization was not reported to the police, are not included in these tables. Generally speaking, their responses were similar to those who were satisfied with police action. Most of those who did not report the incident indicated that it was not a very serious matter or that they did not want to bother the police.

If satisfaction with police response to a report of victimization is a major determinant of victims attitudes toward the police, it is important to know what police actions lead to citizen satisfaction with the police response. One factor noted in a number of studies is the quickness of police response when called. Incidents that may not seem important to a veteran police officer are likely to be a very unexpected and disheartening shock to the victim. Where there is a long wait for the police, this delay may so alienate the victim that any further police activity will have little effect on resulting satisfaction. Very rapid response, however, may convince victims that the police care about their problems, even if there is little that can be done.

Perceived speed of response has a substantial association with citizen satisfaction. The data presented in Table 5-5 indicate a marked drop-off in satisfaction with police action in response to reported victimization as the length of time taken to respond increases.

Skogan suggests that the lower evaluations of police services typically found among black respondents may be partly explained by a slower police response to reports of victimizations from blacks than to such reports from whites.[22] In the St. Louis study, blacks who were victimized or who had a household member who was victimized generally indicated that the police took longer to get to the scene than did whites. Although only 17 percent of whites reported response times of over twenty minutes, 36 percent of blacks reported that police took more than twenty minutes to arrive. The statistical relationship between longer response times and a respondent's race is a moderate one (gamma = +0.38). Together with the findings relating response time to satisfaction with response

Table 5-5. Satisfaction With Police Response When Summoned, Speed of Police Response and Action Taken by Police: Victimization in Own Neighborhood

Percentage of Respondents Who Report Satisfaction by Speed of Police Response				*Strength of Relationship (Gamma)*
0 to 4 minutes	*5 to 10 minutes*	*11 to 20 minutes*	*Over 20 minutes*	
90 (57)*	87 (173)	75 (68)	43 (83)	−0.61

Percentage of Respondents Who Report Satisfaction by Action Taken by the Police						*Strength of Relationship (Gamma)*
Recovered Property	*Checked Premises*	*Questioned Suspect*	*Took Report*	*Questioned Complainant*	*Took No Action*	
100 (27)	91 (100)	88 (26)	80 (148)	56 (36)	13 (30)	−0.72

*Number of respondents.

Source: Computed from St. Louis survey data collected by the author and others in 1972.

and those linking satisfaction with evaluations of police service, these data provide support for Skogan's suggestion.

In addition to responding rapidly, it is likely that what police do upon arrival is related to citizen satisfaction. Negligible or perfunctory action on the scene could easily negate the favorable effect of a rapid response. The data in the lower portion of Table 5-5 address this point.

An interesting feature of these data is the marked increase in satisfaction when the police take positive action. Filling out a report resulted in satisfaction for 80 percent of the respondents. Further actions, such as questioning a suspect, checking the premises and recovering stolen property, resulted in even higher levels of satisfaction. On the other hand, merely questioning the complainant about the incident without taking a report satisfied only about half of those so treated, and no perceived action resulted in dissatisfaction for 87 percent.

In contrast to the response time findings, there was little difference in the distribution of type of action taken by police after arrival when controls for race of respondent were made. Blacks were slightly more likely to indicate that the police did nothing (12 percent versus 7 percent for whites), but were also slightly more likely to have their property recovered (10 percent versus 7 percent for whites). While police response may have been slower where the victim was black, officers were even-handed in taking positive (or negative) actions upon arriving.

For all respondents who indicated that the police were called, the relationship between satisfaction and action taken by police after arrival is slightly stronger than the relationship between satisfaction and the speed of response (gamma = –0.61 with increasing response times; gamma = –0.72 with decreasing levels of action). This difference is not significant, either statistically or substantively. Because of the limited number of cases available, only preliminary investigation can be made of the relationship between response time and satisfaction, controlling for subsequent actions; or of the relationship between actions taken after arrival and satisfaction, controlling for speed of response.

Examination of the satisfaction-police action relationship while controlling for speed of response shows hardly any difference in the strength of relationship between police actions and satisfaction except when the response time was more than twenty minutes. There, the strength of the relationship increases considerably. This suggests that, if the police are very late in arriving, they had better take positive action in order to satisfy the complainant. Further, as the degree of favorability of police activity increases, the relationship between satisfaction and speed of response diminishes quite markedly. This supports the notion that favorable actions after arrival may ameliorate the negative effects of a slow response. Both sets of controlled relationships are based upon a small number of cases, however. In order to investigate these and other relationships resulting from direct police-citizen encounters, it will be necessary to sample populations known to have had such encounters, rather than the general public. A research project currently underway at Indiana University will collect and analyze information from such a sample.[23]

SUMMARY AND POLICY IMPLICATIONS

This chapter has explored the relationships between victimization—either personal or that of a household member—and citizen evaluations and perceptions of the police service that followed. While the apparent relationships between victimization, evaluations and perceptions were quite weak, a detailed analysis found that police responses to victimization act to mask a stronger relationship. When citizens were satisfied with the police response, evaluations were unrelated to their experience. On the other hand, citizens who were unsatisfied with their police contact were much more likely to give their local police unfavorable evaluations.

The character of police responses to victimizations—the speed of their response and actions taken after their arrival—was substantially related to citizen satisfaction. Some preliminary exploration, limited in power by the small number of victimizations, indicated that favorable actions taken after arrival may overcome ill feelings caused by a longer response time.

The findings reported here indicate that there may be significant payoffs in citizen satisfaction in return for relatively little additional commitment of police time. If officers responding to reported victimizations expend some additional effort, thus indicating to the complainant that they are concerned about the incident, evaluations and perceptions of the local police should improve considerably. One can speculate that those who have had direct experiences with the local police as a result of victimization may be more attentive to police matters in the future and that the direction of their support or hostility may depend upon their experiences. If this is the case, extra effort at the time of response could pay large dividends.

NOTES

1. Among these are Jennie McIntyre, "Public Attitudes Toward Crime and Law Enforcement," *The Annals* 374 (November 1967): 34-46; Richard L. Block, "Police Action, Support for the Police, and the Support for Civil Liberties" (Paper read at the annual meetings of the American Sociological Association, Washington, D.C., August 1970); Elinor Ostrom and Gordon P. Whitaker, "Community Control and Government Responsiveness: The Case of Police in Black Neighborhoods," in David Rodgers and Willis Hawley, eds., *Improving the Quality of Urban Management* (Beverly Hills, California: Sage Publications, 1974), pp. 303-34; Elinor Ostrom, William H. Baugh, Richard Guarasci, Roger B. Parks and Gordon P. Whitaker, *Community Organization and the Provision of Police Services* (Beverly Hills, California: Sage Professional

Papers in Administrative and Policy Studies 03-001, 1973); Paul E. Smith and Richard O. Hawkins, "Victimization, Types of Citizen-Police Contacts, and Attitudes Toward the Police," *Law and Society Review* 8 (Fall 1973): 135-52; and Roger B. Parks, "Complementary Measures of Police Performance," in Kenneth M. Dolbeare, ed., *Public Policy Evaluation* (Beverly Hills, California: Sage Yearbooks in Politics and Public Policy, 1976), pp. 185-218.

2. A simple discussion of how one variable can mask or "suppress" the relationship between two other variables in this way can be found in James A. Davis, *Elementary Survey Analysis* (Englewood Cliffs, New Jersey: Prentice-Hall, Inc., 1971), pp. 95-96. I am indebted to John McIver for this citation.

3. McIntyre, pp. 36-37.

4. Ibid., p. 37.

5. Block.

6. Smith and Hawkins, p. 140.

7. Ostrom et al., p. 40.

8. Ostrom and Whitaker.

9. Smith and Hawkins, p. 140.

10. David J. Bordua and Larry L. Tifft, "Citizen Interviews, Organizational Feedback, and Police-Community Relations," *Law and Society Review* 6 (November 1971): 155-82.

11. Frank F. Furstenberg, Jr., and Charles F. Wellford, "Calling the Police: The Evaluation of Police Service," *Law and Society Review* 7 (Spring 1973): 393-406.

12. For a detailed description of this study, see Elinor Ostrom, Roger B. Parks and Dennis C. Smith, "A Multi-Strata, Similar Systems Design for Measuring Police Performance" (Paper read at the annual meetings of the Midwest Political Science Association, Chicago, Illinois, May 1973). The author wishes to thank the Center for Studies of Metropolitan Problems of the National Institute of Mental Health, whose grant number 5-RO1-MH-19911-02 supported the St. Louis data collection.

13. The "most similar systems" research design is discussed in Chapter Two of Adam Przeworski and Henry Teune, *The Logic of Comparative Social Inquiry* (New York: John Wiley & Sons, 1970), pp. 31-46.

14. The study team believed that interviews dealing with local police might appear somewhat threatening to some respondents. To begin such an interview by requesting a complete list of all adult household residents could certainly aggravate any such feelings.

15. The demographics and simple breakdowns of findings for each of the jurisdictions in the study are provided in a series of reports prepared by Nancy M. Neubert and Virginia Dodge Fielder. These reports, entitled "Law Enforcement in [Name of Jurisdiction]: Citizen and Police Perceptions," were provided to each of the cooperating police chiefs. Copies are available from the Workshop in Political Theory and Policy Analysis, Indiana University.

16. Philip H. Ennis, *Criminal Victimization in the United States: A Report of a National Survey, Field Surveys II* (Washington, D.C.: U.S. Government Printing Office, 1967), p. 5.

17. Smith and Hawkins, p. 136, for example, report that 55 percent of their

respondents from Seattle were victimized within the previous twelve months. The Law Enforcement Assistance Administration reports a 40 percent household victimization rate in the cities of Dayton-San Jose. See their *Crimes and Victims: A Report on the Dayton-San Jose Pilot Survey of Victimization* (Washington, D.C.: National Criminal Justice Information and Statistics Service, 1974), p. 10. In their subsequent surveys of victimization in the larger American cities, there are differences in the base used for reporting that prevent direct comparisons with the St. Louis data. See their *Criminal Victimization Surveys in the Nation's Five Largest Cities*, and *Criminal Victimization Surveys in 13 American Cities*, both (Washington, D.C.: U.S. Government Printing Office, 1975).

18. The wealth strata were restricted to less than the full range available using a criterion based on median value of owner-occupied housing. The upper stratum included neighborhoods where this ranged from $15,000 to $24,999, the middle stratum from $10,000 to $19,999 and the lower stratum included neighborhoods where the median was below $10,000. The top two strata were further differentiated where they overlapped by a median contract rent criterion. See Ostrom, Parks and Smith.

19. Due to the design of the St. Louis research, various combinations of in-person, mail and telephone interviews were used across the forty-four neighborhoods. This resulted in some questions not being used for the full set of respondents. This, in turn, accounts for most of the variation in number of respondents from question to question on Table 5-1 and subsequent tables. See Ibid.

20. See L.A. Goodman and W.H. Kruskal, "Measures of Association for Cross Classification," *Journal of the American Statistical Association* 49 (December 1954): 732-64. The phraseology used to describe the strength of relationship is taken from that suggested by Davis, p. 49. A gamma with a magnitude greater than 0.7 will be called a very strong relationship, one from 0.5 to 0.69 a substantial relationship, 0.3 to 0.49 a moderate relationship, 0.1 to 0.29 a low relationship, 0.01 to 0.09 a negligible relationship, and a gamma of zero, no relationship. As Davis notes, these are essentially arbitrary designations made a priori for the sake of consistency.

21. All of the relationships in Tables 5-1 and 5-2 are statistically significant ($p > .01$) except for the evaluation of police courtesy. That is, there is less than one chance in a hundred that relationships this large would have been found if in fact there were no relationship between victimization and evaluations and perceptions. But statistical significance is partly an artifact of the number of cases involved. The large number of respondents in the St. Louis study means that relatively low gammas are statistically significant. In any case, statistical significance is never a sufficient reason to argue that a relationship has any *substantive* significance. Thus, the data reported here are generally consistent with previously cited studies that found little or no relationship between the experience of victimization and citizen attitudes and perceptions of police service.

22. Wesley G. Skogan, "Public Policy and Public Evaluations of Criminal Justice System Performance," in John A. Gardiner and Michael A. Mulkey, eds. *Crime and Criminal Justice*, (Lexington, Massachusetts: D.C. Heath, 1975), pp. 43-61.

23. The project, entitled "Evaluating the Organization of Service Delivery: Police," is funded by the Advanced Productivity Research and Technology Division of the National Science Foundation. The first phase of the project, in which a detailed overview of the police service delivery systems in eighty metropolitan areas was compiled, is completed. The overview is reported in a comprehensive volume co-authored with Elinor Ostrom and Gordon P. Whitaker, *Patterns of Metropolitan Policing*, to be published in the spring of 1976 by Lexington Books. The second phase will entail a concentrated investigation of police activities undertaken under various forms of police organization in agencies found in three to four metropolitan areas.

Chapter 6

Crime and Crime Rates*

Wesley G. Skogan

Victimization surveys were conceived to provide new and more accurate measures of the incidence of crime. Direct interviews with victims enable us to bypass the fallible data-gathering activities of local police departments and gather wide-ranging and detailed information on the experiences of citizens both with crime and with the criminal justice system. One of the first uses of the victimization survey data collected for the federal government by the Bureau of the Census was to compare them with the official crime statistics published yearly by the FBI. This was an obvious first step, for the discrepancy between crime estimates made through surveys and crime reports filed with the FBI was quite large. The Census Bureau's National Crime Survey uncovered about three times as many crimes as had been recorded by the police.[1] The media focused on the differences between official and survey crime figures for specific cities. The *New York Times*, for example, printed the two side by side for eight large cities. In a front page article, David Burnham argued that the publication of such statistics would increase pressure on local criminal justice agencies to improve their performance and end FBI and local police department domination of crime statistics.[2]

This chapter examines the relationship (1) between official and survey measures of crime and (2) between each type of measure and the "true" crime rate. The chapter also examines the consequences of these observations for criminal justice planning, management and evaluation.

There are three factors that make the relationship between crime statistics

*This chapter was prepared under Grant Number NI-99-0032 from the National Institute of Law Enforcement and Criminal Justice, Law Enforcement Assistance Administration, U.S. Department of Justice. Points of view or opinions stated in this document are those of the author and do not necessarily represent the official position or policies of the U.S. Department of Justice.

and the crime rate problematic: variations in the rate at which citizens report their experiences to the police; differences in the way police departments receive, evaluate and account for citizen's reports; and methodological quirks that make each measure a less than accurate indicator of the crime rate. The quantity each of these methods is trying to measure—the true crime rate—is always unknown. It can only be observed through one or another pair of methodological spectacles. The method that gets us closest to those events is the victimization survey. Such surveys have been conducted in a number of communities, both in the United States and abroad. Richard Sparks' chapter in this volume discusses his work in London, and Anne Schneider's essay is based upon a survey that she carried out in Portland, Oregon.[3] The federal government's surveys have been conducted by the Bureau of the Census with the support of the Law Enforcement Assistance Administration (LEAA). Since 1972, the Bureau has carried out a series of surveys designed to produce yearly estimates of the national victimization rate. Dodge, Lentzner and Shenk summarize some of the Bureau's findings in the first chapter of this book. Between 1972 and 1974, the Census Bureau also conducted special surveys in twenty-six major cities, using a somewhat different methodology. Barbara Boland's essay is based upon those interviews. City residents were asked questions focusing on six major crimes: rape, assault, robbery, burglary, simple property theft and motor vehicle theft. In addition, local businessmen were questioned about the incidence of burglary and robbery in their places of business. The commercial and household surveys together give us a fairly thorough enumeration of the frequency of robbery and burglary.[4] This chapter uses the data for these two crimes in examining the relationship between survey and official crime rates.

CITIZEN REPORTING TO THE POLICE

Interviews with victims indicate that many incidents uncovered by surveys are not reported to the police. Burglary and robbery are about average in that respect. The national victimization survey conducted by the Bureau of the Census in 1973 found that about 49 percent of all personal robberies reported in the survey had also been reported to the police. About 46 percent of the household burglaries uncovered in the interviews had been brought to the attention of the authorities. Crimes affecting commercial establishments were reported at a higher rate—robbery in 86 percent of all cases and burglary in 79 percent.[5] In contrast, some crimes, e.g., auto theft, were reported at a higher rate. Personal thefts (picked pockets, snatched purses) were reported only about 32 percent of the time.

It has always been known that underreporting has an effect on official crime statistics. The crimes chosen by the FBI for inclusion in the Crime Index were selected, in part, because they seemed *relatively* well reported. At the same time, everyone involved in collecting and analyzing official statistics was aware that crimes as diverse as rape and simple property theft often went unreported. The issues were, Are we being led astray by *systematic* errors? Is underreporting patterned in ways that systematically bias studies that use crime statistics to measure relative rates of crime, studies that use changes in reported crime to evaluate the effects of crime prevention programs or decisions about how the criminal justice system ought to allocate its resources? The fact of undercounting may be less important than its distribution in time and space.[6]

These issues played an important role in the federal government's decision in the early 1970s to launch a program of research and methodological development in the area of crime measurement. The federal victimization surveys included questions to determine which incidents recalled during an interview were reported to the police. The survey's results have a bearing on several important questions:

–Does nonreporting work to the disadvantage of minorities and the poor, who may be receiving less police protection than they require?
–Might crime prevention programs increase reporting rates at the same time they reduce the incidence of victimization, thus confounding the evaluation of those programs?
–Do different citizen reporting practices affect police crime statistics in various locations in different ways?

The victimization surveys indicate that reporting practices do differ from city to city. The reporting rate for robbery (including personal and commercial offenses) was very high in Miami (76 percent), Washington (73 percent) and Atlanta (71 percent); but the robbery reporting rate was only 52 percent in Portland and San Francisco and 55 percent in Los Angeles and Newark. Only 51 percent of all burglaries were reported in Houston, while Miami again topped the list at 67 percent.[7] Overall, only about 60 percent of all big city burglary and 62 percent of all robbery was reported to the police, thereby becoming *eligible* for inclusion in official crime statistics. Crimes like these almost always come to the attention of the police through citizen complaints; the national data for 1973 indicated that only 1.6 percent of personal robberies and 0.4 percent of household burglaries were discovered at the scene by the police. Any analysis of the differences between official and survey crime rates must begin with this basic source of discrepancies between the two.

The reasons for nonreporting are numerous. People may not call the police because they feel that nothing can be done about the incident or because they plan to pursue private revenge.[8] They may fear their assailants may return to harass them after appearing before a magistrate; or they may be afraid of the police; or they may be afraid of what the police might discover once summoned. People also fail to report crimes to the authorities because they seem trivial. The time and effort involved may seem to exceed any potential gain.

Understanding the reasons for underreporting is important. As we have seen, nonreporting is a major factor shaping official crime statistics, and it may be important to know if the conditions affecting it are changing and what this portends for reported crime levels. It also is necessary to understand the dynamics of crime reporting because those practices may be influenced by the very programs we institute to fight crime and insure justice. If fear of retaliation is an important motive for nonreporting, then policies that return offenders to the streets may have important implications for citizen cooperation with the police. On the other hand, a primary consequence of crime prevention programs is an increase in the rate at which victimizations are reported to the police. Communities which "get tough on crime" may end up looking worse for their efforts.

My analysis suggests that the primary determinant of most reporting and nonreporting is the seriousness of the offense. Individual attributes such as race, sex, income and (although it did account for something) age are secondary in importance to the nature of the incident itself. In both national and city data, the controlling factors were the amount of financial loss involved in a crime, whether force was used, whether a weapon was employed, the extent of physical injury and whether the assailant was a stranger. Factors such as invasion of one's home or being threatened with death have a major impact on crime reporting.[9]

A crucial question is whether these factors vary enough from community to community to affect aggregate levels of crime reporting. Apparently many do. The data collected in twenty-six communities indicates that intercity variations in levels of violence, stranger crime, use of weapons, financial loss and racial fear are sufficient to explain much of the variation across cities in the "willingness" of citizens to report crime. Guns, for example, play an important role in crime, especially in offenses against commercial establishments. They enable lone offenders to control merchants, customers or truculent victims they accost on the street; they are "equalizers." Cities vary in the extent to which guns are employed in robbery. In Cleveland, 38 percent of all personal robbery involved a gun. New York City was a knife town, and Milwaukeans enjoyed the good fortune of experiencing mainly unarmed, "strong-arm" robberies. Nationally, 68 percent of all personal robberies in which a gun was used were reported to the police as compared with 40 percent of those not involving weapons. Not surprisingly, the correlation at the city level between the robbery reporting rate and the proportion of all robberies involving the use of a gun was +0.50.

Measures of the seriousness of interpersonal violence also correlate strongly with reporting rates at both individual and city levels. The surveys collected a great deal of data on the extent of the personal injury suffered in rapes and assaults. Such injuries varied in seriousness from very slight (in unsuccessful attacks or assaults yielding only minor scratches) to very consequential (leading to broken bones, internal injuries, loss of teeth and hospitalization). Victims in some survey cities were more seriously injured than in others. The proportion of assaults falling into the "aggravated" category because of injury (those leading to the serious consequences described above) ranged from only 11 percent in San Francisco and 13 percent in San Diego, Portland, Milwaukee and Minneapolis to 21 percent in Philadelphia, St. Louis and Baltimore, and 25 percent in Newark. Nationally, 82 percent of all serious assaults were reported to the police, as compared to only 43 percent of all minor ones.[10] The correlation at the city level between the proportion of rapes and assaults in the serious category and the reporting rate for the same set of crimes was a powerful +0.73.

Similar differences appear when we examine another element of the seriousness of interpersonal violence—the relationship between victim and offender. Assaults by strangers, which almost invariably occur on the street or in some other public place, are among the most feared crimes, and the reduction of stranger crime was a primary goal of LEAA's high impact city anticrime program of the early 1970s. The survey data have methodological weaknesses in measuring the extent of crime among friends, neighbors or relatives, but they show substantial variation in the proportion of rapes and assaults attributed to strangers.[11] At the top were New York (84 percent) and Boston (79 percent); at the bottom, Atlanta (59 percent) and Houston (60 percent). The correlation at the city level between reporting to the police and this measure of seriousness was +0.34. Multivariate analysis of the joint effect of weapon use and stranger attacks upon the proportion of rapes and assaults reported to the police indicates that each is a significant predictor of victim behavior; together they explain 66 percent of the variance in reporting (a multiple correlation of +0.81).

Other measures of seriousness were also related to reporting practices. The correlation between the proportion of simple property thefts reported to the police and the proportion involving losses of over $50 was +0.49. The correlation between the proportion of household burglaries reported and the proportion involving forced entry was +0.54.

One of the strongest relationships, and one that seems to portend badly for the urban condition, reflected the racial fears of whites. There is considerable evidence that a high proportion of crimes in the survey cities were committed by blacks. In most cases, the victims were other blacks, who, in general, suffer substantially higher victimization rates than whites. However, some crimes involved white victims and black offenders. The proportion of such black-white crimes varied by city; it was low in Minneapolis and Denver (38 percent in each), and high in Washington (79 percent), New Orleans (77 percent) and Detroit (74 percent). The rate at which whites reported crimes to the police was higher in cities where blacks were more likely to be involved. The reporting rate for black victims was not significantly affected. The city level correlation between the proportion of whites victimized by blacks and crime reporting was +0.66 for whites and +0.04 for blacks. The racial characteristics of offenders appear to be a powerful predictor of white reporting behavior in the twenty-six cities.

It should be clear that this measure was related to the racial composition of the cities. As the contrast between Minneapolis and Washington illustrates, the proportion of crimes committed by blacks should be higher in towns with larger black populations. The correlation between the percentage of blacks in a city and the reporting rate was also positive, suggesting that whites may report more frequently in largely black communities. Even when we control for the racial composition of the city, however, the proportion of white victimizations involving black offenders continues to independently affect the reporting practices of whites.

POLICE RECORDING PRACTICES

A second set of factors affecting the relationship between crime rates and official crime statistics are the practices of local police. Police departments act as political and organizational filters through which citizen complaints must pass before becoming part of the official count of "crimes known to the police." There are several devices for accomplishing this end. Offenses reported to the police can be shifted from one statistical category to another, they can be "downgraded" or they can be ignored. The police may choose not to fill out required forms, not to file them or not to account for them when reporting to the FBI. These activities can occur at various levels within the organization: patrolmen, their immediate supervisors or top administrators "downtown." Whatever their locus, such practices should have a powerful impact upon the official crime rate for a jurisdiction. Relatively thorough police departments should publish figures that coincide with survey measures of the crime rate. Where policies or practices discourage honest accounting, larger discrepancies should be expected.

A substantial amount of police underreporting can be attributed to the beat patrolmen who observe or respond to complaints. Part of the filtering process is official. Only complaints in which a legally actionable incident has occurred should be recorded. The remainder are considered "unfounded" and are not included in official reports. Observational studies of patrol operations indicate that a number of extralegal criteria also are applied to this decision. The police generally attempt to avoid unnecessary or unproductive work, to forestall complaints about their behavior and to maintain control of situations on the street. The most serious victimizations are usually recorded, but many never become officially "known."[12]

Pressure on patrol officers to discount or ignore potentially bona fide complaints usually comes from the district commander's office. This pressure may become intense when the performance of middle level managers in police organizations is evaluated by their ability to keep the crime rate down. It was easier to disguise crime reports before the days of centralized radio dispatching systems. Then, complaints were received and filed in district stationhouses and only summary reports were sent downtown.[13] During the 1920s, the prosecutor in Chicago would occasionally "raid" local stations and publish the discrepancies he found between those figures when it seemed politically profitable to embarrass the city administration.[14] Now that citizens call central dispatch centers, it has become necessary for district commanders to see that their men ignore or downgrade more incidents.

Connivance in underrecording of crime often extends to the top of the department. Top administrators in police departments must be sensitive to political winds, which usually carry the message that crime rates should be kept low. When reformers take office, however, the official rate often rises rapidly; complaints that formerly were disregarded are recorded, and the police tend to become more energetic in searching out crime and making arrests. The Crime Commission documented some of these flurries of crime recording, as well as their frequent decline as the new order becomes more settled in office.[15] The commission argued that longer range, more fundamental processes were also at work in police departments. They noted the rise of police professionalism throughout the nation and suggested that a consequence of this movement might be an apparent increase in the crime rate.[16] Professional departments are more interested in data collection and recordkeeping, for they use such information to allocate resources and evaluate personnel. Professionalism also implies a greater reliance on formal rather than informal disposition of complaints, which should increase the proportion of police-citizen encounters resulting in written reports.[17] Together, these long range forces should enhance the correspondence between survey-generated measures of "reported" crime and official crime data.

With a few assumptions, data collected in the victimization surveys can be used to test this hypothesis. The measure of police-recording practices used here is the ratio between the robbery and burglary counts presented for cities in the *Uniform Crime Report* (UCR) and the (projected) number of crimes that survey respondents claimed they reported to the police.[18] These figures are indicators of the discrepancy between survey data and published crime figures that *may* be attributable to police nonrecording. The major assumptions are: (1) the universe of crimes that each purports to measure is (approximately) the same, (2) the survey-based incident count is (relatively) accurate, and (3) we can trust most victims to tell us which crimes were and were not reported to the police. The next section of this chapter examines these methodological problems in some detail; for now, suffice it to say that the resulting measures of police practices vary substantially by city, and the readings they give for individual police departments correspond with other impressions we have about their operational style.

Table 6-1 presents the data upon which this analysis is based. For each of the twenty-six surveyed cities, it notes the percentage of personal and commercial robberies and burglaries that were reported to the police and the ratio of the number that appear in police records to that total.[19] The cities are ranked

Table 6-1. Measures of Police Recording and Citizen Reporting Practices

City	Police Recording		Citizen Reporting	
	Robbery	Burglary	Robbery	Burglary
Newark	100	75	56	65
Washington, D.C.	98	65	73	64
St. Louis	95	79	66	61
Cleveland	74	47	60	59
Detroit	73	62	66	62
Los Angeles	71	67	55	55
Baltimore	71	51	66	66
New York City	69	50	60	62
Miami	64	79	76	67
Chicago	64	39	58	57
Boston	61	45	65	63
Pittsburgh	60	57	70	56
Portland	59	64	52	57
Buffalo	59	48	58	58
Dallas	56	61	64	57
Oakland	55	63	66	64
Houston	55	63	62	51
New Orleans	51	56	61	53
San Francisco	51	59	53	56
Denver	49	61	57	62
Atlanta	46	57	71	61
Minneapolis	44	54	62	56
San Diego	40	49	57	55
Cincinnati	39	41	58	67
Philadelphia	38	35	59	59
Milwaukee	19	22	61	58

Source: U.S. Department of Justice, Law Enforcement Assistance Administration, *Crime in Eight American Cities* (Washington, D.C.: U.S. Government Printing Office, July, 1974); U.S. Department of Justice, Law Enforcement Assistance Administration, *Crime in the Nation's Five Largest Cities* (Washington, D.C.: U.S. Government Printing Office, April, 1975); U.S. Department of Justice, Law Enforcement Assistance Administration, *Criminal Victimization Surveys in 13 American Cities* (Washington, D.C.: U.S. Government Printing Office, June, 1975).

according to the police recording rate for robbery. The two measures of police cheating are strongly related ($r = +0.66$), indicating that the ranking is not an artifact of a particular type of crime and that honesty in recording may be a general rather than crime-specific characteristic of police departments. The scores of some of the highest and lowest departments fit the stereotypes of those agencies. At the top, Washington, D.C., has a vigorous and professional department, and St. Louis has long conducted internal audits of its crime-recording practices.[20] Both Philadelphia and Milwaukee produce notoriously unbelievable crime reports each year, and they appear at the bottom of this ranking.

The distorting effect of recording practices on official crime statistics is of the ame relative magnitude as that of citizen reporting practices. For the twenty-six cities, the proportion of reported robberies that were recorded by the police averaged 63 percent and that for burglary, 56 percent. About the same proportion of events are lost from the system at each stage, although the effect of citizen reporting on the number of events is greater because it acts as "first filter" in the crime measurement process. It is also important to note that the variation among cities is much greater regarding police recording than it is for citizen recording. City level reporting rates for robbery vary by only about 20 percent, and reporting rates for burglary vary even less. However, recording practices differ dramatically from city to city. As we shall see, this has important implications for the use of official crime statistics in research and evaluation.

The determinants of recording practices are difficult to measure. The politics of crime, political responsiveness of the police chief, actual reward structure of the department and professionalism of beat patrolmen are hard to observe even in one city.[21] Moreover, these determinants are subject to rapid reversals. It is possible, however, to explore some of the hypotheses advanced by the Crime Commission and to consider the relationship between basic indicators of department organization, resources and policies and police recording practices.

For example, the commission speculated that increased police professionalism should lead to increased crime recording, lending greater accuracy to official crime data.[22] Professionalism in police departments is a complex issue, but two indicators of the extent to which police organizations pursue modern personnel policies can be measured directly: the departments' recruitment of minority personnel and their employment of civilians.[23] The former reflects openness to change, responsiveness to external demands and the ability of departmental administrators to enforce controversial policies; the latter indicates a desire to raise the level of skill applied to specialized tasks within police departments. The two are positively correlated, suggesting that innovation is a general characteristic of some police departments. When the two measures are combined to form an innovativeness index, the resulting measure is correlated +0.49 with robbery recording and +0.57 with burglary recording.[23] For the twenty-six cities, innovation in personnel policymaking is significantly related to the production of more accurate crime statistics.

The problem may also be one of resources. Systematic recordkeeping, data production and the use of those tools for planning and evaluation are expensive activities. Perhaps only departments with ample resources are capable of collecting higher quality crime data or are interested in the use of these data within the organization. At the city level, the correlation between recording rates for robbery and resource measures is strong and positive: +0.66 for the number of departmental employees for each 10,000 residents and +0.44 for dollar expenditures per capita. The correlations between these resource measures and recording rates for burglary are much lower, however, which may suggest that the relationship represents merely a quirk in the data. Somewhat surprisingly, the correlation between recording practices and the extent to which computers are used by the departments is negative.

Just as citizens are more likely to report more serious victimizations, police departments are somewhat more likely to record incidents as crimes in their community become more serious. Departments in cities where crimes are more frequently serious generally recorded more incidents relative to the victimization survey estimate. Not all of the correlations were statistically significant, but they pointed consistently to higher recording levels in cities where guns were employed, where forcible entry burglaries were the norm, where thefts involved higher financial losses and where whites were victimized more often by blacks.

METHODOLOGICAL DIFFERENCES

The relationship between survey estimates of the crime rate and official police accounts also is affected by the manner in which the data are gathered. The survey figures include methodological artifacts, or miscounts introduced by the measurement process itself. There were also differences in what the two enumerations covered. They measure incidents affecting slightly different populations and, therefore, there always will be some discrepancies between the resulting estimates. The major technical difficulties with the survey data probably do not affect the relative ordering of the twenty-six cities on either the reporting or recording dimension. If their effects are spread randomly across the cities, the relationships reported here will describe accurately the dynamics of reporting and recording.

One methodological issue is "temporal telescoping" by victims. The surveys asked respondents to recall victimizations that occurred in the "past year." There is a strong tendency for victims of crimes that occurred more than one year ago to misrecall the date of those events and mentally pull them forward into the suggested reference period.[24] This "forward telescoping" leads to an overstatement of the crime rate for the reference year. Since reports to the police are more accurately placed in time (most complaints come immediately after the incident), telescoping artificially increases the ratio of survey crimes to officially recognized crimes. However, telescoping is a psychological process, and there is no evidence that it is more frequent in some cities than in others. Thus, this phenomenon probably does not affect the relationship between our measure of police recording and the distribution of other key variables.

Victims also do not report some of their experiences to an interviewer. Studies of the ability of interviewers to elicit accurate recollections indicate that the Census Bureau's victimization surveys substantially undercounted incidents of interpersonal violence involving friends and relatives.[25] Moreover, simply because memories of incidents fade with time, distant events were undercounted as well.[26] Undercounting seems unlikely to vary dramatically by city and should not affect the cities' relative rankings. Nevertheless, if the ability or willingness of respondents to recall events is affected by factors such as race or class, patterns of nonrecall may be city-specific. There is some evidence that this may be the case for incidents of assault, but there is no evidence that such is the case for robbery and burglary.

The final question concerning the survey data involves the veracity of victims' claims that they (or someone else) reported their experiences to the police. There has been no methodological research on the validity of these claims. In some social circles, reporting may be expected and desirable. Nonreporters from such groups may tend to exaggerate their public-spiritedness. The opposite also may occur, and the aggregate effect of these distortions is unknown.

A serious methodological issue is the comparability of coverage of victim surveys and police reports, for they gather data from somewhat different groups. Police figures cover crimes that occur (and have been reported and recorded) *within a city*. Thus, complaints from victimized commuters, tourists, convention delegates and other transient visitors to the central city are included in the published reports. Victim surveys, on the other hand, gather data from city *residents* and business representatives. They were questioned about their experiences during the preceding year, wherever they occurred. The two reference populations generally overlap, but the degree of correspondence differs from place to place. In some communities (Newark, Miami, Washington, Boston), over half of the labor force commutes into the city, while commuters make up a relatively small proportion of the labor force in Houston, San Diego, Baltimore and Chicago.[27] Extensive commuting should affect our measure of police recording practices for personal crimes, for it will "artificially" (from the survey's point of view) increase the ratio of official crimes to survey crimes. Police departments in cities with extensive tourism or commuting should score well on the robbery measure, for they are in fact recording unsurveyed victimizations fairly frequently. The correlation between the relative size of the commuter work force and police recording is indeed positive ($r = +0.38$ for robbery). While not statistically significant (a correlation of this size could occur by chance fairly frequently with only twenty-six cases), it tends to back the hypothesis that comparisons between survey and official crime counts are confounded by differences in their reference populations. Any systematic attempt to compare data collected by surveys and by the police must take this crucial incongruity into account. There are a number of other minor technical differences between the data-gathering techniques used in survey and police measures, but none appear to be important.[28]

THE CONSEQUENCES OF REPORTING AND RECORDING PRACTICES

This chapter has examined the relationship between crime rates as measured by victim surveys and crime rates gathered and published by local police departments. Citizen reporting and police recording practices seem to deflate official reports by about the same proportion, although the net effect of citizen nonreporting is greater than that of police nonrecording because it serves as a "first filter" on the information flow. The discrepancy between the survey crime rate and police figures is fraught with consequences, for the community and for the police. Recording practices affect the apparent effectiveness of the police–when departments encourage the collection of more accurate crime statistics, they suffer as a result. Thorough police recording practices may also encourage more citizen reporting, which further erodes their apparent effectiveness. Finally, the fact that some police departments manipulate their official statistics more blatantly than others indicates that those figures are even less useful for planning and evaluation than we had suspected.

Table 6-2 presents some correlations between measures of police recordkeeping accuracy and measures of the effectiveness of the twenty-six police departments. One of the strongest effects of complete recording is that it *decreases the clearance rate* for robbery and burglary. The clearance rate is the proportion of offenses in a crime category that the police believe they can attribute to a particular offender. It is safe to assume that police departments record and process crimes in which an identification is made or a suspect arrested and that many of the crimes that are not recorded are impossible to solve. Thus, more accurate crime recordkeeping raises the ratio of crimes to suspects, making the organization look less effective. It also strongly affects the official crime rate for cities. Table 6-2 indicates that cities where the ratio of recorded to reported crimes is high were also the "highest crime" areas based on published statistics. Each measure of effectiveness "builds in" these relationships because official crimes are a numerator or denominator on each side of the ratios being correlated–which simply restates the dilemma facing police administrators.

The data collected in the Census Bureau's surveys also suggest that high recording levels may affect another measure of departmental performance,

Table 6-2. The Consequences of Police Recording Practices

	Recording Rate for	
Indicators	*Robbery*	*Burglary*
Traditional Effectiveness		
Crime clearances	–0.61	–0.60
Official crime rate	0.78	0.70
Citizen Perceptions		
Percent think crime has limited their behavior	0.48	–
Percent feel unsafe in their neighborhood	0.50	–
Percent rate the police "good"	–0.53	–
Citizen Reporting Rates		
Interpersonal violence	0.60	0.32
Personal theft	0.45	0.25

Source: Calculated from unpublished tabulations supplied by the Bureau of the Census.

citizen attitudes and perceptions. At the city level, perceptions of crime and ratings of police performance are highly related to official crime statistics. Those figures are the only way that most of us form general impressions on the safety of our community and how it stands relative to other places. In the surveyed cities, the official robbery rate was positively correlated with aggregate responses to questions about the lack of safety in the respondents' neighborhoods at night ($r = +0.70$) and changes in their behavior due to crime ($r = +0.63$). Cities with high official robbery totals were also less likely to give their local police a good rating ($r = -0.42$). One way cities qualify as "unsafe" is by recording more accurate crime statistics; hence the relationship between the robbery recording rate and measures of fear and ratings of the police illustrated in Table 6-2.

Table 6-2 also indicates that departments that record most of the crimes coming to their attention may thereby encourage their citizens to report more incidents to the police. Table 6-2 indicates the positive correlations between police recording rates and citizen reporting of two distinct personal crimes that often go unreported–interpersonal violence (rape and assault) and personal theft (pocket picking and purse snatching). (We cannot use robbery and burglary reporting rates, as they were used to calculate the recording measures in the first place.) The measures in Table 6-2 are independent and suggest that honest departmental behavior may encourage increased citizen cooperation. A consequence of having this reputation for honesty in processing complaints may be an "inflation" (relative to other communities) of the crime rate.

One of the most important implications of the data in Table 6-1 is the serious threat that variations in department recording procedures pose to the validity of comparative measures of the crime rate. Differences in how departments handle complaints have a larger effect on the ranking of cities in the UCR than intercity differences in citizen reporting rates. There have been proposals to develop "correction" formulas for official crime data that would generate more accurate measures of the true crime rate. Proponents of this strategy have focused upon the filtering effect of citizen reporting, arguing that surveys could generate estimates of nonreporting for very specific types of crimes. Those corrections could then be applied to reported events, yielding data comparable to that collected in expensive victimization surveys. The difficulty is that it is the departmental nonrecording of complaints, not citizen nonreporting, that determines how cities will eventually be ranked with regard to crime. Corrections applied to published figures will not reveal the proper ordering of communities. Official crime statistics seem to tell us more about police departments than they do about crime.

NOTES

1. Wesley G. Skogan, "The Victims of Crime: Some National Survey Findings," in Anthony L. Guenther, ed., *Criminal Behavior in Social Systems* (Chicago: Rand McNally, 1976), ch. 9.

2. David Burnham, "Federal Surveys to Gauge Crime Levels in Big Cities," *New York Times*, January 27, 1974, p. 1.

3. See also, Paul Smith and Richard Hawkins, "Victimization, Types of Police Contacts, and Attitudes Toward Police," *Law and Society Review* 8 (Fall 1973): 135-52 (Seattle study); and A.A. Congalton and J.M. Najman, "Who Are the Victims?" Statistical Report 13, Department of the Attorney General and the New South Wales Bureau of Crime Statistics and Research, 1974 (Sydney study).

4. For a general discussion of all the surveys, see Wesley G. Skogan, "Sample Surveys of the Victims of Crime," *Review of Public Data Use* 4 (January 1976): pp. 23-28.

5. These and other national statistics are based upon my own computer analysis of the victimization survey data for 1973.

6. Wesley G. Skogan, "The Validity of Official Crime Statistics: An Empirical Investigation," *Social Science Quarterly* 55 (June 1974): pp. 25-38.

7. Data on reporting rates for cities were calculated from figures in official publications. U.S. Department of Justice, Law Enforcement Assistance Administration, *Crime in Eight American Cities* (Washington, D.C.: U.S. Government Printing Office, July, 1974); U.S. Department of Justice, Law Enforcement Assistance Administration, *Crime in the Nation's Five Largest Cities* (Washington, D.C.: U.S. Government Printing Office, April, 1975); U.S. Department of Justice, Law Enforcement Assistance Administration, *Criminal Victimization Surveys in 13 American Cities* (Washington, D.C.: U.S. Government Printing Office, June, 1975).

8. Eduard Ziegenhagen, "Individual Responses to Criminal Victimization," in William McDonald, ed., *Criminal Justice and the Victim* (Beverly Hills, California: Sage Publications, forthcoming).

9. Wesley G. Skogan, "Citizen Reporting of Crime: Some National Panel Data," *Criminology* 13 (February 1976): pp. 535-49.

10. These and other statistics are based upon my own computer analysis of incidents in the surveys.

11. Anthony Turner, "San Jose Methods Test of Known Crime Victims," *Statistics Technical Report No. 1* (Washington, D.C.: Law Enforcement Assistance Administration, 1972).

12. Donald Black, "The Production of Crime Rate," *American Sociological Review* 35 (August 1970): pp. 733-47; Donald Black and Albert J. Reiss, Jr., "Police Control of Juveniles," *American Sociological Review* 35 (February 1970): pp. 63-77; and Harold Pepinsky, "Police Decisions to Report Offenses" (Ph.D. dissertation, University of Pennsylvania, 1972).

13. David J. Bordua and Albert J. Reiss, Jr., "Organization and Environment: A Perspective on the Police," in David J. Bordua, ed., *The Police: Six Sociological Essays* (New York: John Wiley, 1967), pp. 28-40.

14. *Criminal Justice* 54 (March 1929): p. 10 (a monthly newsletter published by the Chicago Crime Commission).

15. The President's Commission on Law Enforcement and Administration of Justice, *Task Force Report: Crime and Its Impact–An Assessment* (Washington, D.C.: U.S. Government Printing Office, 1967), pp. 22-25.

16. Ibid.

17. Ibid.; and James Q. Wilson, *Varieties of Police Behavior* (Cambridge, Massachusetts: Harvard University Press, 1968).

18. The official data were drawn from yearly issues of the *Uniform Crime Report* (Washington, D.C.: U.S. Government Printing Office, yearly). The data were selected to match the reference periods covered by the surveys, which ranged from mid-1971 to 1973.

19. All of the figures in Table 6-1 were calculated from data in published sources. See note 7, above.

20. Arthur C. Meyers, Jr., "Statistical Controls in a Police Department," *Crime and Delinquency* 8 (January 1962): 58-64.

21. For an excellent study of Washington, D.C., see David Seidman and Michael Couzens, "Getting the Crime Rate Down: Political Pressure and Crime Reporting," *Law and Society Review* 8 (Spring 1974): 457-93. While they document the sins of the city, especially for larceny recording, these data suggest that in context the district does well.

22. The President's Commission, p. 22.

23. Each was *Z* scored, then added together to form the index.

24. See a discussion of this process in Chapter Eight. See also Albert Biderman *et al., Report on A Pilot Study in the District of Columbia on Victimization and Attitudes Toward Law Enforcement, Field Surveys I* (Washington, D.C.: U.S. Government Printing Office, 1967).

25. Anthony Turner, "San Jose Methods Test of Known Crime Victims," *Statistics Technical Report No. 1* (Washington, D.C.: Law Enforcement Assistance Administration, June, 1972).

26. Biderman, et al.

27. These figures were calculated from data in U.S. Bureau of the Census, *Subject Reports 6-D: The Journey to Work* (Washington, D.C.: U.S. Government Printing Office, June, 1973), table 1.

28. These differences include coverage by age (the surveys gathered data only for those twelve years of age and older, while the UCR includes all age groups), and the fact that eight cities had reference periods that did not correspond with calendar years (I averaged UCR figures over the relevant years).

Chapter 7

Measuring a Program's Impact: A Cautionary Note

Sumner N. Clarren and
Alfred I. Schwartz

Can victimization surveys be used to evaluate police programs? The Urban Institute's experience in Cincinnati argues against the use of broadly defined citizen victimization surveys for program evaluation, while supporting a more focused use of victimization surveys.

The argument and evidence to date from Cincinnati suggests that, beyond the methodological considerations, the broad victimization surveys rely heavily upon the FBI *Uniform Crime Report* for definitions of crimes. Those definitions, in turn, allow for a set of variables that are extremely sensitive to individual discretion on the part of both trained interviewers and respondents. The definitions focus upon the perceived intent of the perpetrator, and not upon a shared behavioral description of events or upon some minimum level of seriousness.

However, when "crimes" are narrowly defined (and the survey population is homogeneous), as in the commercial surveys, stable measures of crime may be obtained that appear useful for evaluation. Examples of broad and narrow victimization surveys in the context of program evaluation are available in Cincinnati, and are the subject of this report.

BACKGROUND

From 1971 to 1975, the Urban Institute was involved in evaluating a team policing program in Cincinnati, Ohio. The evaluation and major portions of the program were funded by the Police Foundation of Washington, D.C.

The goals of the team policing program were to reduce crime, to improve police-community relations and to improve the working environment of police officers. This chapter reviews methodological issues that have grown from attempts to measure the reduction in crime. In particular, we discuss:

–the systematic attempt to relate victimization surveys to measures of crime reported by the police; and
–the use of victimization reports to measure the program's impact on crime.

In a team policing program, the team commander and a group of police officers are given twenty-four hour responsibility for delivering service to a specific neighborhood. By organizing effort in this way, and by giving the team as much responsibility as possible, an attempt is made to strengthen the relationship between the police and the community. The expected result is an increased flow of information from the neighborhood residents to the police, which is expected to contribute to the control of crime in that neighborhood. Consequently, the importance of informal interaction with neighborhood residents and of sharing of information between team members is stressed. Teams in Cincinnati are expected to provide all police services (except homicide investigations). Unlike many police departments where numerous specialized units provide specific services, Cincinnati has attempted to develop a "generalist" role for officers–patrolmen are encouraged to perform a broad range of investigative and patrol activities. This chapter describes our experience concerning the application of victimization surveys to program evaluation.

THE DECISION TO USE VICTIMIZATION STUDIES

A major goal of the team policing program was to reduce crime. The problems of using reported crime, as defined for the FBI's Uniform Crime Report (UCR) for program evaluation, are well known.[1] A change in reported crime often seems related to the way the police handle information about crime. Moreover, since the studies conducted by the President's Commission on Law Enforcement and Administration of Justice in the mid-1960s,[2] it has become clear that there are many unreported crimes that never come to the attention of the police. Consequently, a team policing program, or any other police program that attempts simultaneously to reduce crime and to improve police-community relations, may find that a reduction in victimization is masked by a corresponding increase in the proportion of crime reported. The President's Commission believed victimization surveys offered "a great untapped potential as a method for providing additional information about the nature and extent of our crime and the relative effectiveness of different programs to control crime."[3] Such considerations led the Urban Institute to use victimization surveys as a means of obtaining an independent estimate of the crime level in Cincinnati. In carrying out its study, the Urban Institute benefited from the extensive field testing of experimental victimization surveys carried out by the Census Bureau for the Law Enforcement Assistance Administration (LEAA) of the Department of Justice. Not only did the Census Bureau provide the Urban Institute with extensive documentation, field reports and the victimization questionnaires themselves, but Cincinnati was one of twenty-six cities to be surveyed in the National Crime Survey initiated in 1972. Consequently, when the team policing program began in Cincinnati in 1973, citizen victimization questionnaires were administered to 1,200 households.* In 1974, approximately one year later, the Census Bureau conducted additional victimization surveys in 9,600 Cincinnati households.

During the same period, with the Urban Institute's encouragement, the Police Foundation funded a random digit dialing (RDD) telephone victimization survey adapted from the same survey instrument that had previously been used in Cincinnati. This was an attempt to determine whether a telephone survey could provide reliable victimization data at less cost. The RDD experiment was conducted by several University of Cincinnati political scientists. Their comparison of RDD victimization with the Census Bureau's surveys conducted about the same time in Cincinnati should be available in 1976 from the Police Foundation. An overview of that research is provided in Chapter Twelve.

WHAT DOES A VICTIMIZATION SURVEY MEASURE?

UCR provides the usual frame of reference for discussing crime or changes in crime in the United States. The FBI's *UCR Handbook* provides the definitions for crime used in recent victimization surveys. Although the categories for crimes used by the census expand on the detail in the UCR categories, census uses UCR's basic definitions as well as UCR's method of hierarchical scoring.

At first glance, UCR and victimization surveys appear to measure the same events. The surveys were developed from the UCR's definitional framework and the results are often reported as population projections of rates for UCR crimes. However, there are reasons to suspect large and systematic biases when the results from UCR and victimization surveys are compared.

As previously noted, victimization surveys are expected to more accurately measure crime. It has been estimated that more than 50 percent of all incidents that could be classified as crimes are not reported to the police. Still, one might expect that reported crime and victimization surveys would be highly correlated across cities. A high correlation would exist if the ratio of reported to unreported crime were relatively similar from one city to the next, and if the differences between UCR rates and victimization rates were largely the result of differences in reporting. If this were true, cities with relatively high rates on the UCR would have different but relatively high rates on the victimization surveys. Although generally this has been true, there are notable exceptions. LEAA's recently published victimization rates for twenty-six cities[4] allow a comparison between UCR-reported crime and crime as revealed through victimization surveys. Correlations between UCR data and corresponding estimates from victimization surveys are shown in Table 7-1.

---

*Survey was conducted by the Institute for Metropolitan Studies, Inc. (IMS), an affiliate of the University of Cincinnati.

Table 7-1. Index Crimes: A Comparison Between UCR and Victimization Rates for Twenty-six Cities*

		Range in Offenses Per 1,000 Population	
Crime Type	*Correlation*	*UCR High-Low*	*Victimization High-Low*
Rape	0.056	0.9-0.2	2.6- 0.7
Robbery	0.664	12.3-1.5	26.7- 8.5
Aggravated Assault	−0.556	8.6-1.0	12.6- 2.6
Burglary	0.761	42.6-8.0	105.7-37.9
Auto Theft	0.850	28.8-6.0	28.6- 5.2

*Abbreviated from an unpublished memorandum entitled "Comparison of UCR and Victimization Survey Crime Rates in 26 Cities," by Thomas White and Katryna Regan, The Urban Institute, 1975.

It is difficult to argue that UCR and victimization reports consistently measure the same phenomena, especially in cases of rape and aggravated assault. At one extreme, there are cities like Washington, D.C., Miami, New York and Newark where there are more UCR-reported aggravated assaults than are estimated by the victimization surveys. On the other hand, in cities such as Cincinnati, census victimization estimates of aggravated assaults for 1973 are almost ten times larger than the amount reported through UCR.

One partial explanation for this negative correlation may lie in the different base underlying victimization surveys and police records. Cities with high UCR aggravated assault rates have large numbers of transients (commuters and visitors) in comparison to their total populations. Those transients may be as subject to assaults as residents. However, victimization surveys provide the aggravated assault experience of residents only, while UCR provides some measure of the assault experience of anyone living in or passing through the city.

To some extent, this explanation can be tested with data from census decennial surveys and from UCR. The ratio of a city's population to the population of the larger urbanized area that encompasses the city could be used as an indicator of the size of the potential source of nearby transients. Cities surrounded by relatively large, high density areas would be expected to have higher UCR assault rates because they would be more likely to have a larger proportion of transients. That is the case for the twenty-six cities cited above. The correlation is −0.43 between the city to urbanized area ratios (1970) and the UCR aggravated assault rates ($t = 2.34$ d.f. $= 24$, $\rho < 0.05$).

Cincinnati represents a city whose incorporated area includes a relatively high proportion of the total urbanized area population. A sample of 111 assault records from Cincinnati for 1973 indicated that only 10 percent of assaults are reported by individuals who are not city residents and hence would not be picked up by victimization surveys. This proportion is expected to be much higher for many of the other cities mentioned above.

The large discrepancy in Cincinnati between aggravated assault in UCR and the surveys may come from at least two other sources as well. First, many citizen complaints were handled directly by the courts in 1973. Such cases were often not represented in UCR, although warrants were issued directly by the court. Second, in 1973, Cincinnati Police Division (CPD) procedures did not require officers to distinguish between aggravated and simple assault. Such distinctions, for UCR purposes, were made by coding clerks at the police records section. Their decisions had to be based on the written crime report where the full extent of injury (one element in differentiating between simple and aggravated assault) was often difficult to determine. It is likely that the need to translate from officers' crime reports to UCR also contributed to some of the differences between UCR and victimization estimates of aggravated assault. In Cincinnati in 1973, many aggravated assaults would probably have been misclassified as simple assaults even if they had been reported to the police.

Conversely, rape is likely to be subject to distortion or omission on the part of the respondent. The collection of information describing the victimization incidents was preceded, in the interview, by a small set of "screen questions" to identify individuals who might have sustained a scoreable event. No screen question on the victimization survey asked if the respondent had been raped. It was hoped that during the course of the interview, sufficient information would be volunteered to allow classification of an assault as a rape, if appropriate. For this to occur, the respondent would have had to volunteer the information in answer to such questions as: How did the person attack you? or How were you threatened? Clearly, a variety of factors could affect responses; and since rape is not well reported, and is a relatively rare event, it is doubtful that much additional insight will be gained from victimization reports in that area. Given the likely sources of random error for both UCR and victimization surveys, it is not surprising that the correlation is effectively zero between UCR and victimization rates for rape.

Burglary would appear to be one crime allowing a good comparison between UCR and victimization surveys, since the site of the incident is generally the residence.* Cincinnati codes and reports residential burglaries in the CPD's annual report, making such comparisons easier. Unfortunately, even here it is difficult to relate UCR burglary to burglary as estimated from victimization surveys. The 1974 census victimization survey estimates 22,000 burglaries occurred "at home" to citizens in Cincinnati. In the interviews, respondents indicated that 55 percent of these crimes were reported to the police. Thus, one would expect the police to have a record of 12,100 residential burglaries. However, only 6,700 residential burglaries were noted in CPD's annual report for 1973. What accounts for such a difference? What is missing from police records or being added by the victimization surveys? A partial answer was obtained from a sample of 175 burglaries drawn from 1973 police records. From Table 7-2, it is

*Actually, census victimization surveys also obtain reports of burglaries that occurred "elsewhere" (e.g., at a hotel or vacation home), but these can be identified in analysis.

Table 7-2. Percent Dollar Loss for Residential Burglaries for Police Records and Victimization Reports

Net Dollar Loss	*Percent Police Records (N = 170)*	*Percent Victimization Reports (N = 750)*
Nothing Taken	12.4	29.2
1-9	1.7	3.6
10-49	14.1	8.5
50-99	9.4	9.7
100-249	22.9	15.8
250+	39.4	33.3

Source: Calculations based upon data drawn by the authors from Cincinnati's police files and from unpublished tabulations of the Census Bureau's 1973 Survey of Cincinnati.

clear that the "nothing taken" class is underrepresented in police records in comparison to the census surveys. That class alone could account for half the difference between police records and estimates of reported crime based upon victimization reports. Many of the "nothing taken" burglaries could be described as "attempted forced entry." While only about 1 percent of the police-recorded burglaries were in this class, 18 percent of the census burglary victimizations were "attempted forced entry." On the surface, it would appear that either citizens are misrepresenting their reporting of incidents to the police or that the police reporting system is selectively screening, reclassifying or omitting reports that, under UCR definitions, should be classified as UCR Part I offenses.

Some experts have argued that the police should record all reported incidents without any use of discretion. Our purpose is not to review arguments for "forced reporting," but to indicate some of the difficulties that remain in understanding what the victimization surveys (or even what reported crime) tell us about the magnitude of Part I crimes in this country.

Data from Cincinnati have provided some evidence that the difference between UCR reports and victimization surveys may be partially accounted for by:

- the different base upon which the estimate is constructed (home of respondent as compared with place of occurrence);
- the victim's ability to remember and his or her decision to tell; and
- the discretion employed at numerous points within the police reporting system.

These factors and others appear to affect estimates of crime differentially, depending on the type of crime. However, despite these difficulties, the magnitude of the problem can be estimated and accounted for assuming that victimization surveys provide a stable estimate of actual crime.

STABILITY OF VICTIMIZATION ESTIMATES IN CINCINNATI

In order to measure the impact of team policing on crime, a set of measures was used that included both UCR and victimization survey data. Included were UCR data aggregated on a weekly basis—from mid-1971 through late 1974; neighborhood business victimization surveys—conducted in March 1973 and repeated at six month intervals through September 1974; and household victimization surveys—conducted in March 1973 and March 1974.

Before the data were gathered, it had been hypothesized that decreases in the level of actual crime might be masked by increases in the proportion of crime reported to the police. Simple tests of differences between means for the UCR data revealed statistically significant *reductions* in the average number of crimes per week in the team policing area for some crime types—notably burglary and auto theft.[5] Thus, the hypothesis was not supported.

The victimization survey of neighborhood businesses, which estimated only the incidence of burglary and robbery, indicates that the proportion of businesses reporting one or more incidents remained stable (differences between proportions were not so large as to be unbelievable) from one six month period to the next. Over an eighteen month period, however, significant differences could be measured.

In addition, the Urban Institute compared its estimates of household victimization (1973) for separate geographic areas in Cincinnati with later census estimates of victimization for the same areas (1974). The team policing experiment was carried out in Police District 1; the remainder of the city served as a comparison area. When the census estimates were received, the differences between the two surveys, conducted a year apart, were compared. Table 7-3 indicates the proportion of households reporting one or more incidents in the experimental and comparison areas for the two surveys.

Table 7-3 does not indicate the full extent of the differences between the two surveys. Many more households in the census surveys gave multiple incidents. Consequently, for burglary, the Urban Institute estimate from the 1973 survey was 56.5 burglaries per 1,000 households while the census rate was 143.2 per 1,000. Moreover, the preliminary impression from the RDD victimization rates, gathered while the Census Bureau was completing its fieldwork in Cincinnati, suggests that the RDD rates may be systematically higher than the Census Bureau's victimization rates, although the magnitude of the difference is not as startling as the differences noted above. The differences between the Urban Institute and Census Bureau surveys appear too large to attribute to actual

Table 7-3. Percent of Households Reporting Victimization Incidents

Urban Institute 1973 Victimization Survey	*Percent of Households Reporting One or More Victimization*	*Number of Households Interviewed*
Experimental Area	24	480*
Comparison Area	17	297
Census Bureau 1974 Victimization Survey	*Percent of Households Reporting One or More Victimization*	*Number of Households Interviewed*
Experimental Area	36	756
Comparison Area	38	8,852

*Effective sample size for stratified sample.

Source: Computed from the Cincinnati survey data collected for the Urban Institute in 1973 and the Census Bureau's 1973 Cincinnati survey.

changes in crime in Cincinnati.* For a number of crime categories, the victimization rates in the census survey were more than double those in the Urban Institute survey taken twelve months earlier. The differences between Anne Schneider's victimization survey and the census survey in Portland (see Chapter Eight) also seem surprisingly large, depending on the way incidents are counted. She counted series incidents as single incidents in computing the burlgary rate from her 1974 survey. The census did not include series incidents in computing their rates. Consequently, without those series incidents, the Census 1972 burglary rate of 151 per 1,000 would have been compared with a rate that drops below 100 per 1,000 for her 1974 survey. Would a difference that large have been attributed to a real change in crime or to differences in methodology and definitions?

The obvious sources of error in the Cincinnati survey (i.e., sampling methodology, estimation procedures, field procedures, coding and computer software) have been examined and reexamined. Consultants from the University of Michigan and Polytechnic Institute of New York have reviewed the procedures and documentation and interviewed field staff. No obvious flaws could be detected.

Perhaps the differences between the Urban Institute, census and RDD surveys will yet be accounted for by methodological differences or interviewer effects. However, we wish to present an alternate hypothesis to explain the differences. We hypothesize that the UCR definitions of crime, as operationalized in the survey instruments themselves, contribute substantially to these differences. Determining that a crime has occurred requires complex judgments by each respondent concerning the meaning of numerous events in their surrounding and the inferred intent behind the events. One implication of our hypothesis is that,

*UCR reported that Part I crimes for the period covered by the Urban Institute surveys (March 1972-February 1973) were 63,450. For the following year (the period measured by census surveys), reported Part I crimes were 63,474 in Cincinnati.

given a large representative sample from an American city, *the upper bound for the number of "crimes" that could be elicited is limited only by the persistence of the interviewer and the patience of the respondent.* The implications of this hypothesis may need to be explained if the Census Bureau finds that similar differences occur when cities are resurveyed for the LEAA studies. A review of UCR definitions will indicate why this hypothesis may be true.

The victimization surveys were designed to follow UCR definitions of Part I crime.* UCR defines attempted assaults (including threats) as assaults, and attempted burglaries (e.g., a door jimmied or a lock apparently forced) are included as burglaries. In the survey, the respondent is asked a series of screen questions concerning possible crimes. If the respondent answers "yes" to a screen question, a full incident report is taken. The type of crime is determined from information of the incident report. For example, the extent of personal injury or presence of a weapon determines whether an assault is "simple" or "aggravated." A bottle or rock may be a weapon, since UCR defines a weapon functionally.

"Burglary" is defined as unlawful entry with intent to commit a felony or a theft.[6] Included are cases where nothing was taken as well as those where an object or money was lost. Who is to determine whether (1) someone entered or tried to enter and (2) the actual intent of the presumed burglar? UCR uses "police experience" as the criterion; the victimization reports necessarily shift these judgments to the victim or interviewer. The difficulty in determining the intent of an unobserved person is obvious. Forcible entry need have no evidence to support it. Similarly, the belief that an object was taken or moved, that a lock was "picked" or that someone attempted to raise a window is a scorable UCR burglary.

Assault presents similar problems, since a threat (if the victim believes that bodily harm is intended) is an assault under UCR. UCR scores such categories as intimidation and coercion as simple assaults.[7]

We are not presenting these problems as a rehash of the usual arguments about UCR's shortcomings (e.g., all crimes, whatever the seriousness are counted equally), nor is this an argument against police discretion. Rather, we suggest that, given the current UCR definitions, there will be individuals who have a great many experiences that fall within the definitions of a "UCR crime." Violence, threats and the belief that objects have been or are in danger of being stolen are a part of the lives of many Americans. The relatively "low seriousness" end of UCR categories of assault, burglary and larceny include many incidents that can be recalled and that could flood the survey. Alternately, auto theft is an example of a UCR crime type with a very close correspondence between UCR and victimization reports. To be sure, the requirement of

*In 1974 nonaggravated assault became a Part II crime; but for the purpose of this study, the definitions current during 1972-1973 are used, and simple assault is treated as a Part I crime.

reporting for insurance claims contributes to the close correspondence; but, beyond that, there are apparently few incidents detectable in any way that could be classified as "attempted auto theft."

In summary, UCR definitions only partially measure the actual degree of crime. In part, these definitions measure inferences made by citizens about their surroundings and the interpretations they place on events. An individual who reports a "burglary" because he believes objects in a room appear to have been moved while he was away, is reporting a legitimate incident. Moreover, threats, minor violence and minor losses are frequent characteristics of some subcultures; and if one also includes those situations where a citizen feels threatened with violence or loss, then a great many "victimization incidents" or "crimes" could be measured given the willingness to tell and a good memory.

If these assumptions about UCR definitions of crime are accurate, then (1) on the average, victimization incidents should be less serious than reported crime and (2) incidents should be associated with individuals and subcultures and *not* randomly distributed among households. Both these hypotheses appear to be true in Cincinnati. The Sellin-Wolfgang seriousness index[8] has been applied to the victimization incidents generated by the Cincinnati surveys. In those data, reporting of victimization incidents to police is positively correlated with the level of seriousness (+0.36). In fact, half of the "unreported" incidents are at the lowest level on the seriousness scale (comparable to a larceny with a loss of less than $10). For burglary victimization reports, the average seriousness of nonreported burglary incidents was significantly lower than the average seriousness of reported burglaries ($t = 3.46$, d.f. = 130, $\rho<0.01$). Moreover, the average seriousness of burglaries in the Urban Institute victimization report was lower than the average seriousness sample of 1973 burglaries from police records ($t = 3.31$, d.f. = 303, $\rho<0.01$).

The census victimization reports in Cincinnati indicate 0.606 Part I residential crimes per household. Treating crime as an uncommon yet random event, the Poisson distribution can be used to predict the likelihood of a household experiencing multiple incidents.[9] A comparison of the two distributions in Table 7-4 indicates the relatively high number of multiple incidents and relative concentration of "crime" beyond what would be expected if crime were randomly distributed.

In fact, the concentration of incidents per household is even greater than Table 7-4 indicates. Census also collected "series incidents"–victimization incident reports where the same type of incident occurred more than three times in a year to the same person or household. Such incidents were not reported in detail in LEAA publications and would have raised the victimization survey estimate of noncommercial Part I crimes in Cincinnati by over 30 percent. Table 7-4 shows only the "single" incident reports.

What we are suggesting is that UCR definitions of crime be reexamined. If our assumptions are correct, UCR defines a set of variables that are extremely

Table 7-4. A Comparison of the Frequency of Multiple Incidents per Household With the Expected Distribution

Incidents per Household	*Poisson Expected Theoretical Distribution by Chance*	*Actual Distribution by Census Victimization Surveys*
0	0.549	0.627
1	0.329	0.213
2	0.099	0.091
3	0.020	0.032
4	0.003	0.014
5	–	0.006
6-7	–	0.004
8-10	–	0.002
11+	–	0.001

Source: Computed from survey data collected by the Census Bureau in 1973.

sensitive to individual discretion, whether that discretion is on the part of police officers, trained interviewers or citizens. At least for policy decisions, it may be helpful to redefine "crime" to establish:

–a minimum level of seriousness; and
–a behavioral definition for crimes, so that an independent observer would make the same judgment concerning its occurrence and classification.

AN EXAMPLE OF A STABLE VICTIMIZATION SURVEY

Results from the commercial victimization surveys in Cincinnati support the suggestion that "crime" be more narrowly defined for purposes of program evaluation. The commercial victimization surveys measured a subset of more serious and more behaviorally defined crimes in contrast to citizen victimization surveys. The survey questions concerning commercial victimization were also developed by the Census Bureau. Unlike the citizen victimization surveys, the information requested related to incidents of burglary and robbery only. Our commercial victimization surveys (part of a more comprehensive set of survey questions) were administered during February and March 1973 to gather baseline data and at six month intervals thereafter through the first eighteen months of evaluation. The businessmen in the sample operated "neighborhood businesses" (small groups of stores spread throughout the city, excluding the central business district).

The commercial survey asked businessmen whether an actual or attempted burglary or robbery had occurred within the past year. For each incident uncovered, a full incident report was obtained. Each survey wave, therefore, summarized the experience of neighborhood businessmen over an entire year. Not surprisingly, it took from one year to eighteen months before changes in victimization rates were observed. When businessmen in the experimental district described their victimization experience during the survey conducted six months after team policing began (September 1973), they were describing only six months of team policing experience. The incidents they reported also included observations from the six months prior to the start of team policing.

The evaluation included victimization surveys because it was anticipated that increased reporting of incidents to police might mask a real change in crime. Such a change would go undetected if reported crime was the only measure of the program's impact on crime. The survey data from this select group of businessmen support that expectation. The percent of businesses in District 1 experiencing one or more victimization incidents within the past year decreased from 40 percent at the start of the experimental program to 27 percent at the end of the eighteen months, as shown in Table 7-5. No significant changes were noted outside of the experimental area. During the same period, reporting of incidents to police apparently increased significantly within the experimental area. Again, no change in reporting of crime occurred elsewhere.

Robbery and burglary rates for District 1 and the area outside were examined. As might be expected, robberies comprised less than 15 percent of the total incident reports for the commercial establishments. Consequently, the decrease in the victimization rate in District 1 consisted largely of a decrease in the relative numbers of burglary incidents. The crime rates for burglary and robbery in District 1 and outside are shown in Table 7-6.

It seemed possible that the decrease in commercial victimization rates in District 1 might be due to a decrease in the number of relatively less serious incidents reported to interviewers in the later waves of surveys and that the relative level of serious crimes had remained the same. One index of seriousness would be to determine the percentage of "attempted" robberies and burglaries as compared to all incidents reported in the surveys. Table 7-7 shows the percent of attempted crime incidents in each wave of surveys for District 1 and the area outside.

Table 7-5. Proportion of Businesses Reporting One or More Incidents of Burglary or Robbery

	Survey Wave			
Area	*March 1973*	*September 1973*	*March 1974*	*September 1974*
Experimental	0.40 (N = 80)	0.41 (N = 146)	0.34 (N = 138)	0.27 (N = 154)
Comparison	0.27 (N = 97)	0.32 (N = 147)	0.29 (N = 154)	0.24 (N = 168)

Source: Computed from Cincinnati survey data collected for the Urban Institute in 1973-1974.

Table 7-6. Commercial Victimization Crime Rates for Neighborhood Businesses (rate per 1,000 businesses)

		Survey Wave			
Area	*Crime Type*	*March 1973*	*September 1973*	*March 1974*	*September 1974*
District 1	Robbery	37.5	41.1	58.0	32.5
	Burglary	637.5	513.7	384.1	337.7
	(Businesses)	(80)	(146)	(138)	(154)
Outside District 1	Robbery	61.9	95.2	39.0	41.7
	Burglary	340.2	435.4	337.7	309.5
	(Businesses)	(97)	(147)	(154)	(168)

Source: Computed from Cincinnati survey data collected for the Urban Institute in 1973-1974.

Table 7-7. Attempted Burglary and Robbery (percent victimization incidents)

		Survey Wave			
Area	*Attempted Crime*	*March 1973*	*September 1973*	*March 1974*	*September 1974*
District 1	Percent	23.8	21.0	31.0	29.8
	(Number Incidents)	(54)	(71)	(61)	(57)
Outside District 1	Percent	15.4	23.1	14.7	25.4
	(Number Incidents)	(39)	(78)	(68)	(59)

Source: Computed from Cincinnati survey data collected for the Urban Institute in 1973-1974.

There is no indication in Table 7-7 that later incidents were more serious than incidents reported in earlier surveys. In fact, the trend is in the opposite direction, although the changes are not statistically significant.

The Urban Institute's experience in using victimization surveys for program evaluation suggests that for broadly defined victimization surveys, the variance resulting from the different administrations of the same instrument may be quite large. On the other hand, careful selection and definition of incidents and survey populations appear to allow stable estimates from which valid inferences about the effect of crime reduction programs can be made. Examples of both were provided from the evaluation of the Police Foundation-funded team policing experiment in Cincinnati.

NOTES

1. Wesley G. Skogan, "Measurement Problems in Official and Survey Crime Rates," *Journal of Criminal Justice* 3 (Spring 1975): pp. 17-31.

2. Philip H. Ennis, Criminal *Victimization in the United States: A Report of a National Survey, Field Surveys II* (Washington, D.C.: U.S. Government Printing Office, 1967); and Albert J. Reiss, Jr., *Studies in Crime and Law Enforcement in Major Metropolitan Areas, Field Surveys III, vol. 1* (Washington, D.C.: U.S. Government Printing Office, 1967).

3. President's Commission on Law Enforcement and Administration of Justice, *The Challenge of Crime in a Free Society* (Washington, D.C.: U.S. Government Printing Office, 1967), p. 22.

4. U.S. Department of Justice, Law Enforcement Assistance Administration, *Crime in Eight American Cities* (Washington, D.C.: U.S. Government Printing Office, July, 1974); U.S. Department of Justice, Law Enforcement Assistance Administration, *Crime in the Nation's Five Largest Cities* (Washington, D.C.: U.S. Government Printing Office, April, 1975; and U.S. Department of Justice, Law Enforcement Assistance Administration, *Victimization Surveys in 13 American Cities* (Washington, D.C.: U.S. Government Printing Office, June, 1975).

5. Alfred I. Schwartz et. al., "Evaluation of Cincinnati's Community Sector Team Policing Program, A Progress Report: After One Year, Summary of Major Findings," Working Paper 3006-18 (Washington, D.C.: The Urban Institute, March 17, 1975), p. 24.

6. FBI, *Uniform Crime Reporting Handbook* (Washington, D.C.: U.S. Department of Justice, 1974), p. 22.

7. Ibid., p. 19.

8. T. Sellin and M. Wolfgang, *The Measurement of Delinquency* (New York: John Wiley and Sons, Inc., 1964).

9. Emanuel Parzen, *Modern Probability Theory and Its Applications* (New York: John Wiley and Sons, Inc., 1960), p. 105-108.

 *Chapter 8*

Victimization Surveys and Criminal Justice System Evaluation

Anne L. Schneider

Evaluations of local criminal justice system programs often are handicapped by a lack of adequate data to assess the effectiveness of programs in achieving outcome objectives. Data generated from victimization surveys have the potential of expanding the types of evaluations that can be undertaken and increasing the accuracy of conclusions concerning program effectiveness. The purpose of this chapter is to illustrate a few of the ways in which victimization data can be used in local criminal justice system evaluation.

The chapter describes how a victimization survey in Portland, Oregon, was used to supplement project-specific evaluations undertaken as part of the $20 million federally funded impact program.[1] Summarized are our findings on four topics of interest to evaluators and other criminal justice officials:

–change in the residential burglary rate attributable to the impact program;
–the effect of a neighborhood-based property-marking program;
–the importance of citizen attitudes toward police, citizen participation in crime prevention activities and crime seriousness in citizen decisions to report crimes to the police; and
–citizen perceptions of a street lighting program implemented in 1973.

The questionnaire and sample were designed specifically to meet local evaluation needs. The survey instrument was a slightly modified version of the standard Census Bureau screening questions and detailed incident report.[2] In addition, a series of attitudinal, behavioral and perceptual questions were asked prior to the victimization questions. A 10 percent sample of all census blocks in the metropolitan area was drawn and each living unit in each block was enumerated. The final sample was chosen by selecting each *n*th household from among those enumerated. All interviews were conducted in person with one respondent from each household. Certain sections of the city were oversampled to insure a sufficient number of respondents from a street lighting project area and from an area in which the Crime Prevention Bureau conducted door-to-door canvasses to increase the use of property-marking equipment. The final sample was weighted to correct for the oversampling (when analyzing the city as a whole) and for a slight overrepresentation of women and underrepresentation of persons aged sixteen to twenty.

In addition to the local survey, conducted during the summer of 1974, data were available from a victimization survey conducted in 1972 by the Census Bureau for the Law Enforcement Assistance Administration. Information from both surveys concerning the frequency of burglaries will be used in the first section of this chapter.

CHANGE IN THE BURGLARY RATE

A serious problem in measuring the amount of crime and changes in crime rates is that many incidents never become known to the police and, therefore, are not counted as part of official police statistics or reported in the Uniform Crime Reports (UCR). Of particular concern to policy analysts and evaluators is the possibility that improved performance by the police or the criminal justice system as a whole could increase the proportion of victims who report crimes to the police, thereby resulting in an apparent increase in the crime rate.

During the three years beginning in 1971 and ending in mid-1974, official crime data in Portland indicated that the residential burglary rate had climbed from fifty per 1,000 households to fifty-six per 1,000 households. In contrast, data from the two surveys for the same period indicate that the rate actually *declined* from 151 per 1,000 households to (at least) 127 per 1,000.[3] In addition, the proportion of surveyed burglary victims who said that they reported the incidents to the police increased from 50 percent in the first time period to 70 percent by the time the second survey was taken.

These two surveys encompassed a period during which the federal impact program was implemented in Portland. In early 1973, an extensive neighborhood-based, antiburglary program was begun. By summer 1974, when the second survey was taken, more than 27 percent of the households had engraved their property and 19 percent said that an antiburglary neighborhood meeting had been held on their block. Obviously, evaluators of these programs would reach very different conclusions concerning the programs' effectiveness depending upon whether they relied on the official data or the survey data.

Relying solely on the official data, an evaluator would either conclude that the programs were ineffective or that they increased victim willingness to report burglaries to the police. The survey information indicates that reporting increased *and* burglaries decreased. However, the nonexperimental nature of the research (it was a crude before-and-after study) leaves much to be desired in terms of drawing strongly worded conclusions about the programs' effectiveness. There is no way to establish beyond all reasonable doubt that the survey results accurately represent what actually happened during the three year period. Nevertheless, several procedures can be used in an attempt to discount or provide further support for the conclusions based on the survey data. These will be briefly reviewed here.[4]

The most plausible alternate explanation for the simultaneous observance of a drop in victimization incidents and an increase in the victim reporting rate is that the second survey failed to elicit the proper number of "trivial" incidents. This explanation is based on the following reasoning: interviewers who are tired, lazy or in a hurry may fail to record some seemingly trivial incidents in which no loss or injury occurred. Likewise, respondents who are tired, lazy or distrusting of the interviewer may fail to mention some of their less important experiences on the screening questions or they later may refuse to cooperate in the completion of the ten minute detailed report about the incident. Obviously, this would result in fewer victimization incidents for the survey as a whole. In addition, there is ample evidence that serious crimes tend to be reported more frequently than trivial ones. Thus, if one survey group fails to elicit the "proper" number of trivial incidents, the result will be a reduced victimization rate *and* an increased proportion of victims who reported crimes to the police.

In order to test this alternate explanation, the two surveys were compared in terms of the proportion of each type of crime that was trivial rather than serious. Of the nine comparisons that could be made, the 1974 survey had more trivial incidents in three of the tests and fewer trivial incidents in one comparison; the surveys were not significantly different in five of the comparisons. On this basis, it seems reasonable to conclude that failure to elicit the proper number of trivial incidents could *not* account for the reduced victimization rate and the increased reporting.

A second plausible explanation for the difference lies in the composition of the two samples. If the second sample contains fewer members of groups that are more apt to be burglarized, then this could explain the apparently low burglary rate. Although there were some differences in sample composition, the respondents were markedly similar. When differences did occur, they were of the type that should have produced more (not fewer) burglaries in the second survey.[5]

Thus, neither of these arguments plausibly discredits the conclusion that reporting increased and burglaries decreased. However, one may still question the apparent increase in reporting, for it may not seem plausible that reporting tendencies can fluctuate so dramatically. One method to investigate this question is to examine changes in the proportion of incidents reported to the police on a monthly basis, using data from the second survey (no monthly data were available from the first survey). Complicating the problem, of course, is the fact that sampling variability alone will produce marked variations in the percentage of burglaries reported to the police during each month of the 1973-1974 recall period. On the other hand, it seems reasonable to assume that if "real" reporting changes occur (and if the total burglary rate remains relatively stable), then reporting changes should correspond closely to changes in the number of burglaries known to the police.

The percentage of burglaries reported to the police during each two month segment of the twelve month recall period is plotted in the upper portion of Figure 8-1. If the changes in reporting were simply sample variability, and not a reflection of the "real" world, one would expect that the official data (lower portion of Figure 8-1) would change independently of the reporting percentage. In contrast, each increase in percentage reporting is accompanied by an increase in the official rate. The marked decline in reporting percentage is accompanied by a decline in the official data. And, when the reporting change is slight, the change in the official data is slight.

Another way to examine the plausibility of the conclusion that burglaries declined and reporting increased is to seek explanations as to *why* this occurred. As explained in a subsequent section, the survey data indicate that participants in the crime prevention programs (property marking, antiburglary stickers, neighborhood meetings) tend to experience fewer burglaries than nonparticipants. Also, participants tend to report a much higher percentage of the burglaries committed against them.

Thus, evidence from the Portland survey indicates that an evaluation based solely on changes in official burglary statistics would have arrived at a dramatically incorrect conclusion concerning the effectiveness of crime prevention programs implemented in 1972-1973. Further, evidence suggests that victim reporting is not stable enough to justify the assumption made in many evaluations that reporting tendencies are an unchanging factor. It is possible, of course, that fluctuations in reporting of the magnitude found in Portland will be very rare. The problem, however, for evaluators lies not in the likelihood of such changes, but in their timing and in the fact that crime reduction programs may affect the victim's inclination to report incidents to the police.

EFFECTIVENESS OF A NEIGHBORHOOD-BASED PROPERTY-MARKING PROGRAM

The Portland property-marking program was implemented in 1972 and focused initially on providing crime prevention information and marking equipment to residents of specified high crime areas. Personnel from the Crime Prevention Bureau went door to door and cosponsored (with community residents) coffees and other types of small meetings to discuss neighborhood crime prevention activities. After approximately six months of this type of activity, the neighborhood focus was largely abandoned. The program began providing citywide service to interested persons and began mass media advertising to encourage participation.

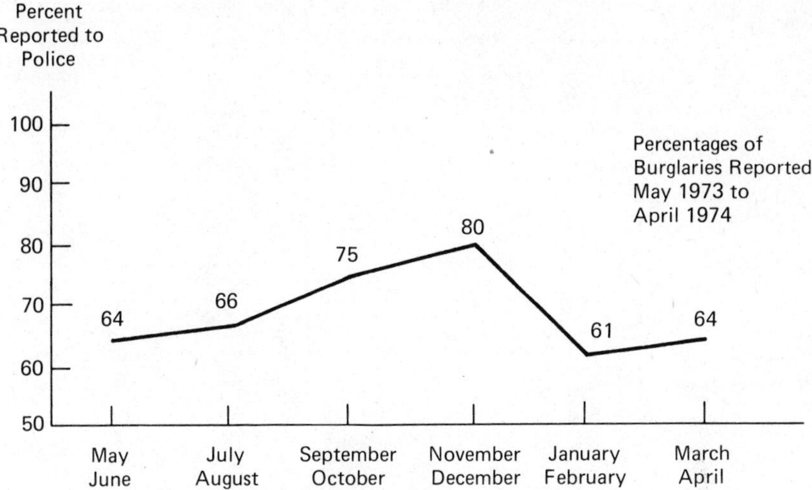

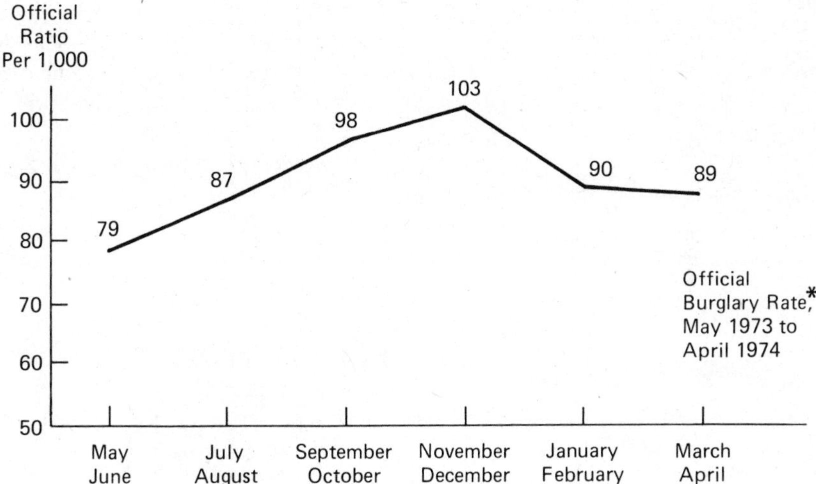

*These burglary figures include commercial burglaries. Residential burglaries constitute about 60 percent of the total.

Source: Computed from the Portland household-sample survey data collected by the Oregon Research Institute in 1974, and from Portland UCR data.

Figure 8-1. Burglary Rate and Percentage Reported, 1973-1974

Victimization survey data are especially useful in evaluating crime prevention programs that involve individual (or households) efforts to reduce crime because the victimization experiences of participants and nonparticipants can be directly compared.

As shown in Table 8-1, homes that display antiburglary stickers tend to have

Table 8-1. Effect of Antiburglary Stickers on Burglary Frequency[a]

Area	*Homes with stickers: percent of homes, per year, with one or more burglaries after display of sticker*	*Homes without stickers: percent of homes, per year, with one or more burglaries*	*All homes: percent with one or more burglaries*
Portland (totals)	6.87*	10.1*	9.65
Street Lighting Area	8.4*	24.0*	21.0
CPB High Priority Area	7.7*	21.0*	17.3
N.E. Portland	7.9	11.3	10.8
Remainder of City	6.6	9.4	9.0
CPB Block and Participants	(only three homes burglarized, too few for analysis)		

[a]For homes with stickers, the number of burglaries after display of the sticker was used to calculate the percentage. The date of display was used to correct (adjust) the figures to a yearly percentage. The rate per 1,000 households can be computed by moving the decimal one place to the right. Asterisks indicate a statistically significant difference at the 0.05 level. The total number of homes in each area and the number with stickers is: Portland (2,227; 267 with stickers); SL area (320; 54 with stickers); CPB area (116; 31 with stickers); N.E. Portland (430; 52 with stickers); remainder of the city (1,024; 102 with stickers); CPB special sample (87; 41 with stickers).

Source: Anne L. Schneider. "Evaluation of the Portland neighborhood-based anti-burglary program," *Occasional Papers in Applied Policy Research* (Eugene, Oregon: Oregon Research Institute, 1975).

lower burglary rates than homes that do not. The lower burglary rates are most marked in areas of highest crime prevention activity. For the city as a whole, slightly less than 7 percent of the participating homes were burglarized one or more times after they displayed the sticker, whereas slightly more than 10 percent of the nonparticipating homes were burglarized. Although these data indicate that the program is effective at the household level, they do not indicate whether the actual number of burglaries declined or whether burglaries were simply displaced from a participating to a nonparticipating household in the same area. It is possible that the program inconveniences burglars only temporarily and encourages them to find a nonparticipating home. In this event, burglary rates for participating homes would be markedly lower than for nonparticipating homes, even though the areawide burglary rate would remain about the same. Although this possibility cannot be ruled out, the previous evidence that burglaries for the city declined between 1971 and 1974 indicates that some citywide reduction occurred. Whether the program displaced burglaries into suburban areas is not presently known.

Data from the survey indicates that persons participating in antiburglary activities such as property marking, sticker display and neighborhood meetings are more apt to report burglaries to the police than are nonparticipants. As shown in Table 8-2, more than 80 percent of the burglary victims who participated in the program said that they reported the incidents to the police, as compared to 65 percent of the nonparticipants.

Before concluding that the program was responsible for the higher reporting rates, one must consider the possibility that people who tend to report crimes may be more likely to participate in the program in the first place. Thus, one could observe higher reporting with higher levels of participation due to self-selection rather than to motivation imparted by the program. It should be recalled that the door-to-door canvassing began in the Crime Prevention Bureau's high priority area and continued there, as well as in parts of the street lighting area and in other sections of northeast Portland that have the city's highest crime rates. If the difference in reporting is due entirely to self-selection rather than to program impact, there should be less improvement in reporting in areas where door-to-door canvassing took place since the degree of self-selection for persons in these areas is not as great as in other areas. The data in Table 8-2 indicate that the higher levels of reporting correspond to higher participation even where the least amount of self-selection would be expected to have occurred. Thus, although the self-selection argument cannot be ruled out entirely, the evidence suggests that self-selection does not entirely explain the difference in reporting percentages.

Consider what would have happened had this property-marking program been evaluated without victimization data. A common evaluation procedure for such programs involves comparing before and after official burglary rates on an area basis. Given the higher levels of reporting by victims who are participating, it is

Table 8-2. Effect of Involvement in CPB Activities on Willingness to Report Burglaries to the Police[a]

Area	*No Involvement, No Information*	*Information Only*	*One Activity*	*Two Activities*	*Three Activities*
	(percent of burglary victims who said they reported the crime to the police)				
Portland (total)	65	67	79	83	87
(Percentages below are based on very small numbers)					
Street Lighting Area	55	60	63	66	75
CPB High Priority Areas	50	100	100	100	–(too few burglaries)
N.E. Portland, excluding above	45	80	71	100	100
Remainder of city	68	66	80	83	100
N =	1,024	484	188	101	64

[a]Percentages represent the percent of burglary victims who said that they reported the incident to the police. The headings are defined in this way:

No involvement, no information: Person has not heard of any special crime prevention programs and has not participated in any activities.

Information only: Person has heard of one or more special crime prevention programs, but has not participated in any activities.

One activity: Engraved property *or* displayed sticker *or* attended a meeting.

Two activities: Any two of the three activities.

Three activities: All three (engraved, sticker, attended meeting).

Source: Anne L. Schneider. "Evaluation of the Portland neighborhood-based anti-burglary program," *Occasional Papers in Applied Policy Research* (Eugene, Oregon: Oregon Research Institute, 1975).

quite likely that one would observe increases in the official burglary rate for areas with higher participation rates. Suppose the evaluation was based on observation of police-burglary incidents combined with telephone surveys to determine whether the victims (who reported crimes) were program participants. Again, due to the markedly higher reporting tendencies of participants, police records are likely to contain more burglaries from participants than from nonparticipants. Even if the number of participants in the city is known, the higher reporting percentage will greatly reduce the observed impact of the program for individual households.

CITIZEN DECISIONS TO REPORT CRIMES TO THE POLICE

Although numerous studies indicate that many victims do not report incidents to the police, the meaning of nonreporting has not been dealt with extensively.

Criminal justice officials do not have sufficient information about nonreporting to know whether this phenomenon should be a major concern or whether it should be dismissed as an interesting, but relatively unimportant, phenomenon in crime analysis, planning and evaluation.

One could argue that nonreporting serves a useful function in the criminal justice system. Citizens may not define certain acts as "crimes" and, therefore, may not report them to the police. Thus, the victim serves as an initial screening mechanism to separate important crimes (as defined by victims who report the incidents) from unimportant ones (those not reported to the police). One could argue that if all suspicious or suspected incidents, even the most trivial, were reported, the police would not be able to handle the magnitude of the demands and the more important crimes would be given less attention.

On the other hand, if nonreporting is due to a lack of trust in the police, fear of retaliation or other perceptual factors, then "screening" by victims exacerbates the inequitable distribution of police services to the public. That is, alienated segments of society, and persons who do not trust the criminal justice system, will be less likely to report crimes and, therefore, will not receive their fair share of the services provided by the criminal justice system.

In order to examine the importance of crime seriousness and citizen attitudes, the 1974 survey contained a series of questions dealing with alienation, attitudes toward the police and courts, and perceptions of the effectiveness of the police and courts. (For this part of the analysis the entire metropolitan area sample was used rather than just the city residents.)

The analyses first scored each victimization incident on the basis of its seriousness, using the Sellin and Wolfgang system.[6] Because these scores were highly skewed, both for property and personal crimes, the incidents with more extreme scores were grouped into a "high seriousness" category (see Table 8-3).

Clearly, the seriousness of a crime greatly affects whether it will be reported. For property crimes, the correlation (gamma) is 0.65 between seriousness and whether the incident was reported. For personal crimes, the correlation is 0.52.

The important question, however, is not whether crime seriousness influences reporting decisions, but whether reporting decisions are based on attitudes toward the criminal justice system rather than on the nature of the offense. Correlations illustrating the bivariate impact of several independent variables on the victim's decision to report or not report the incident, controlling for crime seriousness, are given in Table 8-4.[7]

Minor Property Crimes

As indicated in the first column of Table 8-4, minor property crimes are more apt to be reported by victims who are more trusting of the police, who live in an area where the police enjoy good relationships with the community, who are more integrated into the community (i.e., able to understand most of the local issues rather than only a few or none of them) and who have participated in

Table 8-3. Property and Personal Incidents

Type of Crime	*Number of Incidents*	*Percent Reported*	*Percent in Each Seriousness Category*	*Definitions*
Property Crimes				*Property Crime Definitions:*
Low Seriousness	283	25	35	*Low Seriousness.* Lowest possible score on seriousness scale was "1" and all cases with this score are considered "low." Incidents in this category involve no loss at all or loss not greater than $10, and in no instance is a forcible entry involved.
Moderate	352	49	44	*Moderate Seriousness.* Scores of "2" on the scale. Incidents include those with loss of $10 to $250 *not* involving forcible entry; or loss of less than $10 *with* forcible entry.
High	171	84	21	*High Seriousness.* Scores of "3" or greater include loss greater than $250 (with or without forcible entry); or forcible entry with a loss of $10 or more.
Personal Crimes				*Personal Crime Definitions:*
Low Seriousness	42	52	53	*Low Seriousness.* Scores of 1, 2, or 3 on the seriousness scale. No incident in this category involved use of a weapon, none involved injury requiring doctor's treatment, none were sex offenses and none involved loss of more than $250. These incidents, then, involve a combination of verbal threats, small losses, minor injuries.
High Seriousness	38	77	47	*High Seriousness.* Scores of 4 or higher on the scale. In this category are rapes, any offense involving a dangerous weapon, any injury requiring doctor's treatment, any monetary loss of $250 or more and combinations involving threat of harm with monetary loss or threat of harm and minor injury combined with any monetary loss.

Source: Computed from the Portland survey data collected for the Oregon Research Institute in 1974.

Table 8-4. Strength of Relationship Between Attitudes and Decisions to Report Crimes[a]

	Independent Variable	*Property Crimes Seriousness* *Low* *gamma*	*Moderate* *gamma*	*High* *gamma*	*Personal Crimes* *All* *gamma*
1.	Trust in Police	0.32	0.25	0.15	0.31
2.	Police-community Relations	0.32	0.08	0.13	0.11
3.	Chance Police Catch Offender	0.02	0.14	0.32	0.08
4.	Chance Police Recover Property	−0.04	0.02	0.07	0.32
5.	Chance Court Punish Offender	0.10	0.04	−0.28	0.25
6.	Attitudes Toward Court	0.10	0.03	0.07	0.12
7.	Understand Local Issues	0.30	0.17	−0.07	0.48
8.	Length of Residence	0.11	−0.09	0.34	0.08
9.	Involvement in CPB Program	0.24	0.35	0.09	0.04
10.	Insurance	0.10	0.05	0.25	0.08
11.	Stranger	0.02	0.29	0.40	0.08

[a]Tests of significance for the gamma values are not readily available and were not conducted.

Source: Computed from the Portland survey data collected for the Oregon Research Institute in 1974.

more community crime prevention activities.[8] It also is interesting to note that the victim's perception of whether the police are apt to catch the offender and/or recover the property are not correlated with decisions to report minor incidents.

Moderately Serious Property Crimes

Decisions to report moderately serious property crimes correlate with the independent variables in much the same way. However, the victim's perception of whether the police will catch the offender is more important for moderately serious crimes than for minor ones. And, when the crime is quite serious (column 5), this becomes one of the most important variables. Likewise, if the crime was committed by a stranger, it is more apt to be reported.

Highly Serious Property Crimes

The most serious property crimes are more apt to be reported by victims who:

1. trust the police (although the importance of this variable obviously *declines* as seriousness *increases*),
2. believe the police will be able to catch the offender,
3. have lived in the area for a longer time,
4. have insured their property and
5. who believe that the crime was committed by a stranger.

The one negative relationship (court punishment) indicates that victims who think the likelihood of punishment is small are more apt to report incidents than are persons who believe the court will punish the offender. Perhaps the direction of causality should be reversed: persons who have reported incidents to the police are less confident the courts will punish the offender than are persons who were victimized but did not have the experience of reporting the incident.

Personal Crimes

(Personal crimes were analyzed within each seriousness level, but since the results were almost identical, the categories were combined.) As with the less serious property crimes, attitudinal items are quite important. Trust in the police, a belief that the police will catch and the court will punish the offender, and the victim's ability to understand the nature of local issues (an indicator of community integration) were all relatively important in victim decisions to report crimes.

Although the relationships shown in Table 8-4 are not particularly strong, predictions are being made to a dichotomous dependent variable (reported or not reported) and, with the exception of the trust in the police attitudinal scale, all of the independent variables are based on single item responses. Thus, the reliability of these data will be relatively low. The low reliability and the dichotomous dependent variable both operate to depress the observed strength of association between independent and dependent variables.

The implications of the analysis are:

1. Efforts to improve residents' attitudes toward the police or to increase citizen perceptions of police effectiveness can be expected to increase the proportion of victims reporting crimes.
2. Victims who distrust the police and who are not as well integrated into their communities generally do not report crimes to the police as often as other persons, even though the crimes are of the same level of seriousness.
3. Serious property crimes are more apt to be reported than any other type of crime, and the percentage of those reported to the police is influenced much less strongly by victim attitudes toward the police.

4. Increased participation by citizens in crime prevention programs can be expected to increase the proportion of citizens who will report victimizations to the police.

CITIZEN PERCEPTION OF STREET LIGHTING

A high crime area in northeast Portland received approximately $180,000 worth of improved or new street lighting during 1973. The most desirable evaluation of such a program would enable us to determine whether the crime rate decreased below what it would have been had the lights not been installed. Further, that evaluation would determine whether crime was displaced into adjacent areas. Such an evaluation cannot be conducted with official police data. The use of official crime rates in before and after evaluations can produce highly misleading conclusions about a program's effectiveness because increases in crime can be attributed either to increases in total crime or to increases in victim reporting to the police. Official crime data should not be used unless the researcher is confident that the proportion of victims reporting crimes to the police is stable over time. In Portland, there is substantial evidence that victim reporting increased as a result of participation in crime prevention programs. Thus, analyses of program effectiveness based on official data are extremely difficult to interpret.

Although victimization data for Portland are available for time periods before and after implementation of the lighting program, the earlier data (from the LEAA survey) cannot be disaggregated to characterize the victimization rate within a particular section of the city. For these reasons, it is not possible to determine whether crime has been reduced and/or displaced. On the other hand, a preliminary reconnaissance can be undertaken with data from the 1974 survey to provide some information concerning the likelihood that street lights would reduce crime.

Consider the logic of street lighting programs: Better-lighted areas presumably will result in residents feeling safer and using the streets and parks more frequently. An increase in the number of law-abiding persons who use these areas presumably makes them less-inviting locations for criminals because of the increased likelihood that someone will observe the crime and aid the victim. Survey data can be used to examine these linkages between street lights and crime reduction.

Awareness of Street Lights

The first question is whether people living in the street lighting area were aware that the lighting had been improved. Only 25 percent of the approximately 350 residents interviewed in that area were aware of the lights; 62 percent said that no lights had been added or improved and 13 percent said that they did not know. Each respondent was asked whether he or she was aware of any special crime prevention programs in the city (an open-ended question); only one person out of more than 3,900 interviewed in the metropolitan area mentioned the street lighting program.

Respondents were asked whether they considered their area to be very well lighted, fairly well lighted, poorly lighted or very poorly lighted. For this analysis, the metropolitan area was divided into fifteen "social areas" representing relatively homogeneous groupings of census tracts. Of the respondents in the street lighting area, 43 percent said that the area was very well lighted—the lowest percentage of individuals giving such a response across the fifteen social areas of the city. Thus, in spite of the additional lights, residents judged their area to be more poorly lighted than did residents of any other area in the city.

Interviewers in the 1974 survey were instructed to count the number of street lights that they could see from the front entrance of each household or apartment. For households in the street lighting area, the interviewers' coding revealed that 75 percent of the households were within sight of two or more street lights, making it the third *best* lighted area among the fifteen. (Gamma values were calculated, within each area, between the interviewer's assessment of the number of lights and the respondent's subjective judgment of how well lighted the area was. All correlations were positive and most were between 0.25 and 0.45.)

Lighting and Feelings of Safety

Only in the street lighting area were there enough people who knew that lighting had been improved to permit an analysis of responses to a direct question concerning whether the improved lighting made them feel safer. Of the 79 persons who said that the lighting had been improved, 28 percent said they felt much safer, 14 percent said they felt somewhat safer and 58 percent said the improved lighting had not changed their feelings of safety.

Respondents also were asked how safe they felt outside, at night, in the area where they lived. Responses were correlated with subjective perceptions concerning how well lighted the area was and the interviewer's estimate of the number of street lights in the area. The analysis of subjective perceptions was conducted within each of the fifteen areas and resulted in fifteen coefficients that were very close to zero (only in one of the fifteen areas was the relationship significant using a 0.05 significance level). Using the interviewer's estimate of the number of lights, the analysis again revealed fifteen coefficients that were very close to zero (one was statistically significant).

Regarding the question of feeling safe at night within the neighborhood, 45 percent of the persons in the street lighting area said they felt reasonably or very safe at night. Although this might seem to be a relatively high percentage, in only one of the other fourteen areas did residents feel less safe. In most parts of the metropolitan area, more than 60 percent of the residents said that they felt reasonably safe or very safe at night.

Since one would expect street lights to reduce crime, primarily because of increased numbers of law-abiding citizens in the area, combined with a willingness on their part to assist victims, it is not likely that the lights reduced crime in the Portland target area. Most persons (75 percent) did not know that the lights had been improved. Of those who did, only 25 percent said that they felt safer because of the improved lighting. Very low correlations were found between subjective perceptions about how well lighted an area is and statements concerning how safe one feels at night in the neighborhood. One could argue, of course, that offenders do not have such information. Offenders or potential offenders might believe that improved lighting increases the risk of committing a crime, even if there are no more persons in the area to observe or prevent the incident. If so, then lighting might reduce crime in spite of its apparent lack of impact on the perceptions or behavior of area residents.

CONCLUSIONS

This chapter has illustrated a few of the uses that could be developed for victimization data. In relation to systemwide studies of change in the crime rates, victimization data may be essential to an adequate understanding of whether the total crime rate has changed or whether changes in the proportion of victims reporting crimes have produced an apparent change in the frequency of crime incidents recorded in the official data. In addition, the type of information that can be obtained from victimization surveys permits evaluators not only to examine the effectiveness of crime reduction programs, but in many instances to examine the logic of the program itself. This type of analysis, exemplified by the study of citizen perceptions of street lighting, can provide important information to decisionmakers and planners concerning how programs could be altered to increase the likelihood that the program will reduce crime.

Victimization data are not, of course, complete substitutes for officially recorded crime. Police departments and some other law enforcement agencies must respond to the crime incidents reported to them. The evidence reported here, however, adds to the growing belief among evaluators that victimization data should be considered as a substitute for official crime data in evaluations that seek to assess change in the total crime rate.

NOTES

1. Funding for the survey and the evaluation were provided by Contract No. 74-NI-99-0016-G from the Oregon Law Enforcement Council and the National Institute of Law Enforcement in Criminal Justice, LEAA.

2. The revisions were very slight and most pertained to placing less emphasis on the parameters of the recall period in order to reduce the tendency of victims to telescope incidents into the most distant month or two of the recall period.

3. There are many problems in the computer analysis of victimization data, particularly problems involved in counting the number of incidents. In order to

make the second survey results as comparable as possible to the first, we attempted to use the same rules for counting incidents, but in relation to counting incidents coded as a "series" of incidents it was not possible to achieve complete comparability because the interviewers in the second survey probably used the "series" option slightly more often than interviewers in the first survey. LEAA does not count any of the incidents recorded as a "series." Because there were more incidents of this type in the second survey, they *were* counted. Thus, the 127 burglaries per 1,000 households represents all single incidents plus each incident within a series counted as one additional burglary. If the series are excluded from the 1974 data (as they were in 1972), the estimated burglary rate would be less than 100 per 1,000.

4. A more complete explication of the procedures used to examine alternative explanations for the findings can be found in Anne L. Schneider, "The Portland Victimization Study: Analysis of Trends, 1971-1974," *Occasional Papers in Applied Policy Research* (Eugene, Oregon: Oregon Research Institute, 1974).

5. For example, the second survey was composed of 63 percent homeowners and 37 percent renters whereas the first had 55 percent homeowners and 45 percent renters. The burglary rates for homeowners, however, is higher than for renters. Thus, the difference in sample composition would produce more burglaries in the 1974 data rather than fewer. See Anne L. Schneider, "Evaluation of the Portland Neighborhood-Based Anti-Burglary Program," *Occasional Papers in Applied Policy Research* (Eugene, Oregon: Oregon Research Institute, 1975).

6. Thorsten Sellin and Marvin E. Wolfgang, *The Measurement of Delinquency* (New York: John Wiley, 1964), pp. 292-307.

7. Trust in the police is an attitudinal scale composed of five items. Police-community relations is a statement of satisfaction with this type of police service. Attitudes toward the courts refers to the general satisfaction with court operations. See Anne L. Schneider, Janie Burcart and L.A. Wilson, "The Role of Attitudes in Decisions to Report Crimes to the Police," in William F. McDonald, ed., *Criminal Justice and the Victim* (Beverly Hills, California: Sage Publications, 1976), forthcoming.

8. Participation in community crime prevention refers to marking property, using anti-burglary stickers, or attending neighborhood meetings.

Chapter 9

The Limits of Victim Surveys: A Community Case Study

Fredric L. DuBow
and David E. Reed

Victimization surveys were developed to meet some of the deficiencies of official crime statistics.[1] They provide a means for discovering crimes that were not reported to the police. To the extent that victimization surveys provide a more complete picture of the nature and amount of some types of crimes, they can be an important tool for the evaluation of crime programs. Only in the past few years have they begun to be used for this purpose. The first study to integrate before and after victimization surveys into the design and evaluation process was the Kansas City Preventative Patrol Experiment.[2] Since the Kansas City study, a small number of other evaluations of crime programs have included victimization survey data as one of several strategies for determining impact.[3] This chapter will discuss the utility of using victimization surveys for a particular type of crime program that has become an increasingly important part of the contemporary response to the problem of crime–the small scale community-based program devoted to reducing "street crimes." There are a wide variety of such programs, including citizen patrols, more generalized surveillance programs and escort services.[4] These comments will address common issues in these programs, but will rely most heavily on a study of the WhistleSTOP program in the Hyde Park area of Chicago. We focus on street crime programs because, while there is widespread concern about all types of crimes, street crime engenders the greatest fear and has the greatest impact on patterns of daily existence. Small scale programs are important because of the wide variations in both the nature and extent of crime across different localities. These programs provide the closest fit between specific problems and means intended to address them. Local programs are also most likely to involve the sort of citizen participation that has recently been heralded as the most practical solution to the major crime problems in our society.[5]

Operation WhistleSTOP was initiated by the Hyde Park Kenwood Community Conference (HPKCC) in early 1972. It was a response to declining community businesses, the emigration of some longtime community residents and the general feeling that residents were afraid of being victimized in the course of their daily activities within the community. The goals were to reduce street crime incidence and to make residents less afraid to make use of the streets and, therefore, the community's resources. The program called on residents to use whistles to call for help. Those hearing whistles were to respond by first calling the police and then seeking to assist the victim by going to the street and proceeding toward the victim-whistleblower while blowing a whistle themselves. It is a program that stresses the responsibility of residents for one another's safety. In the first month of program operation, 7,000 whistles were sold in an area with a population of 45,000 to 50,000. By the end of the year, the area had absorbed close to 17,000 whistles. However, beyond the data on whistle sales and an awareness that there were many instances of whistle use, WhistleSTOP, like other local programs, lacked a systematic evaluation of its impact.

In the WhistleSTOP case as in most crime programs, the most typical measure of success would be a change in the reported rate of targeted crimes after the program intervention. With all such evaluations, the official crime statistics pose problems of interpretation where it cannot be determined whether a change in the crime rate is due to changes in the number of crime incidents or to changes in the percentage of incidents that are reported to the police.[6] If the *direction* of change in the percentage of crimes reported were known then, under certain circumstances, it would be possible to infer the *direction* of change in the incidence of crime from the official statistics. Thus, in Table 9-1, if it were known that a given program would be likely to increase or leave unchanged the level of crime reporting, any downward change in the rate of reported crimes (see Table 9-1, box 2) could be taken as an indication that the rate of incidents had decreased. Conversely, if there is good reason to believe that reporting rates are decreasing, an increase in reported crimes would be a reflection of increases in the rate of incidents (Table 9-1, box 3). However, under the other two conditions represented by boxes 1 and 4, no such inferences about the direction of change could be made.

When the program being evaluated attempts to increase the number and frequency with which citizens report crimes, the percentage of crimes reported will increase to the extent that the programs are successful in mobilizing

Table 9-1. Changes in the Reported Crime Rate

		Increase	*Decrease*
Likely Changes in the Rate of Crime Reporting	Increase	1	2
	Decrease	3	4

participants. Thus, if we could assume that WhistleSTOP was successful in improving citizen reporting of crimes, the 40 percent decrease in purse snatchings during the first year of its operation illustrated in Table 9-2 would reflect a substantial decrease in the rate for that crime.[7] Table 9-2 presents yearly purse-snatching data for the WhistleSTOP area, comparing the first intervention year with three prior years. If the incidence of purse snatching had increased, it would be impossible to know whether the assumed increase in the rate of crime reporting could have canceled out a decrease in the number of incidents.

Assumptions about the direction of change in the percentage of crimes reported may be reasonable for programs like WhistleSTOP, but to date there are no studies that have measured the change in reporting patterns over time for programs specifically aimed at increasing reporting. The closest approximation to this data comes from evaluations of antiburglary programs in Portland and Seattle.[8] Those findings suggest that general citizen involvement tends to increase crime reporting, even though, in both of these cities, the increases occurred in programs where expanded crime reporting was not a primary goal.[9]

Victimization surveys have made a major contribution to the understanding of reporting behavior. Their advantage is that they identify many crimes previously unreported to police, and the results in a number of different surveys have always shown substantial differences between police statistics and their tabulations. They provide a measure of crime that is unaffected by changes in reporting to police and give some indication of the percentage of crime incidents that are reported. To date there is considerable data on reporting rates in different communities but little on reporting rates over time.[10] Only Portland and Seattle have collected and analyzed reporting rates over time and, as we have already noted, found substantial changes. The Portland victimization studies provide the first concrete piece of evidence that changes in reporting patterns can be substantial enough even over a relatively short period of time to effect

Table 9-2. Purse Snatchings in the Hyde Park-Kenwood Section of the Twenty-first Police District Before and After the Introduction of WhistleSTOP

Years	*Incidents*	*Yearly Percentage Change*
3	152	–
2	223	+46.7
1	276	+23.8
	WhistleSTOP introduced	
1	165	–40.2

Source: Unpublished data supplied by the Chicago Police Department.

the picture of crime in a community. Schneider[11] found that between 1972 and 1974 the official burglary statistics rose 12 percent. However, her comparison of the two victimization surveys reveals an increase in the rate at which burglaries were reported to the police from 50 to 70 percent. This change in reporting behavior was associated with a decline in the number of burglary victimizations found in the surveys. Therefore, an increase in reporting had produced a rise in the official crime rate for burglary when the victimization rate may have been declining.

Until information is available on changes in crime reporting behavior, the patterning of relationships over time between victimization and reported crime will remain unclear and the usefulness of official statistics to evaluate many types of interventions will be limited. Fortunately, victimization surveys, applied within a proper longitudinal framework, hold great promise for providing this much needed information.

COMMON PROBLEMS OF VICTIMIZATION AND OFFICIAL CRIME DATA

Victimization surveys have advantages when compared with official crime statistics in their capacity for generating information about crimes not reported to the police, but there are some problems that the two types of measurement share.[12] Where crime programs are designed to affect a particular set of crime activities, it is important to be able to differentiate those activities from the general pattern of crime activity. The legal categories in which crimes are recorded and which are generally used to report official and victimization data may be cross-cut by other distinctions that are more relevant for studying the impact of a crime program. For example, "street crime" has no formal status in the law, but is a definable set of activities that are to be found distributed across several "legal" categories of crime. In most cases, the basic elements of "street crimes" can be identified as crime in which (1) violence is used or threatened, (2) the parties involved are strangers, and (3) the activity takes place or is initiated in a public or semipublic place out of doors. The spatial placement of a crime or the relationship among the parties is not generally part of the legal definition. For example, assaults, thefts and robberies may occur either indoors or out and could involve strangers or persons known to each other. For each crime, it might be possible to state whether it most commonly happens in one type of relationship, but as long as there is a substantial proportion of crimes in the legal category that don't share those characteristics it becomes difficult to use that category.

In the past few years, some researchers and criminal justice organizations have begun to introduce distinctions of this type into the way crimes are recorded and analyzed. Police departments have begun to use similar distinctions in their official statistics. In St. Louis, the police refer to crimes as "suppressible" or "nonsuppressible," and in San Francisco crime policy is discussed in terms of "preventable" and "nonpreventable" crimes. In both cases, the distinction is based on whether a patrolman could discover the crime in the course of normal patrol activities.[13] In at least one study, the distinction between inside and outside crimes was used to assess the impact of policing variations. The use of distinction led to an overall assessment substantially different from what would have been concluded without it.[14] As yet, there have been no systematic studies of crime statistics in which the inside-outside distinction has been studied over time for different categories of crime. Until we have such studies, researchers must continue to be sensitive to the potential importance of this distinction whether they are working with official or victimization crime data.

In our study of WhistleSTOP, we were not able to obtain breakdowns of the relevant crime categories by place of occurrence, but since purse snatching occurs almost exclusively outside, and burglaries, by definition, involve activities inside houses, we could investigate whether measures that approximated this distinction provided any insights. Purse snatching was used as an indicator of "street crimes" while burglary represented all "nonstreet crimes." In Table 9-3, the number of burglaries and purse snatchings over a four year period during which WhistleSTOP was begun is shown.[15] Also included are the purse snatchings for Prairie-Oakland, a part of the same police district in which no WhistleSTOP program was in operation.[16]

In all three categories, the number of reported incidents declines during the period when WhistleSTOP was introduced, but purse snatchings in Hyde Park-Kenwood decreased at the highest rate. The pattern of change for burglaries in Hyde Park-Kenwood is too variable to indicate a trend, while purse snatching in Prairie-Oakland remained at an almost constant level for two years. Time series analysis was also used to analyze trends in the data, using each twenty-eight day reporting period over the four years as data points. When monthly totals are used, however, fluctuations associated with the small number of crimes occurring within each area made it difficult to discern trends. The problem of small crime totals is shared by official statistics and victimization survey data for small areas.[17] Victimization surveys consistently find a higher rate of crime than that obtained by police for those categories where they have been used. This suggests that, when translated to a rate form, the victimization results could be sufficiently higher in numbers that they might be more stable than the official statistics. This would of course make them much more useful for longitudinal or time series analysis.

While official statistics and victimization surveys, in theory, share the problem of small numbers and consequent instability in analyzing trends in local areas, the problem for victim surveys is only theoretical. To date we have no studies that have concentrated on gathering victimization data in a small area for more than two points in time. To date, only Schneider[18] has shown how

Table 9-3. Burglaries and Purse Snatching in Hyde Park-Kenwood and Prairie-Oakland Sections of Chicago's Twenty-first Police District for Periods Before and After the Introduction of WhistleSTOP

Years *Before and After*	*Purse Snatching in Hyde Park-Kenwood*	*Purse Snatching in Prairie-Oakland*	*Burglaries in Hyde Park-Kenwood*
		Incidence	
3	152	296	880
2	223	229	767
1	276	329	864
		WhistleSTOP introduced	
1	165	326	759
		Percentage Change	
3	–	–	–
1	46.7	–22.6	–12.8
1	23.8	43.7	12.6
		WhistleSTOP introduced	
1	–40.2	–0.9	–12.2

Source: Unpublished data supplied by the Chicago Police Department.

monthly totals might be generated from a single survey for the city of Portland. The resources and commitment for conducting a series of surveys focusing on a particular locality have not yet emerged.

DISTINCTIVE PROBLEMS OF VICTIMIZATION SURVEYS

Costs

There are a number of problems that must be confronted, in considering the use of victimization surveys for studies of local street crime programs, that are not shared by official crime statistics. Perhaps the most obvious is cost. Official statistics are collected· as a routine part of police activity. A small area victimization survey implies a significant new financial commitment. Whatever the merits of victimization surveys, they are unlikely to be used to evaluate most crime programs because they are too expensive to administer. Even in high crime areas, low victimization rates per person require that a great number of persons be interviewed to obtain the necessary amount of data on most crimes. When such interviews are done in person by trained interviewers, the costs quickly mount up. Interviews with 200 persons,[19] a number that is questionably small for the purposes of analysis, would easily cost close to $20,000. To be useful for evaluation purposes, it would be necessary to gather this data at a minimum of two points in time. One partial solution may be to use the telephone. Telephone surveys are significantly less expensive than face-to-face interviews. There is some evidence[20] that, with the use of random digit dialing procedures, samples can be generated that are as representative as those that have been obtained in the traditional face-to-face surveys. Further, response rates in both the Cincinnati studies and in pilot surveys in Chicago neighborhoods are as high as or higher than those achieved with face-to-face methods. In a pilot victimization survey of the Northtown community area of Chicago, 83 percent of the English-speaking adult respondents contacted by telephone completed an interview.[21]

Relatively less information is available about the substance of the responses to telephone as opposed to face-to-face victimization surveys. The findings from the Cincinnati study[22] are encouraging on this account, but more research is needed before the differences between the two techniques are fully understood. One source of insight into this might be a comparison of the original face-to-face interviews with telephoned callbacks in the Census Bureau's twenty-six city victimization surveys.

Some additional questions are encountered when the telephone survey idea is applied in local areas. First, the technique has a number of compelling advantages. For the low budget evaluation efforts of local organizations, telephone surveys offer lower costs and less demand for sophisticated personnel. Since the interview process could take place in a contained area, supervision is greatly simplified and problems in maintaining interview consistency and accuracy are more easily monitored without the need for extensive training. In addition, the technique is particularly useful in areas with "high rise" buildings where access to residents is difficult and in areas where the security of face-to-face interviewers is questionable.

Where a small locality with defined boundaries is being studied, problems arise in the ability to draw a sample through random digit dialing effectively and efficiently. The procedure for drawing a sample from a local area begins with a determination of the three digit exchanges serving the area. Once the exchanges are known, a computer program is used to generate random sets of numbers for the last four digits of the phone number. This random pool will include nonassigned numbers, as well as nonresidential phones. Depending on how the exchanges are arranged, it may also be difficult to avoid generating a high percentage of telephone numbers that are outside the target area. In the Chicago area, for example, the number prefixes are geographically bounded only in the most general sense (e.g., north, central, south and west). Estimates of the number of generated numbers that would be outside the geographical boundaries of a given community area range as high as 80 percent. Unless there is technique for determining before dialing whether the generated number is within the target area, the difficulties of reaching a sufficient number of appropriate respondents are immense.

In Chicago, the telephone company has a "name and address service" that gives the caller the name and address for any listed phone number upon request. The service will also indicate whether the number is unassigned or a business phone. This service allows interviewers to screen out a large proportion of geographically inappropriate numbers. Unlisted numbers would require checking as part of an interview to determine whether the residences were located within the appropriate boundaries.

In designing a telephone survey of local area victimization, the researchers must determine the availability of "name and address service,"[23] the geographical distribution of prefixes, the proportion of households having phones, etc., before a decision about feasibility can be made. In cases where major problems in the use of random digit dialing techniques exist, there are alternate means of telephone sampling. In the Hyde Park-Kenwood neighborhood, good results were obtained from a telephone survey using a random selection of phone listings from a street directory. This sampling technique is limited by its exclusion of unlisted numbers and the relatively high proportion of numbers that have recently been changed. However, it has the advantages of building in a geographical distribution and allowing for the exclusion of business numbers. In addition, the selection of numbers can be a fairly expeditious process easily handled by volunteer labor and at low cost when public copies of the directory are used. Despite the errors of the street directory sample, its ease of generation may be sufficient to recommend its use for local program evaluations that lack substantial research funds.

Households as Sampling Units

All of the existing victimization surveys have used households as the sampling unit. Within households, one or all of the adults may be questioned directly or through proxies. Sampling by households has certain built-in biases, particularly when one respondent is used as a representative of the entire household. These biases have been discussed at length elsewhere.[24] To study a neighborhood or community crime program, the use of household respondents with or without the inclusion of a commercial sample poses significant difficulties in obtaining a picture of crimes committed *in* the community. The problems can be summarized in the question: How does the survey deal with the movement of persons in and out of neighborhoods? Victimization surveys interview residents of particular geographic areas about their personal and household victimization experiences. As part of such questions, the survey in a locality (shown by the small square in Figure 9-1) would gather data on the experiences of residents in the neighborhood, but also on those personal victimizations that occurred elsewhere (#1). If the victimization interview includes questions on where the

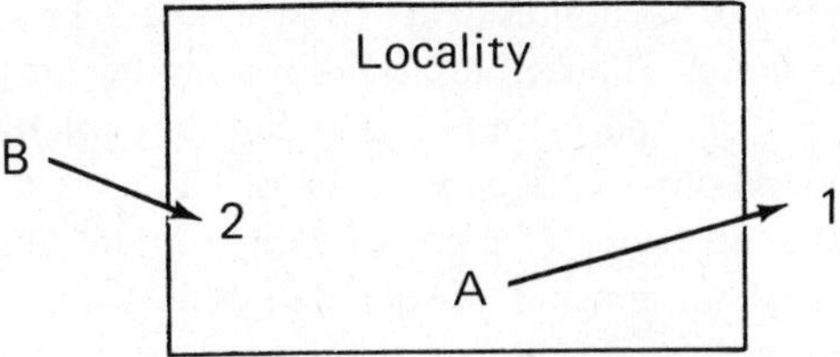

Figure 9-1. The Problem of Mobility for Household-Based Victim Survey

victimization occurs, then it may be possible to differentiate between victimizations occurring inside and those occurring outside the neighborhood. For most purposes, an evaluation of a neighborhood-specific crime program will be most interested in crimes that occur within the neighborhood.

In order to use the information on where a personal victimization has occurred, it is necessary to ascertain whether respondents can give a geographic fix to their victimization. When the victimization did not take place at home or in some familiar place, there may be a vagueness about its exact location. For the purposes of the Census Bureau's twenty-six city victim surveys, it was sufficient to determine whether the crime occurred within or outside the city. In a local victim survey it might be adequate to determine whether the crime occurred within the more familiar locality in which the respondent lives. Therefore, even if the exact location were difficult to recall, this difficulty would not necessarily undermine the ability of the local survey to generate the relevant personal crime estimates.

The possible difficulties of geographic recall could be measured through a reverse record check procedure similar to that used in San Jose,[25] which proved useful in elucidating the extent of recall problems for victimization incidents. A sample of victims could be drawn from police records and included in a victimization survey in which the victims would be asked to specify where they had been victimized. These replies could then be compared with the police records, and this procedure would provide some measure of the ability of citizens to locate the place of their victimization.

This location problem arises primarily for personal victimizations. For household crimes, the residence is generally the site of the crime incident, and the movement of people will not confound these rates. If personal crimes occurring outside the area are not eliminated from the neighborhood rates, they will distort the picture of neighborhood crime and will introduce a source of variation in crime that is not subject to influence by the crime program. For example, the proportion of personal victimizations that occurred outside the city was reported in the National Crime Panel Survey of thirteen cities. The proportions ranged from 4 percent in New Orleans to 19 percent in Oakland.[26] These percentages, however, were not used to adjust the city rates for personal crime.

A more difficult problem is the failure of victim surveys to sample the victimization experiences of nonresidents (B in Figure 9-1) who are victimized while in the neighborhood. The victimizations of nonresidents (#2 in Figure 9-1) may be included in police reports for that area, but they will not be picked up in samples based on households or telephone listings. This undersampling of victims would underestimate the degree of personal victimizations occurring within the neighborhood. The seriousness of this underestimate and the overestimate mentioned above depends upon the pattern and degree of mobility of residents and nonresidents and their relative geographically specific victimization rates.

This problem has been recognized in discussions of the National Crime Panel city surveys. One suggestion for reducing problems at the city level has been to move to an analysis of crime by SMSA. By sampling from this larger area, the amount of in- and outmigration on a daily basis may be decreased as a source of error. Using a larger geographic sampling frame may reduce the errors that are generated from the nonsampling of nonresident victims, but, when considered for a neighborhood level study, it is usually impossible. To study a neighborhood, it would be necessary to sample the larger area from which the majority of visitors to the neighborhood come.

Where neighborhoods are relatively stable, this source of error appears unimportant. But it must be kept in mind that workers, consumers and persons traveling through the area on the way to other areas, as well as those visiting friends and relatives, are all potential victims of crime. If a victimization survey is used, it would be important to have some knowledge about the movement of those categories of people on a daily basis. Techniques for measuring population flows at local levels are not well developed.[27]

From the earliest victimization surveys onwards it has been found that there is a large amount of crime reported to interviewers that is not reported to the police. Only more recently have we become aware that there may be a significant proportion of crimes that get reported to the police, but are not reported to interviewers on victimization surveys. In the San Jose reverse record check study,[28] a sample of victims whose victimizations appeared in police records were interviewed as part of a general victimization survey. This study found that the pattern of "nonrecall" of crimes in the interviews was substantially worse for personal than for household crimes. Ninety percent of the burglaries reported to the police were also mentioned to the victim survey interviewers. By contrast, the "recall" crime rates for robbery, rape and assaults were 76, 67 and 48 percent respectively.[29] Further analysis shows that reported crimes involving relatives or persons known to the victim were much less likely to be "recalled" in the victim survey than was the same type of personal offense when it involved a stranger. Assaults involving relatives are rarely (22.2 percent) reported in the interviews, while less than 70 percent of the robberies in which the offender was known were recalled.

This suggests that the rates for personal victimizations generated by the victim surveys more fully[30] reflect stranger-to-stranger crimes, but even for stranger-to-stranger crimes like robbery, almost one-quarter of the crimes reported to the police go unreported on the survey. This pattern of differential "nonrecall" poses major problems for generating overall personal crime incidence rates, but it is somewhat less of a problem where the principle concern is with "street crimes." However, when the problem of interview recall for personal crimes is considered together with the difficulties of using a household sampling frame to collect data on all personal crimes occurring within a local area, the limitation of victim surveys for evaluating local street crime programs is substantial. At this point in their development, victim surveys may be used more confidently for the study of household victimizations than for personal violence since household crimes are less affected by the geographic sampling and recall problems just described.

ALTERNATE CONCEPTIONS OF PROGRAM IMPACT

Changes in the incidence of crime are not only the most important goal for street crime programs, but they are generally seen as the principle means by which other psychological and behavioral reactions will be affected. Figure 9-2 represents the typical interpretation that is usually offered of the relationship between the immediate and longer range consequences of crime programs. However, in WhistleSTOP and other cases, psychological and behavioral orientations may be changing as a result of the program independent of whether there is a change in the crime rates. Crime programs may alter perceptions of the crime rate, and people may believe that risks of victimization have been altered. These activities may also heighten awareness of the amount of crime, leading people to become more concerned and to feel more threatened. Often increased awareness of crime danger is an intermediate goal of crime programs. It is anticipated that changes in awareness will increase citizen participation in efforts to respond to

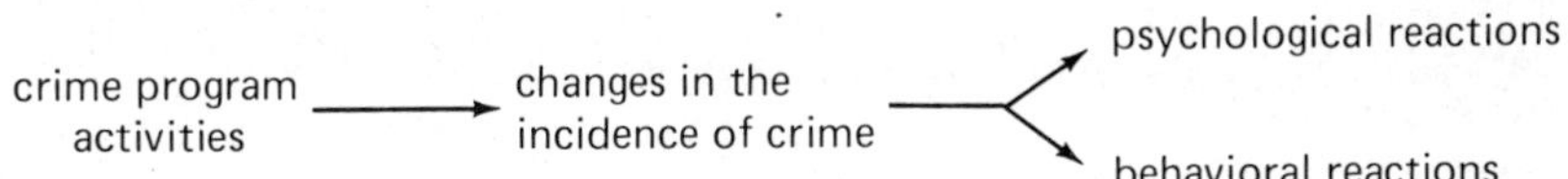

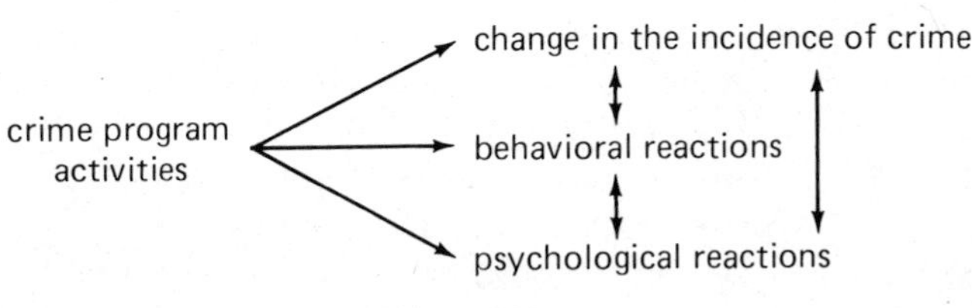

Figure 9-2

crime. Conversely, activities of crime programs may be perceived as effective, thereby justifying less cautious behavior. In either case, crime programs may have significant effects *regardless* of their effectiveness in reaching their avowed goal of crime reduction. WhistleSTOP's originators were aware that they had to deal with perceptions and fears as well as criminal deterrence. They consciously sought to reduce anxieties and to encourage behavior that presumed less vulnerability to crime on the streets.

In measuring the impact of local street crime programs like WhistleSTOP, it is crucial to include appropriate measures that will allow these additional consequences to be studied. Since official and victimization crime data pose the limitations that have been discussed above, it is doubly important to consider additional ways in which an assessment about street crime programs might be reached. The remainder of this chapter will explore some of these possible sources. In terms of importance, we would suggest that they are at least as significant as incident data so long as one accepts our assertion that citizen-based responses to crime are directly related to these factors rather than being related through changes in crime incidence.

Attitude and Behavioral Surveys

Combining these two dimensions of citizen response, survey methods are one of the best known and developed techniques for gleaning information. While the processes of completing surveys, sampling, design, etc., are very similar to those for victimization studies, the two techniques differ in at least one important dimension–size of survey population. The victimization survey technique requires a large enough base to uncover victimizations that are experienced by a minority of the population each year. While crime is a comparatively rare occurrence, every respondent can report on psychological orientations. For example, a relatively small sample of 200 completed interviews may be adequate for developing a picture of attitudes and behaviors for a population but may be insufficient to develop incidence measures for any but the most frequently occurring crimes.

The specific contents of the survey will, of course, be a function of the intended consequence of the program being studied. Since the major cost of these surveys lies in the actual interview process, it is usual practice to maximize the gains of the individual contacts by combining both attitude and behavior inquiries, and even more recently some elements of a victimization survey.[31] In the case of the Hyde Park study, both behavioral and attitude issues were included in the survey because the program was directed at both dimensions of citizen response. The behavioral inquiries focused on familiarity, whistle purchase and incident participation, while the attitude questions dealt with concerns about crime and expectations or evaluations of the potential effectiveness of the program. The problem of interview design may be heightened with this sort of "dual purpose" questionnaire since respondents can be expected to strive toward consistency between reported attitudes and behavior that may affect the validity of responses unless wording and placement are very carefully controlled. Of course, with any survey there are the usual difficulties in insuring reasonable reliability and validity that have been dealt with by many social scientists.[32]

Cognitive Mapping

Another attitude measure that is administered through a survey medium is the newly developed technique of cognitive mapping. This technique is distinctive in the type of information it produces—a map of perceived concern or threat within the environment—but is limited to application in "face-to-face" surveys because of the need for a pictorial response. The principle work in this area comes from geographers and psychologists.[33] The specific techniques have been applied most thoroughly to issues of preferences for and knowledge about different geographical areas. However, Ley's research included the mapping of "stress levels" in a North Philadelphia community, while Springer specifically asked about where the crime dangers in a Seattle suburb could be found. In addition to the type of use that has already been made, this technique might be fruitfully applied to conclusions about the displacement effects of crime and the importance of community and neighborhood areas of security, and in distinguishing the possible correlates of different types of responses to crime.

BEHAVIORAL INDICATORS

Our remaining suggestions of alternate data sources include a range of behavioral indicators that are distinguishable from those above by the fact that they are distinctly "unobtrusive measures."[34] Since attitudes are expressed most succinctly through verbal exchanges, they are usually tapped through the use of survey and interview techniques.[35] Behavioral measures, while confounded by problems of interpretation of the meaning of some types of acts, tend to be relatively straightforward and less subject to the problems of interviewer effects and distortion of data as the respondent struggles toward presenting an image of consistency in responses and compliance with acceptable values.[36]

Use of Public Space

In communities dealing with problems of crime, an early and rather sensitive indicator of local concern is the limitation of use made of public space. The roots of this behavior pattern are still to be clearly delineated, but the hypothesis is that, since citizens are particularly afraid of violent and stranger perpetrated crime, one of the first defensive reactions is to limit contact with the threatening public environment where these incidents are most likely to occur.[37] This is one of the reasons for the focus earlier on "street crime" in the planning of many local crime control programs. In terms of behavioral indicators, there are several areas for potential inquiry, including use of public transportation and street and business activity levels.

Transportation Usage. Communities with well-developed public transportation systems have a valuable data source. The several types of public conveyance—ranging from taxis to buses—suggest a range of citizen responses. Taxis are the most private and secure means since they minimize time spent on the street and generally entail no forced contact with strangers.[38] On the other extreme we have bus service, where the citizen must travel to the stop, wait in a public and unprotected spot for the bus, travel in company with strangers, and finally walk from the stop to his destination. Somewhat less sensitive as an indicator are mass transit systems like subways and elevated trains where frequently the waiting area is less public and overseen by system personnel so that greater security is provided.

Data sources for transportation modes are of two types. Archival records of ridership patterns are kept by transit organizations and, with the proper contacts, this might be accessible to community researchers. The quality and applicability of these records is likely to vary and, consequently, other sources of the information may be called upon. Particularly in the case of bus traffic, where records are not typically kept of entrances and departures, the researcher may be forced to turn to observation. Here the procedures are simple, but the costs are extremely high in terms of time spent by the observers to gather even a limited amount of information. The very problems, for example, that make official records of buses unlikely also make the collection of loading information extremely difficult unless one has the manpower to cover every bus passing through an area. Short of this level of completeness, however, it is possible to collect information about specific areas or stops by observing those locations only. Similar techniques can be used for gauging taxi and rapid transit usage where records are not available.

Street Usage. The most obvious indicators of a behavioral reaction to street crime concerns are changes in the use made of the public ways of a local community. If a population is reacting to the threat of crime, changes will most usually occur in the evening and after dark hours first, but in certain groups within the population such as the elderly, reduced daytime use of streets may also be found. As many authors have noted,[39] fear of crime is in large part apprehension about contact with strangers and unacceptable behavior one confronts on the streets. The threatening aspect of streets relates to a commonly held perception that that is where the most threatening and violent crime is likely to take place.[40] Therefore, the ability of a local crime response program to deal effectively with this concern is one of the more important indicators of their success in addressing citizen concerns. In Hyde Park-Kenwood, street use had become sufficiently diminished (particularly at night) to be a major concern for the WhistleSTOP program. The organizing staff often spoke in terms of "reclaiming the streets" for Hyde Park citizens. Gathering data on this variable poses a series of problems. To date, research on activities in the city has been more highly developed for measuring the time people spend at each activity and the type of places where people spend their time.[41] For eliciting this type of information, interviews have generally been used. A thorough study would entail tabulating street use over substantial periods of time and in different parts of the community. Some information might be obtained just by counting the people who pass different points in the community; in cases like Hyde Park, however, the ethnic composition of pedestrians in the community is an important enough factor for it to also be useful to tabulate race, age (youth or adult) and possibly sex. Since the concern would be changes in street usage, the tabulation would have to be done before the innovation to have any real value, and corrections for weather and time of year would be necessary to make the data relevant. Though the area of most focused concern might be the business districts, the concern about street safety can be even greater in less populous areas of the community. A distribution of sites for the collection of foot traffic data would help to illuminate important differences in the response of different areas and to pinpoint the type of effects that a program might have. To deal with the labor intensity of these observations, some technically sophisticated techniques such as time lapse photography and even infrared photography have been suggested. While these methods might save a great deal of labor, they produce limited types of data and have interpretation problems all their own.

Business Activity

Another indicator of impact is the variation in business within a community as it is related to the tendency of citizens to retreat from full use of public space. In areas where businesses are centralized and alternative shopping facilities limited, this may not be an important consideration, but in older urban neighborhoods like Hyde Park the availability of both a range and quality of local businesses is perhaps critical for the continued viability of the community as a desirable middle class residential area. WhistleSTOP organizers expressed concern that local businesses and particularly nighttime businesses like restaurants, galleries and theatres were leaving the area as patrons decreasingly ventured forth at night.

A census of local businesses, their tenure and the tenure of their predecessors would give the first major indicator of business change. Longitudinal data may be obtainable from records of local business organizations or taxing bodies. More sensitive, and perhaps more interesting, information would come from records of sales volume, but the probability of getting accurate information on this seems very slight unless there is a particularly strong and involved local business organization. It would, of course, be necessary to consider the possibility that business patterns have changed for reasons other than consumer perceptions of the dangers involved in shopping. The opening of new business in nearby areas, and changing transportation facilities, may alter the relative attractiveness of local commercial establishments. In some cases, however, the attractiveness of new shopping malls may include perceptions of greater safety in their more controlled environments.

Insurance records provide another indicator of the business environment. This information would probably reflect both the overall incidence of actual claims and an evaluation by the industry of the relative "security" and "viability" both of the area and of different types of businesses within it.[42] Again, the access problem might be difficult and even impossible both for reasons of confidentiality and because of the likelihood that insurance will be spread throughout a number of firms. On the other hand, there is also the possibility that the insurance industry might keep records in a manner that aggregates by area, or even that some form of these records might be retained in governmental agencies charged with regulating the business.

Residential Mobility

The ultimate response to a concern about crime is to leave the particular area that is perceived as threatening. From the perspective of a community, "exit" is the most threatening possible outcome.[43] Therefore, in communities where the problem is already serious enough to prompt outmigration, indicators of the magnitude and nature of this movement are of particular importance.

In most urban communities, there is a range of residential patterns. The distribution of rooming houses, hotels and single family or multifamily residences suggest not only different types of residents, but very different levels of commitment to a community as well. One might expect to find people in rooming or apartment arrangements generally more mobile than those owning their own house. Unfortunately, the nature and accessibility of records may also be expected to vary for these different types of living arrangements. At one end of the spectrum, records for rooming houses and hotels are likely to be very limited. Apartment records may be more consistently kept in areas where there are large buildings controlled by management firms, though access to these records may be limited. Finally, the change in ownership of single family dwellings is a matter of public record through the recording of deeds and real estate transactions. While these different records indicate the levels of real estate turnovers, one major problem with them is their failure to indicate the new place of residence of the renter or owner. Both normal attrition through deaths and movements within the community would be included in these data and therefore be indistinguishable from the outmigrations that are of principle concern. Again, the probability of this affecting the data would be substantially higher for rooming and rental units than for owner-occupied homes, but the confounding factors still remain an indeterminant quantity.

As part of the Hyde Park study, a survey of the real estate transfers was conducted. Realizing that there would be certain normal levels of turnover, a sample of five years was drawn in an effort to find patterns of change over time that would indicate broader shifts in the community makeup. Though this data has not yet been thoroughly analyzed, an initial examination revealed no clear patterns of change.

CONCLUSION

The interest in systematic evaluation of crime control and prevention programs is relatively recent.[44] This chapter has considered alternative ways to conceptualize and to measure the impact of local crime programs that are concerned primarily with "street crimes." In most evaluations of crime programs, the principle measure is the official crime rate. The relevance of official statistics is enhanced if crimes occurring in public and semipublic places can be distinguished for the purposes of analysis from crimes occurring elsewhere. Even if this can be done, the interpretation of changes in official crime rates over time is hazardous unless information is available on the changing reporting patterns. Where the crime program seeks to increase crime reporting rates, it is even more difficult to ignore this problem. Victimization surveys are valuable because they generate data both on crimes not reported to the police and on patterns of crime reporting. For these reasons they have been described as a powerful new tool for evaluating crime programs. The potential of longitudinal victimization studies is only beginning to be explored, and the studies by Schneider and Schwartz and Clarren in this volume represent two of a very small number of such studies that are presently available.

When the value of victim surveys for measuring the impact of local street crime programs is examined, it is found that the residential sampling frame does not provide data on victimizations that befall nonresidents while visiting the local area. When this difficulty is combined with the recognition that under some conditions a large proportion of personal violent crimes are not being reported on the surveys, the present utility of these surveys for measuring the impact of these local street crime programs must be questioned.

Our acquaintance with WhistleSTOP and other local crime programs leads to the conclusion that alternative psychological and behavioral measures are particularly relevant because these may change even without changes in the crime rate. The way people perceive and experience crime problems is influenced by a number of factors other than crime rates, and their affective and behavioral reactions have as much or more consequence for the quality of life in communities as the crime rate itself. These alternate measures are further called for by the limitations in official and victim survey crime statistics previously described. None of the measures is without its own collection and interpretation problems, but, until further research is conducted, it is not possible to conclude which will be the most fruitful. Moreover, unless new methods are introduced into the design of victim surveys, these alternatives may be more feasible and equally useful evaluation tools for the small scale crime program.

NOTES

1. Philip H. Ennis, *Criminal Victimization in the United States: A Report of a National Survey, Field Surveys II* (Washington, D.C.: U.S. Government Printing Office, 1967); and Albert D. Biderman and Albert J. Reiss, Jr., "On Exploring the 'Dark Figure' of Crime," *The Annals of the American Academy of Political and Social Science* 374 (November 1967): pp. 1-15.

2. George L. Kelling, Tony Pate, Duncan Dieckman and Charles E. Brown, *The Kansas City Preventative Patrol Experiment: A Technical Report* (Washington, D.C.: Police Foundation, October 1974).

3. Anne Schneider, *Measuring Change in the Crime Rate: Problems in the Use of Official Data and Victimization Survey Data* (Eugene: Oregon Research Institute, September 1975); Alfred I. Schwartz, Sumner N. Clarren, Thomas Fischgrund, Eric F. Hollins and Paul G. Nalley, *Evaluation of Cincinnati's Community Sector Team Policing Program–A Progress Report: After One Year Summary of Major Findings* (Washington, D.C.: The Urban Institute, March 17, 1975); John E. Boydstun, *San Diego Field Interrogation: Final Report* (Washington, D.C.: Police Foundation, August 1975); and Floyd Fowler, "Hartford Crime Surveys" (Hartford: Institute of Criminal and Social Justice, 1975).

4. George Washnis, *Citizen Involvement in Crime Prevention* (Lexington, Massachusetts: Lexington Books, 1976); John E. Conklin, *The Impact of Crime* (New York: Macmillan, 1975); and Gary Marx and Dane Archer, "Community Police Patrols and Vigilantism," in H. Jon Rosenbaum and Peter C. Sedenberg eds., *Vigilante Politics* (Philadelphia: University of Pennsylvania Press, 1976), pp. 129-57.

5. National Advisory Commission on Criminal Justice Standards and Goals, *Community Crime Prevention* (Washington, D.C.: U.S. Government Printing Office, 1973).

6. Biderman and Reiss.

7. The available data on crime in Hyde Park-Kenwood included breakdowns by beat for five major crimes and for thirteen twenty-eight day reporting periods for the three years proceeding the introduction of WhistleSTOP and for one year following. The thirteen reporting periods are used to create time units that are equal in length and in number of weekend days. The South-East Chicago Commission from whom this data was obtained collected its crime statistics each week from the district station. This method of collection minimized the effects of clearances, unfoundings and other redefinitions that may occur after the initial report.

8. Schneider.

9. In both programs, the principle effort was made to make homes more secure and to get residents to mark property for identification purposes.

10. Studies that have the potential for yielding such information but have not

been analyzed to address the issue of rates of reporting over time include Kelling *et al.*, Boydstun, the National Crime Survey and the Eight Impact Cities for which two surveys have been collected. An informal examination of the data on crime reporting in the Kansas City report suggests considerable instability over time in reporting rates.

11. Schneider.

12. Wesley G. Skogan, "Measurement Problems in Official and Survey Crime Rates," *Journal of Criminal Justice* 3 (1975): pp. 17-31.

13. Nelson B. Heller and J. Thomas McEven, "The Use of an Incident Seriousness Index in the Deployment of Police Patrol Manpower Methods and Conclusions" (Report to the National Institute of Law Enforcement and Criminal Justice, January 1972).

14. S. James Press, *Some Effects of an Increase in Police Manpower in the 20th Precinct of New York City* (New York: The New York City Rand Institute, 1971).

15. We present data on the absolute number of crimes occurring in Hyde Park-Kenwood and Prairie-Oakland, but since the total number of residents in these two areas was stable during this period they can be interpreted as rates.

16. Prairie-Oakland was some distance from Hyde Park-Kenwood because the 21st Police District has a dumbbell shape. Therefore, there would be less chance of crime displacement or, conversely, an extension of the deterrent effects from Hyde Park-Kenwood to Prairie-Oakland than if they were highly contiguous.

17. In the Kansas City Preventative Patrol Experiment, the yearly totals for repeated and non-repeated samples in each of the three treatment conditions were quite small for most of the crimes reported. Kelling *et al.* If more than two data points had been used it is likely that wide fluctuations in crime occurrences would have been found.

18. Schneider.

19. This is the number interviewed in each sample treatment condition in the Kansas City study. Kelling *et al.*

20. William Klecka and Alfred Tuchfarber, Jr., "The Advantages of Random Digit Dialing Surveys: An Empirical Test" (University of Cincinnati, Draft copy, July 1975).

21. A Chicago citywide telephone survey on crime reporting also achieved a response rate of over 80 percent. See Michael J. O'Neil, "An Examination of Sampling Bias Due to Nonresponse" (Evanston: Department of Sociology, Northwestern University, 1976).

22. Schwartz *et al.*

23. Efforts to locate "name and address" services in other cities met with no success. The staff operating the service in the Chicago area were uncertain whether such a service existed elsewhere. However, a sales representative from the telephone company suggested that he thought the service did exist within every large telephone company in the country, though access to it and the name it might carry would vary widely.

24. Wesley G. Skogan, "Appendix" to "Crimes and Victims" (manuscript, 1975).

25. Anthony Turner, *"San Jose Methods Test of Known Crime Victims,"*

Statistics Technical Report #1 (Washington, D.C.: Law Enforcement Assistance Administration.

26. U.S. Department of Justice, Law Enforcement Assistance Administration, *Criminal Victimization Surveys in 13 American Cities* (Washington, D.C.: U.S. Government Printing Office, June 1975).

27. Stuart F. Chapin, Jr., *Human Activity Patterns in the City: Things People Do in Time and in Space* (New York: John Wiley and Sons, 1975).

28. Turner.

29. Ibid., p. 6.

30. Whether citizen or police accounts of an incident are more accurate is not possible to determine with the existing studies. In some "nonrecall" cases, the police and the respondent may not have agreed on whether there had been a crime committed or on the legal definition of the type of crime. In other cases, subsequent events may have caused the victim to redefine and minimize what had occurred.

31. Increasingly, this practice of "piggy-backing" data collection has been used to decrease survey costs, though the returns are limited as the length of the surveys increases and respondent attention and acquiescence is affected.

32. Morris L. Rosenberg, *The Logic of Survey Analysis* (New York: Basic Books, 1968); Raymond L. Gorden, *Interviewing: Strategy Techniques, and Tactics* (Homewood, Illinois: Dorsey Press, 1969); and Aaron V. Cicourel, *Method and Measurement in Sociology* (New York: The Free Press, 1964).

33. Peter Gould and Rodney White, *Mental Maps* (New York: Penguin Books, 1974); David Ley, "The Black Inner City as a Frontier Outpost: Images and Behavior of a North Philadelphia Neighborhood" (Ph.D. dissertation, University Park, Pennsylvania, 1972); Larry Springer, "Crime Perception and Response Behavior: Two Views of a Seattle Community" (Ph.D. dissertation, Pennsylvania State University, 1974); and Stanley Milgram, "Mental Maps of a City," *New York* 8:45 (November 10, 1975): pp. 49-51.

34. Eugene J. Webb, Donald T. Campbell, Richard D. Schwartz and Lee Sechrest, *Unobtrusive Measures: Nonreactive Research in the Social Sciences* (Chicago: Rand McNally, 1966).

35. The clearest exception to this is the use of participant observation whereby a skilled observer can evaluate nonverbal expressions of attitude in the context of familiar patterns of events. Otherwise, nonverbal evaluations are difficult to execute and even more difficult to justify as valid findings.

36. George J. McCall, *Observing the Law: Applications of Field Methods to the Criminal Justice System* (Rockville, Maryland: National Institute of Mental Health, Crime and Delinquency Issues, 1975).

37. Chapin.

38. The exception to this exists in cities like Washington where cab pooling practices are used, though even in these cases the fact that the driver is present as an observer limits the threat of the stranger contacts.

39. Jane Jacobs, *Death and Life of Great American Cities* (New York: Vintage Books, 1961).

40. This is in spite of evidence that suggests that the most violent crime, murder, most often occurs in private places and between relatives, friends and acquaintances.

41. Chapin.

42. Council on Municipal Performance, "Police Evaluation: I," *COMP News* (December 1975).

43. Albert O. Hirschman, *Exit, Voice and Loyalty: Responses to Decline in Firms, Organizations and States* (Cambridge: Harvard University Press, 1970).

44. Michael Maltz, *Evaluation of Crime Control Programs* (Washington, D.C.: National Institute of Law Enforcement and Criminal Justice, April 1972); Michael Maltz, "Measures of Effectiveness for Crime Reduction Programs," *Operations Research* 23:3 (May-June 1975): pp. 452-74; and Richard B. Hoffman, "Performance Measurements in Crime Control," *Journal of Research on Crime and Delinquency* (1972), pp. 165-74.

Chapter 10

A Strategic Choice Analysis of Robbery*

Philip J. Cook

Victimization surveys are providing criminologists and criminal justice officials with a wealth of detailed information on the incidence of theft and violence and the impact of these crimes on their victims. For crimes involving personal confrontation between victim and offender, these survey data also provide information on readily observable characteristics of offenders and their conduct during the incident. Given these microdata on "inputs" and outcomes of a large number of incidents, we have the empirical base for a process analysis of certain important categories of crime such as rape, assault and robbery. In this chapter[1] I develop such an analysis for noncommercial robbery, taking the view that observed robbery patterns are the aggregative result of choices made by individual robbers, and that these choices can be understood in terms of the robber's need to intimidate his victim and his desire to acquire as much money as possible with a minimum of effort. This viewpoint, which I have dubbed a "strategic choice" analysis, serves to organize the empirical description of urban robbery presented here, and yields some insights into the role of guns in robbery. The concluding section of the chapter suggests the relevance of this perspective to the gun control controversy.

The main alternative source of such data that would be appropriate for this type of analysis is police files; detective reports typically include the complainant's description of the incident and the offender in cases for which the complainant (usually the victim) was an eyewitness. The usefulness of such data was illustrated by the National Commission on the Causes and Prevention of Violence staff report on victim-offender relationships in violent crime, which was based on samples of police reports collected in seventeen cities.[2] Relative to police data, victimization survey data have both advantages and disadvantages. Some of the disadvantages result from the inherent problems with retrospective

*Points of view or opinions stated in this chapter are those of the author and do not necessarily represent the official position or policies of the U.S. Department of Justice.

survey data; such problems (memory lapses, deliberate distortions in reporting) are certainly not lacking in complainant reports to the police, but they may be more severe in survey interview situations. Additional disadvantages of survey data include the lack of any data on homicides and the impossibility of following cases through the police investigation and arrest phases.[3] The principal advantages of victimization survey data are that (1) they provide more detail on victim characteristics and the crime's impact on the victim, and (2) they include reports of crimes that were never reported to the police and, hence, they may more accurately represent the total number of such crimes.

The empirical results in this chapter are based on data generated by victimization surveys of twenty-six U.S. central cities conducted in 1973-1974 by the U.S. Bureau of the Census as part of a program known as the National Crime Panel.[4] The findings reported below focus on the demographic characteristics of victims and offenders, types of weapons used by offenders, and financial losses to victims. These variables by no means cover all the information contained in the NCP data, and this chapter is in that sense preliminary.[5]

NCP DATA ON ROBBERY

The Uniform Crime Report (UCR) defines robbery as any theft from a person by force or violence or by putting in fear. This includes such crimes as strong-arm robbery, stickups, armed robbery, assaults to rob, and attempts to rob. The definition covers a great diversity of events, ranging from a child's strong-arm demand for his classmate's lunch money, to a bank robbery committed by a gang of shotgun-toting bandits. Between these extremes lie such crimes as muggings and "yokings," purse snatches (when the victims resist), residential robberies, and stickups of cab and bus drivers and shopkeepers. All of these crimes have two common elements: violence or the threat of violence, and theft or attempted theft.

The National Crime survey includes reports on 9,946 incidents that can be classified as robberies using UCR's definition; given the sampling method used in the NCP survey, these reports can be viewed as a random sample from a population of 413,397 robberies occurring within the twenty-six cities during 1972-1973.[6] Robberies committed within city limits against nonresidents are not included, since only residents were interviewed; the relatively few robberies committed against respondents outside their city of residence were included in the data set but excluded from our analysis.[7] Finally, the data are limited to incidents involving victims twelve years old or older.

The survey cities had a combined population of thirty million in 1970, 15 percent of the total U.S. population; 55 percent of all robberies known to the police in 1973 were committed within these cities. We can reasonably assume that the NCS data on robberies are representative of all robberies committed against residents of large U.S. cities.

My analysis is limited to "noncommercial" robberies, defined here as robberies committed somewhere besides the premises of a commercial enterprise. (A small fraction of "noncommercial" robberies involve taxi drivers and other victims engaged in commercial activities.) A total of 8,816 such incidents were reported in the surveys, representing a total of 370, 381 noncommercial robberies.

I decided to limit this analysis to noncommercial robberies largely because a Commercial Victimization Survey, conducted by the Census Bureau in the same cities during the same period, will yield more complete and accurate data on commercial robberies.

CHARACTERISTICS OF OFFENDERS AND VICTIMS IN NONCOMMERCIAL ROBBERIES

Offenders

Noncommercial robbery is typically not a lucrative enterprise (the take was less than $50 in 72 percent of all incidents); therefore it is not surprising that robbers generally come from groups that have relatively poor legitimate opportunities to make money. Most incidents (53 percent) involved offenders who were less than twenty-one years old (with 42 percent in the fifteen to twenty age range), and 84 percent of all incidents involved nonwhite offenders. The latter statistic is striking, for nonwhites constitute only 30 percent of the twenty-six cities' total population.

Successful commission of a robbery requires the ability to intimidate the intended victim, a factor which helps explain several other characteristics of robbery incidents:

–Robbers typically work in teams. One-third of all incidents involved three or more robbers, and an additional 30 percent involved two robbers; nevertheless, it was rare for offenders to attempt to rob couples or groups, and in 94 percent of all incidents the victim was alone at the time of the robbery.
–The robbers were armed in 62 percent of all incidents; 21 percent involved a gun, 29 percent a knife and 14 percent one of a variety of other weapons.[8]
–Robbery is a male occupation; 96 percent of incidents involved male offenders (including 3 percent in which male(s) and female(s) worked together).

Victims

Table 10-1 shows robbery incident rates by victim characteristics for the twenty-six cities. The rates (which are virtually equivalent to victimization rates) reproduce well-known victimization patterns: the incidence of robbery incidents is disproportionately concentrated on blacks, males and youths. Victimization rates are presumably the result of (1) exposure, (2) vulnerability (as perceived by the robber) and (3) average amount of cash and other property carried on the

Table 10-1. Noncommercial Robbery Incident Rates by Demographic Characteristics of Victims

Victim Characteristics	*(1) Number of Incidents (000)*	*(2) Population, Aged Twelve and Older (000)*	*(3) Incident Rate (percent)*
1. *Race*			
White	226	16,978	1.3
Black	136	6,605	2.1
2. *Sex*			
Male	240	11,215	2.1
Female	130	12,884	1.0
3. *Age*			
12-15	54	2,094	2.6
16-24	86	4,714	1.8
25-64	191	13,983	1.4
65+	39	3,309	1.2
4. *All Incidents*	370	24,100	1.5

Sources: Column (1) is from National Crime Panel Surveys of twenty-six cities. Column (2) is from various reports of the Decenniel Census for 1970.

Note: An incident rate is not quite the same thing as the more common victimization rate, since 6 percent of all incidents involved two or more victims. (Victimization rates would be about 9 percent higher.) The population figures are not quite appropriate, since they are for 1970 and the victimization surveys counted reports of crimes committed in 1972 or 1973.

person. Victimization patterns suggest that the exposure factor is dominant; all three patterns are compatible with (1), but the sex pattern contradicts (2) and both race and age patterns contradict (3). Clearly a multivariate analysis of victimization patterns is needed to explore these factors further.

PROCESS

One unsurprising conclusion is that both robbers and robbery victims are drawn disproportionately from certain demographic groups. Such analysis is interesting only to the extent that it reveals patterns of concentration. After identifying such patterns, we can begin to understand the phenomenon at hand. The cross tabulations presented in Tables 10-2 through 10-6 yield a more complex view of the robbery process. Three processes are discussed: (1) the "similarity pattern"—the tendency for a robber to choose a victim with similar demographic characteristics; (2) the pattern of weapon use among robbers; and (3) the "intimidation pattern."

The Similarity Pattern

A fairly constant pattern of "likes robbing likes" emerges for each demographic dimension—race, sex and age. A useful statistic for illustrating this pattern is $R_{ij} = \frac{O_{ij}}{V_j}$, where O_{ij} is the percentage of robberies committed by offenders in demographic group i against victims in group j, and V_j is the percentage of the total population that are members of group j. For example, 52.3 percent of all robberies committed by blacks had white victims, whereas whites made up 70.4 percent of the total population of the twenty-six cities; in this case $R_{BW} = \frac{52.3}{70.4} = 0.7$. Demonstration of the similarity pattern for group i requires that $R_{ii} > 1$.

Race. Table 10-2 presents the pattern of racial interactions in robbery. The similarity pattern for race is evident from this table and from the fact that $R_{BB} = 1.3$. Although a majority of black robbers' victims were white, black robbers were nevertheless much more likely to choose black victims than one would expect from the proportion of blacks in the total population. It is this fact, coupled with the relatively high robbery offense rate by blacks, that accounts for blacks' relatively high victimization rates. The high offense rate by blacks also explains the finding that whites are three times as likely to be robbed by nonwhites as by other whites.

Sex. Robbery is an overwhelmingly male phenomenon: 65 percent of victims were males, and 96 percent of all incidents involved male offenders (including 3 percent that involved both male and female offenders). Intrasexual robbery predominates, with $R_{MM} = 1.5$ and $R_{FF} = 1.5$.

Table 10-2. Joint Distribution of Noncommercial Robbery Incidents by Race Of Offender(s) And Race Of Victim(s)
(percent)

Offender Race	*Victim Race*			
	Black	*White*	*Other*	*Total*
Black	34.7	39.3	1.2	75.2
White	1.2	14.8	0.4	16.5
Other	0.6	4.1	0.4	5.2
Mixed	0.6	2.5	0	3.1
Total	36.9	61.0	2.2	100.0

Source: National Crime Panel Survey for twenty-six cities.

Note: Victims did not know the race of the robbers in 5.5 percent of all reports. These missing observations are omitted in calculating the percentages in the first four rows, but not in the last row. Thus the first four rows' entries total to 100 percent, as do the entries of the last row.

Age. Table 10-3 presents the distribution of robberies by age. Over half of the youngest offender group's robberies were committed against victims aged twelve to fifteen, and the propensity to rob this group declines steadily with the offender's age. Other similarity effects are hard to observe given the disparate age categorizations. It is interesting to note that the likelihood that a robbery victim will be from twenty-five to sixty-four years old increases with the offender's age (see below) but the likelihood of an elderly victim being chosen is about constant at 10 percent for all offender age groups.

Table 10-3. Joint Distribution of Noncommercial Robbery Incidents by Age Of Offender(s) And Age Of Victim(s)
(percent)

Age of Robber	*Age of Victim*				
	12-15	*16-24*	*25-64*	*65+*	*Total*
14 and younger	3.6	0.1	2.1	0.7	6.8
15-17	7.6	4.3	7.1	2.0	21.0
18-20	2.7	7.5	12.6	2.6	25.4
21 and older	1.1	11.8	28.7	5.2	46.8
Total	14.5	23.3	51.5	10.7	100.0

Source: National Crime Panel Survey for twenty-six cities.

Note: "Age of Robber" refers to the age of the *oldest* robber if there is more than one involved in an incident. "Age of Victim" refers to the age of the respondent.

Patterns of Weapon Use

Table 10-4 presents the distribution of weapons use in robbery incidents for a number of offender categories. Large differences in the propensity to use weapons are evident within the sex, age and race categories.

The proportion of robberies committed with a "knife or other weapon" does not differ much among categories, lying in the 35-45 percent range in every case but one. The proportion of gun and unarmed robberies varies much more, and either figure serves to characterize the category. If we associate gun use (or the use of any type of weapon) with "professionalism," then the relatively professional categories are made up of males, blacks, adults and robbers working in pairs.

John E. Conklin concluded on the basis of his study of robbery in Boston: "Robbing with accomplices reduces the need to carry a weapon for self-protection, since the group itself acts as a functional equivalent of a weapon."[9] This

Table 10-4. Distribution Of Weapons Used In Noncommercial Robbery Incidents, Conditioned On Offender Characteristics (percent)

Category	*Gun*	*Knife or Other Weapon*	*Unarmed*	*Total*
1. *Number of Offenders*				
1	19	39	42	100
2	27	41	32	100
3 or more	18	41	40	100
2. *Sex of Offenders*				
Single male	20	39	41	100
Mult. male	23	41	35	100
Female	5	35	60	100
Mixed	24	42	34	100
3. *Age of Offender*				
14 or less	2	25	73	100
15-17	7	38	54	100
18-20	18	45	37	100
21 or older	32	41	27	100
4. *Race of Offender*				
Black	24	40	36	100
White	14	35	51	100
5. *Total*	21	41	38	100

Source: National Crime Panel Surveys for twenty-six cities.

Note: Incidents for which the respondent did not know the weapon or relevant characteristics of the offender were excluded from the analysis.

"weapon equivalent" notion, while apparently confirmed for Conklin's Boston data, is contradicted by NCP's data. Table 10-5 shows that guns are *less* likely to be used by single offenders than by multiple offenders and that this pattern holds for subgroups of offenders (classified by age, race and sex) as well as for the entire sample of offenders. While it is plausible that a team of offenders has less "need" of a gun than a single offender for a certain type of victim, the data suggest that teams of offenders tend to choose stronger victims. This pattern of victim choice, explored in the following section, helps explain the apparent anomaly of weapon use by groups.

The Intimidation Pattern

One would suppose that the offender's choice of victim is influenced by the necessity of generating actual or threatened force sufficient to intimidate the victim–to "persuade" him to comply quickly with the robber's demands. If so, we would generally expect to find less potent robbers choosing more vulnerable victims, while more potent robbers would choose less vulnerable victims in a greater proportion of cases. We assume that the most vulnerable victims are the very young and very old, females and people who are alone. The most "intimidating" offenders are adult males, armed (especially with a gun) and working in teams of two or more.

Table 10-5. Percentage Of Noncommercial Robbery Incidents Which Involved Two or More Offenders, Categorized by Offender's Weapon And Demographic Characteristics

Offender Characteristics	*Weapon*			
	Gun	*Knife or Other Weapon*	*Unarmed*	*Combined*
1. *Race*				
White	54	51	54	53
Black	68	66	60	64
2. *Sex*				
Male	66	64	56	62
Female	49	56	56	55
3. *Age*				
14 or less	72	67	62	65
15-17	75	65	67	67
18-20	73	71	62	68
21+	65	58	49	58

Source: National Crime Panel Surveys in twenty-six cities.

Note: Incidents involving groups of offenders that included both male and female offenders (3 percent of the total) were excluded from consideration in row 2. Incidents involving groups of offenders which included both black and white offenders (3 percent of the total) were excluded from consideration in row 1. The "age" category refers to the age of the *oldest* offender if there was more than one. Incidents for which the respondent did not know the relevant characteristics of the offender (5 percent for race, 4 percent for sex and 10 percent for age) were excluded from the analysis.

The statistics presented in Table 10-6 tend to support these suppositions, although the intimidation pattern is not always pronounced. The offenders' propensity to choose relatively well-defended victims (males, groups of two or more, adults) increases consistently with the deadliness of the offender's weapon and number of offenders involved. Furthermore, the offender's propensity to choose victims aged twenty-five to sixty-four increases markedly with the age of the offender; this relationship obtains even when type of weapon is controlled for.

MEDICAL AND PROPERTY LOSSES FROM NONCOMMERCIAL ROBBERY

Robbery is a serious crime. It usually involves a sudden, unprovoked attack by a stranger who threatens bodily harm—a threat that is often realized: 17 percent of all murders occur during the course of a robbery.[10] Most victims also lose some cash or other valuables, and in some cases this loss is considerable. For most noncommercial robberies, however, the victim sustains neither injury nor substantial property loss; the worst part of such incidents may be the trauma of the attack.

Table 10-7 presents statistics on property losses from noncommercial robberies in the twenty-six cities.[11] Thirty-eight percent of all victims lost no property, and half lost less than $10. At the other end of the spectrum we have one-sixth

Table 10-6. Percentage of Noncommercial Robbery Incidents Involving Male Victims, Multiple Victims and Victims Aged Twenty-five to Sixty-four, Categorized by Offender Characteristics

<table>
<tr><th rowspan="2">Offender Category</th><th colspan="3">Victims</th></tr>
<tr><th>Male</th><th>Multiple</th><th>Aged 25-64</th></tr>
<tr><td>1. All incidents</td><td>65</td><td>6</td><td>52</td></tr>
<tr><td>2. Offender's Weapon</td><td></td><td></td><td></td></tr>
<tr><td>Gun</td><td>75</td><td>12</td><td>61</td></tr>
<tr><td>Knife or other</td><td>72</td><td>6</td><td>52</td></tr>
<tr><td>Unarmed</td><td>56</td><td>5</td><td>41</td></tr>
<tr><td>3. Number of Offenders</td><td></td><td></td><td></td></tr>
<tr><td>1</td><td>53</td><td>4</td><td>50</td></tr>
<tr><td>2</td><td rowspan="2">75</td><td>6</td><td rowspan="2">51</td></tr>
<tr><td>3 or more</td><td>9</td></tr>
<tr><td>4. Number of Offenders, Gun Robberies Only</td><td></td><td></td><td></td></tr>
<tr><td>1</td><td>65</td><td>10</td><td>60</td></tr>
<tr><td>2</td><td rowspan="2">80</td><td>12</td><td rowspan="2">60</td></tr>
<tr><td>3 or more</td><td>14</td></tr>
</table>

Source: National Crime Panel Surveys in twenty-six cities.

Note: Missing observations are excluded in the calculation of each of the percentages.

Table 10-7. Victim's Property Losses in Noncommercial Robberies, by Weapon Type

Weapon	*Overall Mean*	*Percent With Zero Loss*	*Mean For Those With Losses*	*Percent Losing $100 +*	*Percent Losing $1,000 +*
Gun	$164	22	$207	30	3.5
Knife	60	34	89	17	0.5
Other Weapon	65	45	119	13	1.4
Unarmed	40	46	75	8	0.4
Weapon Unknown	67	40	111	14	1.0
All incidents	$ 76	38	$122	16	1.2

Cumulative Percentage Distribution of Victim's Property Losses From Noncommercial Robbery

Losses Less Than Or Equal To	*Cumulative Percent of Victims*	*Cumulative Percent of Losses*	*Marginal Percent of Victims*	*Marginal Percent of Losses*
$ 0	38	0	38	0
9	51	1	14	1
49	72	8	21	7
99	84	18	12	11
249	94	38	10	19
999	99	67	5	29
All incidents	100	100	1	33

Source: National Crime Panel Survey in twenty-six cities.

of all victims losing more than $100, and a small fraction (1.2 percent) losing more than $1,000. These high loss groups, although only a small fraction of the total victim population, account for 72 percent of the total reported property losses. Table 10-9 indicates that victims with losses in the $1,000 + range recouped a substantial fraction (47 percent) of their losses from insurance, whereas other victims recovered less than 10 percent. The distribution of medical costs to victims (Table 10-8) is even more skewed, with 94 percent of victims reporting zero costs (suggesting that their injuries, if any, were minor). The remainder of victims averaged $291 in medical costs. Victims suffering losses of $100 or more made up 2.3 percent of the total victim population (but accounted for 92 percent of total medical costs). Very serious injuries ($1,000 +) were sustained by 0.5 percent. (It should be noted that these figures exclude homicides occurring during the course of robbery.) Table 10-9 indicates that insurance coverage for medical losses was more widespread than for property losses; half of the former was recovered from insurance. A third type of

Table 10-8. Victims' Medical Costs Resulting from Noncommercial Robberies, by Weapon Type

Weapon	*Overall Mean*	*Percent Incurring Medical Costs*	*Mean For Those With Medical Costs*	*Percent With Medical Costs Exceeding $1000*
Gun	$17	2.8	$583	0.3
Knife	18	6.6	267	0.4
Other Weapon	27	12.0	223	0.7
Unarmed	12	5.2	221	0.2
Weapon Unknown Residual	23	8.1	283	0.7
All incidents	$19	6.2	$291	0.5

Cumulative Percentage Distribution of Victim's Medical Costs Resulting From Noncommercial Robberies

Losses Less Than or Equal to:	*Cumulative Percent of Victims*	*Cumulative Percent of Medical Costs*	*Marginal Percent of Victims*	*Marginal Percent of Medical Costs*
$ 0	93.8	0	93.8	0
9	94.1	0.1	0.3	0.1
49	96.2	2.8	2.1	2.7
99	97.7	7.8	1.5	5.0
249	98.9	17.2	1.2	9.4
999	99.5	32.4	0.6	15.2
All incidents	100.0	100.0	0.5	67.6

Source: National Crime Panel Surveys in twenty-six cities.

Table 10-9. Percentage of Noncommercial Robbery Victims' Losses Recovered from Insurance

Victim's Gross Loss	*(1) Medical*	*(2) Property*
1-99	23	9
100-249	37	7
250-999	51	11
1000 +	56	47
All Incidents	51	22
		Total Recovery: 28 Percent

Source: National Crime Panel Surveys in twenty-six cities.

Note: Column (1) gives the percentage of the total of all property losses in the specified range which were paid by insurance. Column (2) gives the corresponding percentages for medical costs.

financial loss resulting from robbery—lost wage earnings due to injury—was not estimated.

The statistics in Table 10-10 show an intriguing correlation between medical and property losses. Robberies resulting in large property losses also result in a disproportionate number of serious injuries; robberies resulting in serious injury account for a disproportionate share of property losses. Two (of many) plausible hypotheses compatible with this finding are that (1) victims carrying large amounts of cash are more likely to resist and thereby more likely to be injured, and (2) robbers who can injure the victim are relatively likely to successfully complete the theft.

Table 10-7 reveals a positive relationship between the deadliness of the offender's weapon and the amount of property loss. Robbers wielding guns are much more successful than others, with an average theft of $164 (three times the average theft for other incidents). Their success apparently results both from choosing more lucrative targets and successfully completing the theft in a high proportion of cases. (I am assuming here that "zero loss" robberies primarily result from successful victim resistance rather than from the victim being without valuables at the time of the robbery.) The fact that gun robberies are directed at lucrative targets is consistent with our previous observation that gun robberies disproportionately involve adult victims.

Almost half the unarmed robberies are unsuccessful, and those that are

Table 10-10. Relationships Between Victims' Property Losses and Medical Expenses, Noncommercial Robberies, Twenty-six Cities

	Medical Costs (for those incurring property losses in the indicated range)	
Property Loss	*Mean*	*Percent Incurring Medical Expenses*
$0	$11	4.4
1-99	10	5.5
100 +	56	12.1
All incidents	$19	6.2

	Property Losses (for those incurring medical costs in the specified range)	
Medical Expense	*Mean*	*Percent Incurring Property Losses*
$0	$72	62
1-99	123	67
100 +	168	84
All incidents	$76	62

Source: National Crime Panel Surveys in twenty-six cities.

successful tend to be relatively unrewarding. Armed robberies involving a knife or other weapon (not including guns) are between gun robberies and unarmed robberies in terms of the proportion that were successful and the average theft. Of the two categories here, knife robberies are more often successful and slightly more likely to involve thefts of $100 or more. The average theft for "other weapon" robberies is larger, however, due to a few very lucrative robberies included in this category.

Our picture of how serious these types of robbery are changes dramatically when we examine the injury and medical cost data in Table 10-8. Gun robberies are *least* likely to result in an injury requiring medical care, and a relatively low percentage (0.3 percent) result in serious injuries ($1,000 or more in medical expenses). A gun ordinarily eliminates the need for a robber to physically attack the victim in order to gain his compliance. The very high average medical costs for those victims who *are* injured in a gun robbery is the result of a few reports of extraordinarily high expenses; it may be that a high proportion of critical and fatal injuries occur during gun robberies, but victimization survey data are not appropriate for testing this hypothesis.

CONCLUSIONS

My purpose for this chapter was to present and to begin to document a particular analytic view of robbery that could be dubbed a "strategic choice" or "war game" analysis. In this analysis, robbers make strategic choices of victims (targets) according to (1) the robber's potency ("firepower") in generating a convincing threat and overcoming the victim's resistance, and (2) the perceived vulnerability, availability and attractiveness of the potential victim. The "similarity pattern," in these terms, would result both from differential exposure (youthful targets are disproportionately exposed to youthful robbers, blacks are disproportionately exposed to blacks, etc.) and from vulnerability (females thus become especially attractive targets for female offenders, children are especially attractive targets for youthful offenders). However, offenders can expect a higher "payoff" from less vulnerable targets (e.g., groups of victims and males aged twenty-five to sixty-four); hence, they may seek to increase their firepower by acquiring accomplices or deadly weapons. Such offenders are more likely to select relatively well-defended targets that have a relatively high payoff.

Particular attention was focused throughout this chapter on the role of firearms in robbery. Two patterns of gun use would be compatible with the strategic choice formulation:

1. Guns could be used disproportionately by those offenders who would otherwise be lacking in potency; e.g., youths, females and lone offenders. The opposite pattern was in fact observed.
2. Guns could be used disproportionately by offenders seeking to rob more

> lucrative (and better defended) targets. This was the pattern that actually emerged–for each type of offender (defined by age, sex and number of accomplices), those carrying guns were more likely to rob prime age adult males than those who lacked a gun; robbers armed with a knife or other cutting or bludgeoning weapon were more likely to rob such targets than were unarmed offenders. The value of a gun is suggested by the relatively high success rate for gun robbers and the relatively high average payoff to gun robbery.

Overall, then, it appears that guns are not used as substitutes for other sources of power; rather, they result in the substitution of less vulnerable targets for relatively weak targets.

The fact that the robbery data presented in this paper are compatible with the theoretical "strategic choice" formulation does not constitute proof of a causal process. However, it is useful to suggest how this formulation might be used in policy analysis. Consider the effects on robbery patterns of a successful gun control program. Offenders who otherwise would have used a gun may drop out of the robbery business (because the more lucrative targets become less accessible to them); barring that, at least some would turn to more vulnerable targets, implying a relative (or even absolute) increase in victimization rates for women and youths. The overall property loss from noncommercial robbery would be reduced, but my analysis suggests that the victim injury rate and total medical costs per victim would be increased. If true, these predictions are relevant to the gun control policy debate, but further analysis is required to justify them.

In any event, NCP data are a rich new source of information regarding robbery and other crimes of personal confrontation and offer a good alternative to police files. The potential of these data to generate detailed descriptions of crime patterns should ultimately increase our ability to rationalize criminal justice policy.

NOTES

1. Edward D. Jones III of the Office of Policy and Planning, U.S. Department of Justice, was responsible for the very extensive programming task for this study, and made a number of helpful suggestions.

2. D.J. Mulvihill and M.M. Tumin, *Crimes of Violence*, vol. 12. Staff report submitted to the National Commission on the Causes and Prevention of Violence (Washington, D.C.: U.S. Government Printing Office, 1969), ch. 5.

3. Studies which use police files to do this type of study include John E. Conklin, *Robbery and the Criminal Justice System* (Philadelphia: J.B. Lippincott Co., 1972); Floyd Feeney and Adrienne Weir, eds., *The Prevention and Control of Robbery*, 5 vols. Davis: University of California, The Center on Administration of Criminal Justice, 1973); and Andre Normandeau, "Patterns in Robbery," *Criminologica*, November 1968.

4. The cities are Atlanta, Baltimore, Boston, Buffalo, Chicago, Cincinnati, Cleveland, Dallas, Denver, Detroit, Houston, Los Angeles, Miami, Milwaukee, Minneapolis, New Orleans, New York, Newark, Oakland, Philadelphia, Pittsburgh, Portland, St. Louis, San Diego, San Francisco and Washington, D.C. Results of these surveys are available from a series of publications by the Law Enforcement Assistance Administration, National Criminal Justice Information and Statistics Service.

5. The author and Edward D. Jones III are collaborating on a series of empirical studies dealing with robbery and gun control policies, based largely on the NCP data.

6. The population weights used to estimate the total number of robberies were taken from the 1970 census, and are hence not entirely accurate for the years for which the surveys were taken. The error introduced by these inappropriate weights is no doubt very small.

7. Also excluded from the analysis below are robberies that are part of a series of victimizations reported by a respondent. In most of these cases the respondent was unclear as to the details of any one incident.

8. Eight percent of all incidents in which an offender was carrying a gun also involved a knife. Such incidents are classified throughout this paper as "gun" robberies. Four percent of all incidents in which an offender was carrying a knife (but no gun) also involved some third type of weapon. Such incidents are classified as "knife" robberies.

9. Conklin, p. 108.

10. Derived from statistics presented in Clarence M. Kelley, *Uniform Crime Report 1974* (Washington, D.C.: Federal Bureau of Investigation, 1975), pp. 18-19.

11. While statistical analysis in previous sections employed population weights for incidents, the analysis in this section uses population weights for victims because the focus is on losses sustained by the individual victim in order that total victim losses could be estimated. The difference between incident weights and victim weights results from the fact that some incidents involved more than one victim: 4.88 percent involved two and 1.35 percent involved three or more. There are therefore an average of about 109 victims for every 100 incidents.

Chapter 11

A Cost Analysis of Federal Victim Compensation*

Edward D. Jones III

This chapter utilizes data from the Law Enforcement Assistance Administration's National Crime Survey of personal victimization in twenty-six central cities[1] to assess the cost of a proposed federal program that would compensate victims of assaultive crimes of federal jurisdiction. The data, which include information on incidents beyond those reported to police, are particularly appropriate for calculating risks and costs of victimization. Drawn from samples in an urban environment comprising approximately twenty-two million persons twelve years of age and older, the data include information on degree of injury, cost of medical care, extent of hospitalization, amount of compensation and length of worktime disability for approximately 7,700 assaultive victimizations with injury. These sample victimizations reflect about 293,000 injurious victimizations in the population of the twenty-six cities.[2]

Until recently, analyses of criminal justice programs and criminal events were limited to police-based statistical sources. Injury and cost data relating to victimization, which may not be fully known for months or years after the event, generally are not well covered in those sources. When the President's Commission on Law Enforcement and Administration of Justice (the Katzenbach Commission) was created in 1965, it found in its assessment of crime and the criminal justice system that the lack of knowledge which the Wickersham Commission noted in the early 1930s remained a major problem thirty years later. For example, the Katzenbach Commission stated in its final report that "except in the case of willful homicide, where the figures describe the extent of injury as well as the number of incidents, there is no national data on the likelihood of injury from attack."[3] Indeed, it was forced to rely on a small District of Columbia Crime Commission survey of assaultive violence to infer the

*Points of view or opinions stated in this chapter are those of the author and do not necessarily represent the official position or policies of the U.S. Department of Justice.

risk of attack, and had to commission the National Opinion Research Center to conduct a national survey of 10,000 households to measure, among other things, the cost of injury incurred by victims of assaultive criminal violence.[4]

Recent interest in victim-based statistics reflects an increased concern by the public and the government with crime problems. From 1960 to 1974, the national level of reported violent crime—murder, forcible rape, aggravated assault and robbery—increased 238 percent and the rate of violent crime increased 186.8 percent.[5] Crime became a presidential campaign issue for the first time in 1964, and opinion polls indicate that crime became the most serious domestic issue for the first time in 1968.[6] Because traditional data bases are insufficient for analyzing many complex crime issues, the federal government has committed resources to the development of new sources of information such as the victim-based National Crime Survey that will complement police-based statistics.

The analysis herein relies on both police-based and victim-based information to assess the costs of death and injury incurred by the victims of assaultive criminal violence in federal jurisdiction. Identifying and measuring these costs of victimization are essential if society is to allocate its enforcement resources efficiently; provide appropriate health, social and insurance services for victims; and choose the most desirable program among alternative policy choices. After a discussion of state victim compensation programs and the provisions of the proposed federal program, issues and data problems associated with an analysis of federal jurisdiction offenses are examined. Then, analyses of the costs of victimization and of the projected cost of the proposed victim compensation program are presented.

VICTIM COMPENSATION PROGRAMS

The existence and enforcement of criminal law reflect the notion that society is responsible for protecting its members from victimization. The restoration of damages inflicted by criminal offenders on victims of crime similarly can be viewed as a social responsibility when that protection fails. Although members of society may desire that the risk of victimization be reduced to near zero, the pecuniary cost of providing the required level of enforcement and the concomitant psychic costs of the loss of freedom and of equity may be prohibitive. Restoration by society may be a more cost-effective method of handling victimization, given an affordable level of enforcement.

Restoration by society can be achieved through victim compensation or court-ordered offender restitution. State victim compensation programs were first implemented in the United States in the mid-1960s, and offender restitution has been achieved through court judgments in some instances in the United States. The existing state compensation schemes, federal compensation proposals and restitution judgments have one objective in common, namely, restoring the health, earning capacity and welfare of the assaultive crime victim or his dependents. Compensation is probably more equitable than restitution because not all offenders are identified and many lack the resources or earning capacity to pay damages.

Since 1965, nineteen states have introduced victim compensation programs.[7] Currently, seventeen of these state programs are operational. Among the permissible claims in the operational programs are medical expenses and the loss of earnings (in all states), death benefits (in thirteen states), and pain and suffering (in three states). Several programs have no maximum awards, while maximums in the other states range from $5,000 to $50,000. Nine states have no minimum claim requirement, but others have thresholds ranging from $25 to $500. Eligible recipients include the victim of the crime and, in some states, the dependents of deceased victims and good samaritans.

Other provisions relate to offense coverage, reporting criteria and the sources of funds for compensation. In some states compensable acts include property offenses such as burglary in addition to assaultive offenses. To be eligible for compensation the victim of a compensable offense or his dependent is required by most states to report the criminal incident to the police. The time limit for this report ranges from forty-eight hours in four states to within one year in two states. Finally, most state compensation programs rely upon legislative appropriations for funds. However, one state relies upon court fines, and several on a mixture of court fines or federal funds and state appropriations.

PROPOSED FEDERAL PROGRAM PROVISIONS

The proposed federal program analyzed in this paper is the Criminal Victim Compensation Fund outlined in Senate Bill Number One (S.1).[8] This proposal has provisions similar to those in state programs, but provides coverage only to victims of assaultive offenses that fall within federal jurisdiction. These assaultive offenses include homicide (murder, manslaughter, negligent homicide); assault (maiming, aggravated battery, battery, menacing, terrorizing, communicating a threat, reckless endangerment); kidnapping, (kidnapping, aggravated criminal restraint, criminal restraint); hijacking (aircraft, commandeering a vessel); and sex offenses (rape, sexual assault, sex abuse of minor or ward, unlawful sexual contact).

Generally, a victim would be eligible for Fund consideration in the following federal jurisdiction situations:

- an offense committed in a special territorial jurisdiction (for example, real property of the United States, unorganized territory or possession of the United States, Indian country); in a special maritime jurisdiction (for example, high seas, U.S. waters outside of state jurisdiction, vessel upon Great Lakes or St. Lawrence); or in a special aircraft jurisdiction (for example, aircraft in flight within the United States);

- an offense committed against a U.S. official, a federal law enforcement officer, a foreign dignitary or official, or an official guest of the United States;
- an offense committed in connection with a federal statutory offense such as bank robbery; or
- an offense committed in connection with sending a dangerous weapon or threat through the U.S. mail; transporting a victim across state or U.S. boundaries; holding a person involuntarily; or using facilities of the United States, or of interstate or foreign commerce.

Federal jurisdiction over an offense qualifies it for Fund eligibility. Hence, a victim of a federal jurisdiction offense could be eligible even if, technically, the case were criminally processed in another jurisdiction.

Victims of federal jurisdiction offenses sustaining personal injury may be eligible for compensation to the extent of their actual pecuniary loss, including medical expenses related to physical or psychiatric care, physical or occupational therapy and loss of earnings due to disability. In the event of the victim's death, his or her surviving dependents may be eligible for compensation of funeral and burial expenses and for the loss of support. There is no coverage for losses due to pain and suffering.

A compensation board determines the size of an award after a hearing is held to establish a claim. That claim can be made within a year of an offense, and the maximum award permissible is $50,000. In cases involving disability or death, the award would be paid periodically during the period of disability or over a period of ten years, whichever is less. Further, payment for loss of earnings in the case of a victim's disability, or for the loss of support in the case of a victim's death, cannot exceed $150 per week. Compensation can be paid only over the actual period of loss, and the board can adjust or terminate any award as circumstances warrant.

There are several constraints regarding victim eligibility. First, the victim must report the offense to the proper authorities within seventy-two hours and must cooperate with them during the relevant phases of the criminal justice process. Second, a victim must incur, at a minimum, medical expenses of $100 or loss of earnings for one week, whichever is less. If a victim is to be eligible for loss of earnings compensation, disability must be expected to continue for ninety days or more.

The size of an award is dependent upon several factors. First, if a victim is partially responsible for the occurrence of an offense, the size of an award can be reduced by the proportion of responsibility he bears. The victim can be denied compensation entirely if he is substantially responsible for the occurrence of the offense. Second, the Fund is coordinated on a secondary basis with all other insurance schemes that cover similar losses. If a primary insurer covers some losses that are compensable by the Fund and other losses that are not, it is assumed in determining the Fund's liability that the victim's noncompensable losses (for example, pain and suffering) are offset by the primary insurer prior to its offset of compensable losses. In the case of death, it is presumed that life insurance covers noncompensable losses and that funeral expenses and loss of support will be compensated by the Fund to the extent permissible.

The major revenue sources proposed for the program are criminal fines collected in the United States courts, 20 percent of net profits from Federal Prison Industries and public or private donations. Provision also exists for subrogating a claim against an offender convicted of an offense that gave rise to the claim.

THE FEDERAL JURISDICTION CONSTRAINT

We have identified the Fund provisions that are important for analyzing likely claims and awards and for determining resource availability. Administrative provisions and their implied costs will be discussed briefly following the estimation of the Fund's likely payout. That estimate, which represents a maximum payout, is based upon injury loss information from the National Crime Survey and the Social Security Administration, and federal offense information from the Federal Bureau of Investigation and the Administrative Office of the United States Courts. The data from these sources are discussed later in the chapter.

An alternative estimate of injury loss awards of the Fund could have been based upon the claim and award experiences–adjusted for differences in provisions–of the existing state compensation programs. This procedure was not used because, for the reasons discussed below, the Fund's claim and award experience is likely to be different from that of state schemes that are not constrained by the federal jurisdiction provision. These differences can be accounted for more easily with the National Crime Survey data.

Unlike most offenses occurring in state or local jurisdiction, federal jurisdiction offenses are defined narrowly with respect to targets and the location of offenses (see the definitions above). These crimes are quite visible and their victims readily identifiable. As such, federal jurisdiction offenses are relatively likely to come to the attention of the authorities. For example, we probably would find that a much higher proportion of bank robberies are reported than street robberies. The Fund's police reporting requirement, then, will likely screen proportionally *fewer* federal jurisdiction offenses than an identical requirement in a scheme covering all assaultive offenses.

Federal jurisdiction is frequently defined by the victim's functional capacity. For example, a victim may be a foreign dignitary or a U.S. official acting in the performance of his duties, thereby making an assault functionally one of federal jurisdiction. Such victims are more likely to be covered by primary sources of compensation than victims of similar nonfederal offenses. Consequently, the

Fund's compensation criterion probably will exclude proportionally *more* federal jurisdiction offenses than an identical requirement in a scheme covering all assaultive offenses.

Finally, comparing police-reported federal assaultive offenses with similar nonfederal offenses, there is reason to suppose that the proportion of serious, nonfatal injuries would be different. Many non-federal assaultive crimes are not reported to police because injuries are not serious. For example, the National Crime Survey data for twenty-six cities indicate that for all assaultive crimes in which medical care is required, 76.1 percent are reported to the police. Serious assault cases are reported 77.1 percent of the time, compared with only 49 percent when no medical care is required. Among cases requiring overnight hospital care, 86.5 percent are reported. By comparison, reported federal jurisdiction crimes are likely to include a larger proportion of minor injuries because of the federal nature of the offense, whether relating to circumstance or the capacity of the individual. Therefore, the Fund's minimum claim criterion probably will exclude proportionally *more* federal jurisdiction offenses than an identical requirement in a scheme covering all assaultive offenses.

POTENTIAL FUND CLAIMANTS

Estimates of the frequency of assaultive crimes are available from police-based statistics such as Uniform Crime Reports and from victim-based statistics such as the National Crime Survey. In addition to estimates of the number of events, these sources contain information characterizing the circumstances of the event, including the relationship between offender and victim, the type of weapon used and the location of the offense.

The reliability of these data depends upon several factors. With regard to official data, police organizational structures, crime classification schemes and legal definitions of offenses vary across jurisdictions. Further, events perceived as criminal by victims may not be classified as such by the police, in which case those events are not included in official statistics. In sample surveys of victims, events that the police would regard as unfounded may be included as offenses, while events with foundation may not be reported to interviewers. In addition, because of the time lag between the commission of an offense and the reporting of it in a survey, the recollection of the event and circumstances surrounding it may be impaired. For example, injury costs may be forgotten or (if an insurance company paid for medical services directly) unknown to the victim. According to one analysis, although sample surveys may uncover more events than the police, the estimates may significantly undercount the true frequency of criminal activity.[9]

While these sources include federal jurisdiction offenses, they are not separately identified. However, useful estimates of the true number of federal jurisdiction offenses are readily available as "matters received"[10] by U.S.

Attorneys' offices, and as "cases filed"[11] in U.S. District Courts. Generally, the determination of jurisdiction is made after an offense comes to the attention of an investigative agency. If the offense is a federal violation, it normally will be referred, after preliminary investigation, to a U.S. Attorney's office. "Matters received" data provide an estimate of the number of offenses that office considered important enough for prosecution. An offense also could be referred back to state or local authorities for possible prosecution. If prosecuted federally, a felony offense is filed in a U.S. District Court; a minor offense is within the jurisdiction of U.S. Magistrates.

For an estimate of the true number of federal assaultive offenses, the most desirable sources of data would be investigative agencies. However, there are many such agencies, and referrals to federal prosecutors, based upon quite disaggregate U.S. Code sections, would be costly to aggregate.

Similarly, "matters received" information, although an ostensibly good proxy for the number of Fund claimants, is difficult to employ in the analysis. First, it too is disaggregate at the U.S. Code section level and costly to aggregate. Second, it does not distinguish assaultive offenses by degree of injury. Finally, some nonassaultive offenses—for example, bank robbery—include cases of injury that cannot be isolated.

This analysis relies upon the number of "cases filed" as a proxy for the number of potential Fund claimants. One advantage of this data set is that assaultive offenses are aggregated at a level that permits direct comparison (except for homicide) to the loss data available in the National Crime Survey. Another advantage relates to the attributes of federal assaultive offenses described earlier. Compared with all reported assaultive offenses, reported federal assaultive offenses probably include a greater proportion with minor injuries. With constraints on criminal justice resources, "cases filed" likely represent offenses involving the more serious injuries that would be eligible for Fund compensation.

A disadvantage of the "cases filed" data set is that, like "matters received," cases of injury in nonassaultive offenses cannot be distinguished. Since those offenses generally provide for higher order penalties if death or injury ensues, homicide or assault counts are not separated from the underlying offense and reported elsewhere. In order to account for them we adjust below the homicide and assault "cases filed" data to include death and injury occurring in bank robbery and kidnapping. Aircraft and ship hijacking is not considered because, with increased security in recent years, there are few such incidents. Further, although the potential exists for many victim deaths or injuries in a single incident, damages would likley be compensated from a source other than the compensation program considered here.

Another disadvantage is that, to the extent that the "cases filed" estimates involve multiple victims, the potential set of claimants could be larger than the number of cases. Unfortunately, we cannot correct for this possible undercount.

For fiscal year 1974, 160 homicide cases, 710 assault cases and 127 sex offense cases—excluding white slave traffic cases—were filed in U.S. District Courts.[12] In the same fiscal year there were seventeen deaths and eighteen cases of injury to the victims of crimes like kidnapping, and there were (excluding perpetrators) seven deaths and 142 cases of injury to victims in bank robberies.[13] Adding these figures to the number of homicide and assault cases above, the estimated numbers of potential claimants by offense type for the analysis below are 184 homicides, 870 assaults and 127 sex offenses.

COSTS OF VICTIMIZATION

To individuals and their dependents, the financial and psychic costs of victimization stem from property loss, minor or disabling injury, death, pain and suffering, and altered behavior resulting from the perceived risk of criminal activity. To society, opportunity costs are realized in the impairment of resources that could otherwise be put to productive use if assaultive violence were reduced. The measurement of most of these costs is beyond the scope of this paper. Rather, we concentrate on evaluating several cost factors relevant to the Fund, and note that the Fund provides compensation only for limited individual and social losses, namely, medical and disability losses, and loss of support.

Although nonfatal injury costs derived from the National Crime Survey do not necessarily correspond exactly to those incurred by federal jurisdiction victims, they can be adjusted for the cost analysis of federal crime victim compensation. Prior to that adjustment in the next section, we examine here medical costs and insurance coverage experienced by survey victims, and outline their implications for an assumed victim compensation program which, unlike the Fund, relies on taxes for revenues. This assumed program, with a revenue source similar to that in many state programs, facilitates an examination of victim compensation costs in relation to victimization risks for different population groups.

Medical costs incurred in assaultive crime victimizations are presented in Table 11-1.[14] This table provides costs and risks of injury for the population as a whole and for income groups. Serious assault, minor assault and rape are aggregated to give an overview of assaultive crime costs. Over 60 percent of all injuries uncovered in the survey resulted in no costs. The survey data indicate, further, that costly injuries are relatively infrequent. For example, the data for twenty-six cities indicate that only 0.5 percent of all robbery incidents resulted in medical costs exceeding $1,000.[15]

The risk of victimization resulting in an injury requiring costly medical care is 0.0053 per year. This figure represents the threat of victimization to each resident twelve years of age and older in the twenty-six major American cities surveyed.[16] For this population, the expected cost of victimization with injury

Table 11-1. Medical Costs Incurred in Assaultive Crime Victimizations by Selected Injury Characteristics and Income Classes

Characteristic	*Total*	*Less Than $5,000*	*$5,000-$11,999*	*$12,000-$24,999*	*More Than $25,000*
1. ALL INJURIOUS VICTIMIZATIONS*	292,720	87,734	110,504	56,145	9,459
a. No medical costs incurred (percent)	60.7	57.0	59.5	66.7	74.1
b. Medical care costs incurred (percent)	39.3	43.0	40.5	33.3	25.9
2. MEDICAL CARE VICTIMIZATIONS	115,016	37,692	44,804	18,712	2,453
a. Average medical cost ($)	205.23	117.62	254.44	281.68	94.12
b. Risk of medical care injury (2÷3)	.0053	.0126	.0065	.0024	.0012
c. Expected medical care cost ($) (205.23 x (2b.))	1.09	2.59	1.33	0.49	0.25
3. POPULATION**	21,884,900	2,998,175	6,864,250	7,889,945	1,972,490

Sources: National Crime Survey (NCS) of twenty-six cities; 1974 population by income weights, which were applied to NCS population data, derived from U.S. Department of Commerce, Bureau of the Census, *Statistical Abstract of the United States, 1975* (Washington, D.C.: U.S. Government Printing Office, 96th ed., 1975) Table 640, p. 393.

*Series incidents, a string of events for which the survey respondent was unable to provide complete information, are excluded, as are events that took place outside of the central cities.

**Population figures for income classes do not add to total population. Family income was not identified in 9.9 percent of the survey victimizations. It is assumed that these residual victimizations are distributed in proportion to income class. Population for each income class was reduced accordingly in order to derive proper risk figures. This adjustment reflects a total urban population of 19,724,860.

(medical care only) is $1.09. This can be viewed as the cost to each resident twelve years of age and older in the twenty-six cities to cover and compensate fully the medical expenses incurred by the victims of the nonfatal assaultive crimes surveyed.

When we compare unequal risks with overall risk, as for different income groups in Table 11-1, and for other demographic groups in Table 11-2, different expected costs of victimization emerge. These expected costs are calculated by multiplying the overall average medical expense for the sample—$205.23—and the risk of victimization experienced in each sample group. Although average medical costs vary by group, using the overall average permits us to focus solely on differences in expected costs arising solely from relative risks. In determining the willingness of segments of society to support a public compensation program, these relative expected medical costs can be compared to the overall expected cost of victimization—$1.09—a proxy for each individual's contribution to support the compensation programs. For this comparison we initially assume that each individual is taxed the expected $1.09 to pay for a public compensation program.

Looking first at income and comparing expected costs, only for the income groups under $12,000 would the public compensation program cost be less than the expected medical loss. Although this tax would be regressive in relation to income, lower income groups would benefit on a comparative cost basis from the assumed public compensation program.

Looking now at Table 11-2, we find that only those in the age groups twelve to fifteen years and sixteen to twenty-four years, blacks and males would find the assumed public compensation program beneficial in terms of its costs. To those in the age group twenty-five to forty-nine years, the cost of the program would equal the expected medical loss.

We have assumed a regressive tax structure for funding this assumed program. Under a progressive tax structure similar to the federal income tax, costs and benefits may be somewhat different. For example, lower income groups would bear a proportionally smaller burden of the cost of funding the program as costs would be shifted to higher income groups.

In the absence of public victim compensation, people may avail themselves of private compensation in the form of insurance. However, access to such sources of compensation is constrained by income and demographic factors, in which case some victims must pay all medical costs and other costs resulting from an assault. Table 11-3 presents average medical costs incurred by assaultive crime victims, broken down by insurance coverage and injury seriousness. Coverage includes any type of medical insurance, or benefits from public programs such as Medicaid, Veterans Administration or public welfare. Approximately 35 percent of the victims incurring medical care costs indicated that they had no coverage whatsoever, whereas 65 percent had some type of coverage available.

Average medical costs are presented within a cumulative distribution based

Table 11-2. Medical Costs Incurred in Assaultive Crime Victimizations by Selected Demographic Characteristics

Characteristic	(1) *Twenty-six City Population 1972-1973*	(2) *Survey Victimizations*	(3) *Risk of Injury Requiring Medical Care (2÷1)*	(4) *Average Medical Cost ($)*	(5) *Expected Medical Cost ($) (205.23 x (3))*
1. TOTAL	21,884,900	115,016	.0053	205.23	1.09
2. AGE					
a. 12-15 years	1,971,800	12,808	.0065	104.34	1.33
b. 16-24 years	4,394,500	34,173	.0078	146.44	1.60
c. 25-49 years	8,296,600	43,608	.0053	301.63	1.09
d. 50 years and older	7,222,000	24,427	.0034	168.25	0.70
3. RACE					
a. Black*	6,195,600	46,945	.0076	190.09	1.56
b. White	15,689,300	68,071	.0043	216.83	0.88
4. SEX					
a. Male	9,983,900	67,608	.0068	248.18	1.40
b. Female	11,901,000	47,408	.0040	143.97	0.82

Source: National Crime Survey of twenty-six cities.

*Includes 1,122 victimizations of other races, less than 1 percent of total victimizations.

Table 11-3. Average Medical Costs Incurred in Assaultive Crime Victimizations by Injury Seriousness and Insurance Coverage Characteristics

Victims	10 Percent	25 Percent	50 Percent	75 Percent	90 Percent	100 Percent
			CUMULATIVE			
			MOST SERIOUS INJURIES			
TOTAL	$2219.12	$1116.71	$607.13	$418.17	$351.71	$317.85
With Coverage	2551.56	1309.35	709.58	487.29	408.97	369.69
Without Coverage	1595.58	751.71	413.03	287.20	242.83	219.43
			LEAST SERIOUS INJURIES			
TOTAL	8.90	16.12	28.21	51.37	107.73	317.85
With Coverage	9.20	16.90	29.81	56.47	128.65	369.69
Without Coverage	8.32	14.64	25.18	41.70	67.95	219.43

Source: National Crime Survey of twenty-six cities.

upon an ordinal ranking of medical costs incurred. For example, the average medical cost experienced in the 10 percent most serious injuries was $2,219.12, and in the 10 percent least serious injuries, $8.90. For those with coverage in the 10 percent most serious injury group the average medical cost was 1.61 times greater than the average medical cost incurred by victims without coverage. Unless one believes that offenders inflict greater damages on the insured than the uninsured, this difference in cost cannot be explained satisfactorily by criminogenic factors. However, this difference in cost may be explained by several factors relating to the economics of health care. First, individuals qualifying for compensation may demand higher quality medical care. Second, doctors working with compensable cases may be more likely to practice defensive medicine as one method of minimizing the risk of malpractice. Finally, to the extent that medical care is distributed on an "ability to pay" basis, insurance may be subsidizing the cost of medical care for the uninsured.

To the extent that there is subsidization of the uninsured by the already insured, then the introduction of a public compensation program may result in elimination of the subsidy, thereby reducing the overall program cost to each person sufficiently to make the previously uninsured, as well as the previously privately insured, better off than in the absence of the public program. Again, going back to the initial assumed program-funding assumption, the subsidy is eliminated, but, in relation to income, the cost would be regressive. In contrast, progressive taxation does not eliminate the subsidy, but changes its character. Rather than a subsidy for health care it is a subsidy that eliminates program regressivity.

FEDERAL VICTIM COMPENSATION COSTS

We have estimated 184 homicides, 870 assaults and 127 sex offenses as potentially drawing upon Fund resources. These resources comprise primarily (1) criminal fines collected in U.S. courts, (2) 20 percent of net profits from Federal Prison Industries and (3) public or private donations. Donations are likely to be minimal, and here are assumed to be nonexistent.

Criminal fines collected in fiscal year 1973 in all judicial districts totaled $14,034,546.[17] Under the provisions of S.1, the level of fines are significantly increased for criminal offenses, and collection procedures will be enhanced. Therefore, it is likely that fines that would be available to the Fund would increase markedly. This is, of course, dependent upon the judge's discretion in assessing higher fines. Total net profits of Federal Prison Industries in fiscal year 1973 were $6,610,151.[18] Twenty percent, or $1,322,030, would be available to the Fund under S.1 provisions. In addition, Federal Prison Industries would have greater competitive access to private markets under S.1. Thus, it is likely that net profits—and, hence, the contribution to the Fund—would increase, although the extent of such increases is uncertain. A conservative estimate, then, of revenues available to the Fund, based upon fiscal year 1973 data, is $15.4 million.

The surviving dependents of the 184 homicide victims would be entitled to a maximum award of $50,000. A basis for determining the amount of compensation for loss of support would be the present value of lifetime earnings foregone.[19] Assuming a social discount rate of 6 percent, and adjusting for the age, sex and race of homicide victims according to the national homicide distribution,[20] the present value of lifetime earnings foregone by the average federal jurisdiction homicide victim is $99,043. This exceeds the maximum permissible compensation to a victim's surviving dependents by $49,043.[21]

In order to estimate the maximum draw on the Fund for homicide, assume that each of the 184 claimants is entitled to full benefits of $50,000: $2,500 funeral expenses and $47,500 loss of support. Because payments are periodic, and loss of support is limited to a maximum $150 per week ($7,800 per year), the maximum payout for loss of support will continue for approximately six years and five weeks. First year draws upon the Fund, then, total $460,000 for funeral benefits, and $1,435,200 for loss of support. Under the assumption here, the Fund also commits to loss of earnings coverage of a maximum of $7,304,800 for the 184 claimants over the remaining five years and five weeks. At 6 percent, the present value of this commitment, assuming an annual drawdown of investment to cover one year's payments, is $6,141,330. Thus, the total first year expenses for homicide would be $8,036,530, of which 76.4 percent would be invested for claimants' future annuities. To the extent that each succeeding year sees a like number of claimants and awards, the program would bear similar homicide-related costs.

Unlike homicides, awards from the Fund for assault and sex offenses probably will not be protracted. Injury costs for female rape and serious assault victims are presented in Table 11-4. The average medical costs for rape and serious assault requiring any type of medical care are $67.04 and $271.39, respectively. On the assumption that the more seriously injured would avail themselves of the Fund, perhaps a more accurate approximation of costs is that relating to overnight hospital care. Here, average costs incurred for rape and serious assault are $289.30 and $887.61, respectively. These may still underestimate likely claims. Irrespective of coverage, the average medical cost for the 10 percent most seriously injured assaultive crime victims was $2,219.12 (see Table 11-3).

Because the Fund is secondary to other compensation sources, we must adjust the 870 assault cases and 127 sex offense cases to account for this factor. Based upon the coverage analysis in the previous section, we assume that 35 percent of the rape cases (forty-four of 127) and of the serious assault cases (305 of 870) are not compensated by a primary source. Assuming that all met the $100 threshold, the rape victims would receive at a minimum awards totaling $12,729 (44 x $289.30), and the assault victims would receive awards totaling $270,721 (305 x $887.61). To the extent that the victims received more health care by virtue of having compensation available, these awards probably would be higher. For the eighty-three rape victims and 565 assault victims assumed to have primary coverage of some type, the Fund would coordinate with the primary sources to provide full coverage. We assume that in each case the Fund would coordinate with primary sources to compensate 20 percent of the medical loss. For these rape victims, then, the Fund would provide $4,802 (83 x 0.20 x 289.30) coordinated coverage. For assault victims, the Fund would provide coordinated coverage of $100,300 (565 x 0.20 x 887.61). Adding these coordinated awards to the awards for rape and serious assault above, the expected payout for rape would be about $17,500, and for assault about $371,000, for an overall total of $388,500.

Table 11-4. Average Medical Costs Incurred in Rape and Serious Assault Victimizations by Selected Injury Characteristics

Characteristic	*Rape*	*Serious Assault*
1. All Injurious Victimizations	17,784	147,574
Percent requiring medical care	43.9	52.3
2. Medical Care Victimizations	7,813	77,207
Average medical cost ($)	67.04	271.39
3. Overnight Hospital Victimizations	915	19,226
Percent of medical care victimizations	11.7	24.9
Average medical cost ($)	289.30	887.61

Source: National Crime Survey of twenty-six cities.

With regard to disability, the National Crime Survey data indicate for those rape and serious assault victims hospitalized overnight that 11.3 percent of the former and 43.1 percent of the latter lost more than ten days of work as a result of victimization. Unfortunately, these data do not delineate actual time lost or the lost earnings resulting. Thus, it is not possible to accurately estimate the number of victims that might meet the ninety day disability threshold in the Fund. For a rough order of magnitude, we assume that 1 percent of the rape victims (one) and 5 percent of the serious assault victims (forty-four) meet the threshold, and that disability extends six months in each case. At a maximum of $150 per week for twenty-six weeks, the estimated disability payments would equal $175,500 (26 x $150 x 45).

The total estimated costs of the Fund for coverage of one year's victims is about $8,600,500. This includes $460,000 in funeral benefits and $1,435,200 in loss of support for 184 homicide victims; $6,141,330 as the present discounted value of future loss of support payments to homicide victims; $388,500 in medical coverage for 127 rape and 870 assault victims; and $175,500 in disability payments for one rape and forty-four assault victims. This is well within the $15.4 million allocated to the Fund for awards.

The maximum calculated above may overstate considerably the extent of compensation. For example, dependents of victims killed in the line of duty may receive death benefits from their employers that could be considered payment for loss of support. Similarly, workmen's compensation programs may compensate for injury and disability. To the extent that we have overstated the awards, the costs of administering the Fund, presently unknown, become critical. With the maximum awards estimate above falling well within the estimated revenues available to the Fund, there should be more than sufficient resources to cover administrative costs. However, if claimants are few and awards small, then the administrative costs as opportunity costs are higher. In that case, an alternative program or a broadening of coverage or of benefits may be more desirable then the current Fund structure.

CONCLUSION

We have used the National Crime Survey data to estimate the costs of a federal victim compensation program. The importance of this data is that it enhances the ability of criminal justice planners not only to understand crime characteristics, but also to evaluate alternative strategies to deal with criminal justice problems. In the absence of this data source, the latter could be performed only superficially at best. Even so, the analysis above was of necessity quite assumptive. This highlights the need for the development of new sources of information and for the refinement of existing sources.

NOTES

1. The Law Enforcement Assistance Administration's National Criminal Justice Information and Statistics Service has published several studies relating to the twenty-six central city victimization samples conducted during 1973 and 1974. These studies include: *Criminal Victimization Surveys in the Nation's Five Largest Cities* (Washington, D.C.: U.S. Government Printing Office, April 1975); *Crime in Eight American Cities* (Washington, D.C.: U.S. Government Printing Office, July 1974); and *Criminal Victimization Surveys in 13 American Cities* (Washington, D.C.: U.S. Government Printing Office, June 1975). More detailed information relating to sample design, weighting procedures and variable specification is available in U.S. Department of Commerce, Bureau of the Census, *National Crime Survey, Central Cities Sample 1974: Survey Documentation* (Washington, D.C.: U.S. Government Printing Office, May 1975).

2. Population estimates of injurious victimizations in each city were constructed using the 1970 Bureau of Census demographic weights included as variables in the National Crime Survey computer tape data.

3. President's Commission on Law Enforcement and Administration of Justice, *The Challenge of Crime in a Free Society* (Washington, D.C.: U.S. Government Printing Office, 1967), p. 19.

4. See Philip H. Ennis, *Criminal Victimization in the United States: A Report of a National Survey, Field Surveys II* (Washington, D.C.: U.S. Government Printing Office, May, 1967). The National Opinion Research Center (NORC) conducted its household victimization survey in the summer of 1966. The NORC survey includes information on type of injury, extent of hospitalization, cost of medical care and income loss due to physical disability (see Appendix A, Incident Form, pp. 2-5). Unfortunately, compensation information relating to medical care costs is lacking. By comparison, the National Crime Survey data used in this study include compensation information, but lack estimates of income loss due to physical disability. The NORC survey also covers homicide offenses, whereas the National Crime Survey, limiting sample observations solely to interviewed victims, does not. For an interesting analysis of the incidence of burglary and assault that uses the NORC data, see Neil K. Komesar, "A Theoretical and Empirical Study of Victims of Crime," *The Journal of Legal Studies* II (June 1973): 301-21.

5. U.S. Department of Justice, Federal Bureau of Investigation, *Uniform Crime Report 1974* (Washington, D.C.: U.S. Government Printing Office, 1975), pp. 10-11.

6. Gerald Caplan, "Reflections on the Nationalization of Crime, 1964-1968," *Law and the Social Order* 1973 (3): 583-635.

7. These states with victim compensation programs are Alaska, California, Delaware, Georgia, Hawaii, Illinois, Louisiana, Maryland, Massachusetts, Minnesota, Nevada, New Jersey, New York, North Dakota, Ohio, Rhode Island, Tennessee, Texas and Washington. The information in the text regarding these programs is in Center for Criminal Justice and Social Policy, Marquette University, *Crime Victim Compensation Laws and Programs* (Milwaukee: Marquette University Victim/Witness Project, September 1975). For a bibliographic

source relating to victim compensation in general, see Marvin Marcus, Robert J. Trudel and Robert J. Wheaton, *Victim Compensation and Offender Restitution: A Selected Bibliography* (Washington, D.C.: Law Enforcement Assistance Administration, National Criminal Justice Reference Service, December 1975).

8. United States Senate, *Senate Bill Number One: Criminal Justice Reform Act of 1975*, 94th Cong., 1st sess., January 15, 1975, ch. 41, subch. B, pp. 304-309.

9. Wesley G. Skogan, "Measurement Problems in Official and Survey Crime Rates," *Journal of Criminal Justice* 3 (1975): 17-32.

10. See, for example, U.S. Department of Justice, United States Attorneys' Offices, *Statistical Report* (Washington, D.C.: Office of Management and Finance, Fiscal Year 1975).

11. See, for example, Administrative Office of the United States Courts, *Annual Report of the Director: Fiscal Year 1975* (Washington, D.C.: U.S. Government Printing Office, 1975).

12. Ibid., Table D2, pp. A46-A47.

13. Unpublished data from the Federal Bureau of Investigation.

14. Unless specified otherwise, the costs presented refer only to incurred medical costs. The value attached to pain and suffering is at best difficult to quantify, and work disability is generally treated in insurance schemes differently from medical costs. Another factor is that the National Crime Survey data do not permit a comparative treatment of the losses due to work disability and costs of medical care. See Note 4, above.

15. See Chapter 10, Table 10-8.

16. The risk of victimization varies considerably when we look at different segments of the population, several of which are examined in this chapter. One factor not considered here is the location of the victimization, a factor likely to have a substantial impact upon risk. For example, one study of Oakland found that approximately two-thirds of the occupied city area examined experienced no robberies over a three year span. See Floyd Feeney and Adrianne Weir, *The Prevention and Control of Robbery: A Summary* (Davis: University of California, The Center on Administration of Criminal Justice, February 1974), p. 4.

17. U.S. Department of Justice, United States Attorneys' Offices, *Statistical Report* (Washington, D.C.: Office of Management and Finance, Fiscal Year 1973), table 5.

18. U.S. Department of Justice, Federal Prison Industries, *Financial and Operating Report* (Washington, D.C.: Federal Prison Industries, Fiscal Year 1974), p. 2.

19. This is only one method of calculating economic loss. Besides this commonly used "gross" valuation, there are "net" valuations, voting procedures and "willingness to pay" measures. See, for example, E.J. Mishan, "Evaluation of Life and Limb: A Theoretical Approach," *Journal of Political Economy* 79 (1971): 687-705. A criticism of the gross output measure is that it values life according to a victim's material contribution to society. It neglects the value the victim places on his own life, the value of pain and suffering of dependents and close friends, and the social costs borne by society in dealing with offenders in the criminal justice process. Complexities of calculation dictate that the gross output measure alone be considered here.

20. Unpublished homicide data for 1972 from Department of Health, Education and Welfare, National Center for Health Statistics.

21. It is possible, of course, that some victims would have present value of lifetime earnings below $50,000. For males, this would include age categories under one year of age and over sixty years of age, and, for females, under nine years of age and over fifty years of age. Nationally, the categories include 7.7 percent of males and 25.9 percent of females, for an overall total of 11.4 percent. The figure of $50,000, then, is a maximum, and would be reduced according to the number of victims in these age categories. Present value of lifetime earnings data by age, sex and race is for 1972 (preliminary), and is available in unpublished form from the Department of Health, Education and Welfare, Social Security Administration, Office of Research and Statistics, Division of Health Insurance Studies.

 *Chapter 12*

Reducing the Cost of Victim Surveys*

Alfred J. Tuchfarber, Jr., William R. Klecka, Barbara A. Bardes and Robert W. Oldendick

Accurate information on crime and its consequences is necessary if the criminal justice system is to evaluate crime reduction programs effectively and design new methods for combating crime. The limitations of the Uniform Crime Reports (UCR), especially the fact that they report only a fraction of the crime actually committed, have led the Law Enforcement Assistance Administration (LEAA), working in cooperation with the Census Bureau, to develop new methods for measuring victimization.

The technique employed by the Census team uses a traditional, survey-based approach to measure crime. Under this method, a random sample of households is selected, interviews are conducted with the individuals in these households and from this information inferences are made about the population being studied. This technique provides a more accurate measure of the level of crime than the UCR methodology and also allows the investigator to gather other data that can be of use to planners and evaluators in the criminal justice system.[1] For example, demographic data can be collected as well as data on how respondents feel about the police, the courts or current crime trends. Detailed data about the time, place and perpetrators of the crimes reported can also be gathered. When these data are analyzed it is possible to determine which groups are most likely to be victimized, when crimes occur, which groups do and do not respect the police, and many other questions of interest.

*The research reported here was supported by the Police Foundation. A complete report on the research including detailed instructions on how to conduct an RDD crime victimization survey is available in Alfred J. Tuchfarber and William R. Klecka, *Measuring Crime Victimization: An Efficient Method* (Washington, D.C.: The Police Foundation, 1976). We would like to thank Joseph Lewis of the Police Foundation and Alfred Schwartz and Sumner Clarren of the Urban Institute for their support on this project.

Although a survey-based methodology represents dramatic improvement over the UCR method of crime reporting, it does not solve all of the problems involved in measuring the "true" level of crime. Some of the people who do not report crimes to the police will also not report victimizations to a survey interviewer. They may not want to take the time; they may fear the interviewer is a criminal attempting to "set them up"; they may not want anyone to know about crime committed against them—for example, rape; or they may not know that something which occurred is considered a crime. The crime measured by survey methods is a *lower* limit on the true level of crime.

While the traditional survey methods employed by the Census team represent an advance over previous data collection techniques, they are prohibitively costly for many applications requiring an accurate measurement of crime. At a time when government agencies and public interest groups are finding it increasingly difficult to allocate the resources necessary for any purpose, spiraling inflation and rising energy costs have combined to greatly increase the cost of face-to-face interviews. This problem is especially acute for local programs because local resources are usually inadequate to support the expensive techniques required by the Census approach. Furthermore, it is on the local level that crime can be most effectively combated. The cost of in-person surveys makes them infeasible for most state and local governmental units. As one Census Bureau administrator has stated: "A well-designed, well-executed personal interview survey [crime victimization survey] of 1,000 households would generally be expected to cost $75,000-$100,000, depending upon specifications."[2] Moreover, for many purposes, researchers need samples many times that size.

In light of these considerations, it is surprising to find that face-to-face interviewing is often used without serious examination of its cost effectiveness. We contend that random digit dialing (RDD) telephone surveys provide an efficient, accurate and inexpensive alternative for most applications. The purpose of this chapter is to provide supporting evidence for this point, especially in crime victimization surveys.

WHAT IS RANDOM DIGIT DIALING?

Random digit dialing is telephone interviewing coupled with the use of a sample of telephone numbers that has been generated at random. Although RDD is not new, it is neither widely known nor often used outside of marketing research.[3] While we do not advocate its universal and indiscriminate use, our experience demonstrates that RDD is more efficacious than conventional wisdom would lead one to believe.

As noted above, RDD is simple telephone interviewing which uses a random technique to generate the sample of phone numbers. In general, to obtain an RDD sample, all the operating exchanges in the target area must be determined.

For small area surveys, this information can usually be found at the beginning of the local directory. When a statewide, regional or national sample is sought, working exchanges within area codes can be obtained from the Distance Dialing Reference Guide published by the AT&T Long Lines Department. Once this list of exchanges has been constructed, the procedure for generating the numbers is very straightforward. One of the exchanges is selected at random. Next, a four digit random number is selected to complete the phone number. This sequence is repeated until the desired quantity of phone numbers has been generated.[4]

TELEPHONE INTERVIEWING

Before examining the specific uses of RDD, we will discuss the general advantages of telephone interviewing relative to other methods of survey data collection, such as mail questionnaires and face-to-face interviews. One positive aspect of telephone interviewing is that it increases the amount of supervisory control. With a team of telephone interviewers working from a central location, questions that arise during the survey can be more readily resolved and the information easily transmitted to all the interviewers. In effect, a continual training process takes place. Such a process is not possible in a traditional face-to-face interview situation.

A second advantage of telephone surveys is that they are less threatening both to the interviewer and to the respondent. Telephone interviewers are much safer working from a central location than are personal interviewers who often must work in areas regarded as unsafe or in which they generally feel uncomfortable. Similarly, the respondents' homes are not intruded upon, and the respondents always have the option of hanging up the telephone if the caller appears to be something other than a legitimate interviewer. Telephone surveys also have the ability to penetrate high security apartments and condominiums. On the face of it, these factors appear to support the contention that telephone interviewing generates higher quality data.

While these considerations are of obvious importance, the most distinctive advantage of random digit dialing is its cost effectiveness. One principal saving relates to the cost of sampling. Instead of the lengthy process of enumerating and selecting a complex area probability sample for in-person interviews, representative samples for telephone interviews can be generated by selecting a list of appropriate numbers. A second saving relates to the expense of transporting and maintaining a field team for in-person interviews, a cost which varies according to the area under investigation. In any case, the expenses incurred in a telephone survey will be less than those entailed in the transportation and living costs for in-person interviewers. Although the level of cost savings depends on the specific aspects of the study—for example, a local versus a national survey—telephone interviewing is considerably cheaper. The best general estimate is that an RDD survey will cost one-fourth to one-third as much as a comparable in-person survey.[5]

Telephone interviewing also has certain disadvantages, the most obvious being that visual materials cannot be displayed over the telephone. It is impossible to present interviewer credentials or illustrations in conjunction with survey questions. In addition, many survey researchers believe that telephone interviews must contain far fewer questions than those done face-to-face, although telephone surveys may last as long as an hour if the content is interesting to the respondent and highly skilled interviewers are employed.

THE ACCURACY OF RDD

The advantages of telephone interviewing are meaningless if the results they produce are seriously biased. As we noted, serious criticisms have been leveled at all types of telephone surveys. However, these criticisms were made when telephone subscription was less universal. By 1976, over 90 percent of the households in the United States could be reached by telephone.[6] Less than 10 percent of the population, therefore, is automatically excluded from a telephone survey. The critical question then becomes: Does the exclusion of this small subgroup seriously bias the results of an RDD sample?[7]

In order to test the accuracy of RDD, we replicated a crime victimization survey carried out in Cincinnati by the Census Bureau from February through April 1974. The survey was one of a series the Census Bureau was commissioned to conduct in major American cities. In this study, households were selected according to traditional sampling procedures. The interviewers made their initial contacts in person and interviewed as many people as possible during the first visit. If some member of the household was not present, or if additional information was needed, the interviewers were allowed to call back and complete the questioning either in person or by telephone.

The RDD replication was carried out in April 1974. All interviews, including initial contacts and callbacks, were done over the telephone. The questionnaire developed by the Census Bureau was used in this study, modified for the sake of brevity. In addition to the citywide sample, we drew a supplemental sample from the poorest section of town–an area of low telephone subscription rates–so that an intense investigation could be conducted in an area where RDD would be most likely to produce seriously biased results. The supplemental sample is from Cincinnati's Police District One (PD1).

The survey questionnaires elicited responses to three types of questions. A series of standard demographic questions were asked of all adults. These sought information about the person's age, race, sex and education. In addition, the first responsible adult to be interviewed (the "household respondent") was asked questions about the household in general, such as family income, number of persons in the household and whether the family owned or rented their dwelling place.

A second series of questions were used to obtain information about any crimes committed against the respondent during the previous twelve months. The household respondent was asked to report crimes committed against the property of the household (i.e., burglary or theft of property not kept on the person such as television, car, bicycle, etc.). When any incidents were reported, the respondents were asked to give detailed information about the event. This included details about what happened, the monetary value of any losses, the seriousness of any injuries and descriptive information about the criminals. These details were used to classify the nature and seriousness of the crime.

While the demographic and crime questions dealt with factual information, there were also a few opinion questions dealing with feelings about crime-related matters. Questions of this type included whether the respondent felt the local police were doing a good job and whether crime appeared to be increasing or decreasing.

Our objective was to compare responses to the Census Bureau and RDD surveys on these three types of questions to see if the two survey techniques yielded the same information. Although personal interviewing with complex sampling procedures has its own limitations, survey professionals generally regard it as the best method for collecting most types of opinions and factual information from the general populace. This is the technique against which the RDD data compared. If the data collected in the RDD survey were not significantly different from the data collected primarily by personal interviewing, then it can be said that RDD is at least as accurate as personal interviewing.

This test, of course, makes some assumptions. Its greatest limitation is that there is no completely reliable benchmark. It is assumed that the Census Bureau used the best possible procedures to insure the reliability and accuracy of its survey. We are employing its findings as the "criterion" measures. Yet, its results are not infallible. Despite its complex sampling procedures, the bureau still misses a fraction of the population. Although little is known about these unsampled people, most survey researchers consider this loss relatively unimportant in a survey of the general populace. RDD misses some of this hard to locate group as well; in addition it excludes households without telephone service. However, the question is whether RDD's omission of nontelephone households seriously biases the sample *relative to the best known alternative sampling method.*

The first concern is that both survey methods are reaching the same population of potential respondents. Although the techniques use slightly different sampling frames, the net result should be similar in terms of population characteristics such as race, income, sex, age and education. If these respondent characteristics are sufficiently similar, we can be more confident that RDD is not biased. Table 12-1 presents the evidence from the citywide and low income area (PD1) samples.[8]

One area of potential bias is family income. It seems logical to assume that poor families would be less likely to subscribe to telephone service, because they

Table 12-1. Comparisons of Demographic Characteristics, RDD and Bureau of the Census Samples

	Citywide		*PD1*	
A. Family income (percent)				
	RDD	*CENSUS*	*RDD*	*CENSUS*
Less than $3,000	20.2	21.7	50.7	51.2
$3,000-$7,499	27.1	28.0	29.9	28.5
$7,500-$14,999	35.7	34.1	14.3	14.5
$15,000-$24,999	13.1	12.2	3.9	3.9
$25,000 or more	3.9	4.0	1.3	1.8
	100.0	100.0	100.1	99.9
	(N=635)	(N=8758)	(N=536)	(N=756)
	Chi-square = 1.68 NOT SIGNIFICANT AT 0.01		Chi-square = 0.79 NOT SIGNIFICANT AT 0.01	
B. Household tenancy status (percent)				
	RDD	*CENSUS*	*RDD*	*CENSUS*
Own home	39.9	39.1	7.5	6.6
Rent or no cash rent	60.1	60.9	92.5	93.4
	100.0	100.0	100.0	100.0
	(N=800)	(N=9708)	(N=658)	(N=756)
	Chi-square = 0.19 NOT SIGNIFICANT AT 0.01		Chi-square = 0.37 NOT SIGNIFICANT AT 0.01	
C. Average number of persons twelve and over per household				
	RDD	*CENSUS*	*RDD*	*CENSUS*
Average	2.07	2.05	1.71	1.65
	(N=800)	(N=9708)	(N=662)	(N=756)
	SEdiff = 0.04 NOT SIGNIFICANT AT 0.01		SEdiff = 0.06 NOT SIGNIFICANT AT 0.01	
D. Race of respondent (percent)				
	RDD	*CENSUS*	*RDD*	*CENSUS*
White and other	74.5	72.5	28.8	36.7
Black	25.5	27.5	71.2	63.3
	100.0	100.0	100.0	100.0
	(N=1652)	(N=19903)	(N=1127)	(N=1247)
	Chi-square = 3.18 NOT SIGNIFICANT AT 0.01		Chi-Square = 16.88 SIGNIFICANT AT 0.01	
E. Sex of respondent (percent)				
	RDD	*CENSUS*	*RDD*	*CENSUS*
Male	43.0	44.6	38.6	44.0
Female	57.0	55.4	61.4	56.0
	100.0	100.0	100.0	100.0
	(N=1655)	(N=19903)	(N=1127)	(N=1247)
	Chi-square = 1.48 NOT SIGNIFICANT AT 0.01		Chi-square = 7.22 SIGNIFICANT AT 0.01	

Table 12-1 continued

	Citywide		PD1	
F. Age of respondent (percent)				
	RDD	*CENSUS*	*RDD*	*CENSUS*
12-15	8.1	8.7	10.1	10.9
16-19	9.3	10.0	9.8	9.2
20-34	33.7	30.2	22.1	24.5
35-49	16.0	16.6	15.7	17.3
50-64	17.8	18.7	21.6	19.7
65 +	15.1	15.8	20.7	18.3
	100.0	100.0	100.0	100.0
	(N=1639)	(N=19903)	(N=1118)	(N=1247)
	Chi-square = 9.84 NOT SIGNIFICANT AT 0.01		Chi-square = 5.68 NOT SIGNIFICANT AT 0.01	
G. Education of respondent (percent)				
	RDD	*CENSUS*	*RDD*	*CENSUS*
0-8 years	22.0	26.3	44.2	45.2
9-12 years	48.7	49.4	46.6	43.6
More than 12 years	29.3	24.3	9.2	11.2
	100.0	100.0	100.0	100.0
	(N=1629)	(N=19881)	(N=1106)	(N=1246)
	Chi-square = 25.14 SIGNIFICANT AT 0.01		Chi-square = 3.64 NOT SIGNIFICANT AT 0.01	

Sources: RDD data from *Measuring Crime Victimization: An Efficient Method* (Washington, D.C.: Police Foundation, 1976). Census survey data supplied by the Census Bureau.

would rather spend the money on more basic necessities such as food and clothing. According to the 1970 U.S. census only 74 percent of the households with family incomes below $3,000 have access to a telephone as compared to 84 percent of all American households. These figures are, of course, four years older than the present data, and they do not reveal how Cincinnati may differ from the rest of the country.

Table 12-1 shows that an income bias does not seem to be present. The distributions of family income in both areas from the two surveys are not significantly different. The RDD samples have a slightly lower proportion of respondents in the lowest income group (under $3,000), but the difference is so small that we cannot tell whether it is a systematic bias or a chance occurrence due to sampling variation.[9] This suggests that, if nontelephone households are indeed predominantly low income, their numbers are so small that their exclusion does not significantly distort an RDD sample drawn from a heterogeneous geographic area.

Two other family characteristics that can be tested are tenancy status and family size. Tenancy status refers to whether the family's dwelling unit is owned or rented. Table 12-1 shows that the distributions on this characteristic from the two sets of samples are almost identical. Because both surveys interviewed every household member who was at least twelve years old, the average number of persons in this age range per household can easily be determined. As reported in Table 12-1, the average number of persons was only fractionally higher in the RDD surveys. Again, this difference is not statistically significant.

At the individual level, we were most concerned with the racial distribution—specifically, that RDD might be biased against blacks, because on the average black families are poorer and have a lower telephone subscription rate. Table 12-1 demonstrates that the racial distributions for the citywide samples are not statistically different; the figures from the PD1 samples reveal statistically significant differences, but they are in a direction opposite to that anticipated. Part of this discrepancy may be due to the large concentration of white Appalachians living in PD1. Other data show that they are even less likely than blacks to have telephones.

A large part of this discrepancy may also be due to the inability of the Census Bureau to locate the proper proportion of black respondents. It has been established that the 1970 census underenumerated blacks.[10] Because the sampling and weighting procedures used for the Census survey were based primarily on the 1970 census, it is quite conceivable that the bureau's technique was biased against blacks. This methodological bias may be exacerbated by the fact that we are dealing with a small area that has undergone major demographic changes since 1970. Unfortunately, there is no absolute standard for comparison. Thus, we cannot definitively say which method more accurately measures a community's racial composition. There are good reasons to believe, however, that traditional sampling methods do not include a sufficient proportion of blacks.

A similar phenomenon occurs regarding sex comparisons. The differences discovered in the citywide samples are not statistically significant, yet females are overrepresented in the RDD sample from PD1. These sex differences are somewhat more difficult to explain. Because men are less frequently at home, interviewers have more difficulty finding them; however, this is a problem for the personal interviewer as well as the telephone interviewer. In welfare households, males are often reluctant to be identified as part of the household for fear that the woman of the house will lose some of her benefits. This is especially troublesome for the telephone interviewer, for they have no choice but to believe what they are told about the family's composition. If telephone interviewers are told no adult male lives in the house, they act accordingly, whereas the personal interviewer who finds an adult male in the house has a better chance of including him in the household enumeration. The neighborhood composition may further explain the overrepresentation of females. A disproportionate number of the PD1's male residents are transients and derelicts who are not likely to have a telephone. A personal interviewer may locate some of these individuals. This explanation cannot be verified by our data, but researchers should be aware that telephone surveys may have some difficulty achieving a proper sex balance in neighborhoods of this type. Fortunately, most surveys deal with the general population, where this problem will not occur.

The data from the two sets of surveys on age characteristics show that both techniques yield essentially the same results. The differences on the education variable, on the other hand, are statistically significant for the citywide sample. The bias is in the direction of overrepresenting more educated individuals. The percentage of respondents in the RDD citywide survey with eight or fewer years of education is low by 4.3 percent, while the figure for persons with some education beyond high school is high by 5 percent. In some research situations this discrepancy may be important, but irrelevant for others. The fact that no significant education differences were found in the PD1 sample indicates that an RDD survey does not necessarily produce an education bias and that the differences found in the citywide sample may have been more the result of chance sampling variation than a serious bias inherent in RDD.[11]

CRIME VICTIMIZATION RATES

Because no serious biases were revealed by the analysis of demographic characteristics, there is no reason to expect crime rates to vary greatly between the two surveys. While this expectation is largely borne out by the data for the PD1 samples, the figures in Table 12-2 show differences between the two citywide samples.

Table 12-2 reports victimization rates derived from each survey. "Household crimes" are those committed against the property of the household members when no one is present. They include burglary and theft of property, and attempted as well as completed crimes are counted. As Table 12-2 shows, the respondents in the RDD survey reported about 39 percent more household crimes per thousand than those interviewed by the Census team (378.8 versus 271.7). Although the magnitude of the differences varies from category to category, each major crime category contains a substantially higher rate for the RDD survey. Because of the logic of our experimental design, it was unnecessary to test these differences for statistical significance.[12]

Household victimization rates for the PD1 samples are also presented in Table 12-2. Here, the picture is somewhat different from that of the citywide samples. In PD1, household crimes are reported at essentially the same level in both surveys.

Table 12-2 also reports the victimization rates for personal crimes. "Personal crimes" are those committed against a person in his or her presence, plus larcenies without contact committed away from the home. These include all forms of assault and theft involving contact between victim and offender. Attempted crimes and threats are also included.

For the citywide samples, the total rate of personal crimes reported by the

Table 12-2. Comparisons of Household and Personal Crime Victimization Rates (per 1,000)

	Citywide		*PD1*	
Crime	*RDD*[a]	*CENSUS*[b]	*RDD*[c]	*CENSUS*[d]
Burglary	187.5	143.3	214.5	186.2
Household Larceny	148.8	103.4	72.5	74.1
Motor Vehicle Theft	42.5	25.0	36.3	24.9
Total Household Crimes	378.8	271.7	323.3	285.2
Robbery	15.7	14.6	22.2	38.2
Assault	55.6	46.5	58.6	70.4
Crimes of Theft	143.9	109.9	113.5	116.3
Total Personal Crimes	217.0	172.6	197.8	228.2

a. Household rates based on 303 incidents reported by 800 households. Personal rates based on 359 incidents reported by 1,655 persons.
b. Based on 2,638 incidents reported by 9708 households (estimated from weighted data). Personal rates based on 3,435 incidents reported by 19,903 persons.
c. Based on 218 incidents reported by 662 households. Personal rates based on 209 incidents reported by 1,128 persons.
d. Based on 216 incidents reported by 756 households (estimated from weighted data). Personal rates based on 285 incidents reported by 1,247 persons (estimated from weighted data).

Sources: RDD data from *Measuring Crime Victimization: An Efficient Method* (Washington, D.C.: Police Foundation, 1976). Census survey data supplied by the Census Bureau.

RDD respondents again exceeds the rate reported to Census Bureau interviewers (217.0 versus 172.6). When the personal crimes are broken down into categories, the rates found in the RDD citywide survey are slightly higher in all three categories. In the PD1 samples, personal victimization rates in the RDD sample are slightly lower in all the categories, but none of these are significantly different at the 0.01 level. We suspect that the personal crime rates are lower in the PD1-RDD survey because of the previously documented underrepresentation of men. Men are much more likely to be the victims of most types of personal violence or theft. This may explain why RDD yields higher crime rates in the other cases but appears to underrepresent victimizations in the PD1 personal crime categories.

It can generally be said that the RDD respondents were reporting more crimes. There are two possible explanations for this: persons with telephone service may be more likely to be victimized, or people may be more willing to discuss victimizations over the telephone.

The hypothesis that telephone households are more likely to be victimized is not very plausible. Surveys have shown that blacks and the very poor are generally more likely to be victimized than other groups (although this is not true for every type of crime). While the RDD and census samples have very similar demographic characteristics, RDD does have slightly lower proportions of blacks and poor. We do not feel that these demographic differences are large enough to affect victimization rates significantly; moreover, the observed demographic differences would be expected to produce *lower* rates in the RDD sample. Thus, it seems safe to exclude differential coverage as an explanation for the crime rate differences.[13]

Serious consideration must therefore be given to the possibility that people are more willing to report crime victimizations over the telephone. Unfortunately, the present data do not permit an independent test of this hypothesis. In a practical sense, however, it is not important to know the precise reason for the observed differences. What is important is that the RDD method yielded generally higher crime rates that cannot be attributed to sampling biases or any form of overreporting. This evidence indicates that RDD may be a preferable technique for collecting crime victimization data.

CITIZEN ATTITUDES

The questionnaire used in these surveys included a third type of data–citizen attitudes on crime-related topics.[14] Among other things, respondents were asked for their impressions of the crime trend, neighborhood safety and police performance.

The results for the five attitude questions are reported in Table 12-3. (Data for these attitude questions were not computed by the Census Bureau for the PD1 sample, so PD1 comparisons cannot be made.) The differences between the two surveys are slight for all five questions. Nonetheless, they are statistically significant for one of the five questions (U.S. crime trend). Unfortunately, we have no way of knowing which technique more closely approximates the correct distribution. Indeed, major polling organizations using the same techniques and interviewing at approximately the same time often come up with larger differences on opinion questions than those presented here.[15] The most important finding is that the two methods measured opinions in so similar a fashion that the same substantive conclusions would be reached using either set of data. While the evidence in Table 12-3 is not perfect, we feel that it effectively supports the contention that RDD is as good a survey method as traditional personal interviewing for gathering data on public opinion.

CONCLUSIONS

The evidence from these three types of data supports the contention that RDD is a reliable survey method. The omission of citizens without telephone service does not appear to bias the sample demographically, nor does it adversely affect the substantive information being collected–victimization data and attitudes about crime-related matters. This finding has special significance in light of the

Table 12-3. Comparisons of Attitude Questions (citywide sample only) (percent)

A. Within the past year or two, do you think that crime in your neighborhood has increased, decreased or remained about the same?

	RDD	*CENSUS*
Increased	31.2	32.9
Decreased	6.8	7.7
Same	48.2	45.3
Haven't lived here that long	6.7	5.9
Don't know	6.1	8.2
	100.0	100.0
	(N=1372)	(N=8791)

Chi-square = 7.67
NOT SIGNIFICANT AT 0.01

B. Within the past year or two, do you think that crime in the United States has increased, decreased or remained about the same?

	RDD	*CENSUS*
Increased	72.1	68.0
Decreased	6.0	7.9
Same	16.0	18.7
Don't know	6.0	5.3
	100.1	99.9
	(N=1372)	(N=8789)

Chi-square = 14.08
SIGNIFICANT AT 0.01

C. How safe do you feel or would you feel being out alone in your neighborhood *at night*—very safe, reasonably safe, somewhat safe or very unsafe?

	RDD	*CENSUS*
Very safe	16.7	19.4
Reasonably safe	40.3	39.0
Somewhat unsafe	19.4	20.6
Very unsafe	23.6	20.9
	100.0	99.9
	(N=1371)	(N=8772)

Chi-square = 10.03
NOT SIGNIFICANT AT 0.01

D. How about *during the day*—how safe do you feel or would you feel being out alone in your neighborhood?

	RDD	*CENSUS*
Very safe	59.8	59.9
Reasonably safe	33.0	34.0
Somewhat unsafe	5.1	4.7
Very unsafe	2.0	1.4
	99.9	100.0
	(N=1372)	(N=8779)

Chi-square = 3.25
NOT SIGNIFICANT AT 0.01

Table 12-3 continued

E. Would you say, in general, that your local police are doing a good job, an average job or a poor job?

	RDD	*CENSUS*
Good	56.0	53.2
Average	31.6	34.8
Poor	7.7	8.6
Don't know	4.7	3.4
	100.0	100.0
	(N=1372)	(N=8782)

Chi-square = 7.26
NOT SIGNIFICANT AT 0.01

Sources: RDD data from *Measuring Crime Victimization: An Efficient Method* (Washington, D.C.: Police Foundation, 1976). Census survey data supplied by the Census Bureau.

fact that people without telephone service are more likely to be poor, less educated and non-Caucasian. Although telephone subscription is not universal, there are two reasons why this would not put a telephone survey at a special disadvantage. First, only a small segment of the population is missed when interviewing is done by telephone. This group comprises less than 10 percent of all households, and it is not uniformly poor, black and less educated. Given the small number and the heterogeneity of nonsubscribers, they have only a minor net effect upon the representativeness of an RDD sample. Second, traditional sampling and personal interviewing do not perfectly cover the entire population either. Although these surveys can reach nontelephone households, they have some trouble locating and interviewing the poor, blacks and less-educated members of society. Thus, both tend to underrepresent similar demographic groups. As we have shown, the net result is samples that are demographically similar.

The conclusions based on this research have some hopeful implications for the planner and evaluator in the criminal justice system. The emergence of RDD as an accurate and efficient method of data collection means that the cost of gathering survey data has been brought within the fiscal limitations of many local criminal justice agencies; no longer must they depend upon UCR or attempt to conduct a prohibitively expensive personal interview survey. An RDD survey can be conducted with savings up to 70 or 75 percent over one done by personal interviewing.

This is not to say that RDD should be used indiscriminately. The availability of several techniques provides options to the planner. Before conducting any type of survey, the criminal justice researcher should be certain that the data to be collected will aid in his decisionmaking process. Similarly, if the planner-evaluator does consider conducting an RDD survey, he should be familiar enough with the area under investigation so that he can identify, and hopefully screen for, potential sources of bias.

NOTES

1. For a further discussion see *Measuring Crime Victimization: An Efficient Method* (Washington, D.C.: The Police Foundation, 1976).

2. Anthony Turner, "Victimization Surveying: Its History, Uses, and Limitations," in U.S. Department of Justice, Law Enforcement Assistance Administration National Advisory Commission on Criminal Justice Standards and Goals, *Criminal Justice System* (Washington, D.C.: U.S. Government Printing Office, 1973), Appendix A.

3. The first methodological study of RDD known to us was published by Sanford Cooper, "Random Sampling by Telephone: An Improved Method," *Journal of Marketing Research* 4 (November 1964): 45-48. Although a number of commercial marketing research firms use a form of RDD, a 1973 article reports that only three of the seventeen academic survey research organizations responding to the editor's poll had ever used RDD. See Mary Spaeth, "Interviewing in Telephone Surveys," *Survey Research* 5 (January 1973): 9-13.

4. William R. Klecka and Alfred J. Tuchfarber, "Random Digit Dialing as an Efficient Method for Political Polling," *The Georgia Political Science Association Journal* 2 (Spring 1974): 133-51. Further technical details on using RDD can be found in Tuchfarber and Klecka, ch. 4.

5. For further details on the relative costs of RDD see Tuchfarber and Klecka, ch. 2.

6. This figure is based on a January 1976 survey done by the Census Bureau as part of the LEAA National Crime Survey. Telephone industry estimates place the number of households with telephone service at more than 94 percent, but we feel their data overstate the true level. See "Statistics of the Independent Telephone Industry, 1975 Edition," vol. 1 (Washington, D.C.: United States Independent Telephone Association, 1975), p. 36.

7. It is true that these households without telephones are completely excluded from the RDD sample. However, there are no inaccurate listings or missed households in RDD as there may be when the type of sample associated with traditional methodology is created. For example, it is not hard to imagine more than a few ghetto households not being listed in the typical master sample. It is difficult to say which technique completely excludes more households from any possibility of inclusion in the actual survey sample, but it is clear that all sampling techniques, in practice, exclude some households completely.

8. The low income sample was conducted in the neighborhoods covered by the Cincinnati Police Department's District One (PD1). These neighborhoods include Cincinnati's downtown area, surrounding areas of slum dwellings (including poor blacks and poor whites), and a small neighborhood containing a mixture of working class whites and young professionals. This area was selected because of the high concentration of poor people and because Cincinnati Bell Telephone Company records show that this area has the lowest residential telephone subscription rate for the entire city. If RDD has problems with coverage and biases, it was felt that these would be most pronounced in an area such as PD1.

9. The difference of 1.5 percentage points for the under $3,000 group is

smaller than we would expect from national data. In the January 1976 panel of the National Crime Survey, the difference in this income group between households with telephones and all households was 2.1 percentage points (9.3 percent versus 11.4 percent). Reported in A. Elizabeth Powell and William R. Klecka, "Does It Matter Who is Missed in Telephone Surveys?" (Paper presented at the annual conference of the American Association for Public Opinion Research, Asheville, North Carolina, May 13-16, 1976).

10. See Jacob S. Siegel, "Estimates of Coverage of the Population by Sex, Race, and Age in the 1970 Census," *Demography* 11 (February 1974): 1.

11. In addition, multiple tests of significance such as those conducted here increase the probability that at least one of the differences will be found to be statistically significant. Because seven demographic comparisons were made for each sample, the real probability of one of these seven being significant is 0.07 rather than 0.01. In addition, national data indicate that a telephone sample would not overrepresent the more educated segment of society nearly as much as occurred in our citywide sample. In the January 1976 panel of the National Crime Survey, persons with education beyond high school comprised 28.2 percent of the population (age twelve or more) in households with telephone service. The figure for all households is 27.1 percent, a difference of only 1.1 percentage points. Reported in Powell and Klecka.

12. Because we hypothesized that RDD would yield crime victimization rates equal to or greater than those found by Census, we performed a one-tailed test of significance. Thus, it was necessary to test only when the RDD rates were lower than the Census rates. For details on testing the significance of differences between crime rates, see Tuchfarber and Klecka, ch. 3. The standard errors of the differences are also reported there.

13. National data do not show any difference in the number of incidents reported by households with telephone service compared to all households. Reported in Powell and Klecka.

14. The attitude questions were asked only of persons sixteen years old or older. The Census Bureau included the attitude questions in the questionnaires for a randomly selected half of the households. We asked the attitude questions to all of our RDD respondents who were old enough. However, we asked only five of the questions from the Census Bureau's full list.

15. As a case in point, the Gallup and Harris polls often disagree about the level of voter support for American presidential candidates. Their polls taken in late November and early December 1975 gave opposite indications of President Ford's chances for reelection. See *Newsweek* (January 5, 1976), pp. 16-17.

Index

About the Authors

Barbara A. Bardes is the assistant director of the Behavioral Sciences Laboratory and adjunct assistant professor of Political Science at the University of Cincinnati. A specialist in American national institutions and policy evaluation, she has worked extensively with citizen attitude and victimization surveys.

Barbara Boland is an economist on the research staff of the Urban Institute, Washington, D.C. She recently has completed reports on deterrence and the incapacitation effectiveness of the criminal justice system. She currently is involved in a research project investigating the crime reduction potential of various police strategies.

Sumner N. Clarren is a senior research associate at the Urban Institute. His research interests include the use of information as an intervention in community settings and decisionmaking in complex environments. He has been involved in the Police Foundation-funded evaluation of a team policing experiment in Cincinnati, Ohio. He also has been concerned with evaluation training and the development of local evaluation systems in work for the Law Enforcement Assistance Administration and for the Health Resources Administration of the Department of Health, Education and Welfare.

Philip J. Cook is assistant professor at the Institute of Policy Sciences and Public Affairs and the Department of Economics, Duke University. His research interests include criminal recidivism, deterrence and gun control. He currently is economic consultant to the Office of Policy and Planning, U.S. Department of Justice.

Richard W. Dodge is a survey statistician in the Office of Demographic Analysis, U.S. Bureau of the Census. He was involved in the experimental work leading up to the implementation of the National Crime Survey. He currently is participating in the analysis of the National Crime Panel victimization data and in the program of methodological research associated with victimization surveys.

Fredric L. DuBow is an assistant professor of Sociology and Urban Affairs at Northwestern University. His research focuses upon the fear of crime, the operation of police departments, and lay participation in courts and law enforcement. He recently has conducted an evaluation of the operation of a community-based anticrime program, Operation WhistleStop.

Michael R. Gottfredson currently is a doctoral candidate in criminal justice at the State University of New York at Albany, and a research analyst for the Criminal Justice Research Center in Albany, New York. He has worked on the problem of pretrial release decisionmaking and currently is involved in the analysis of National Crime Survey victimization data.

Michael J. Hindelang is associate professor at the School of Criminal Justice, State University of New York at Albany. His research interests include juvenile delinquency and criminal justice statistics. He currently is directing a research project that is analyzing the findings of the National Crime Survey.

Edward D. Jones III is senior economic adviser in the Office of Policy and Planning, U.S. Department of Justice. His research interests include victim compensation, handgun control strategies and the application of economic theory to the problems of criminal justice.

William R. Klecka is associate professor of Political Science and senior research associate of the Behavioral Sciences Laboratory at the University of Cincinnati. He has spent a year serving as visiting statistician at the Law Enforcement Assistance Administration, studying the potential of telephone interviews for the collection of the National Crime Survey data. His other research interests include the study of computer applications in social research and policy evaluation.

Harold R. Lentzner is a research analyst in the Office of Demographic Analysis, U.S. Bureau of the Census. He has been working with the data from the National Crime Panel for the past three years.

Robert W. Oldendick is a program director for the Behavioral Sciences Laboratory and a PhD candidate in the Department of Political Science at the University of Cincinnati. His primary research interests are methodology and American political behavior.

Roger B. Parks is a research associate with the Workshop in Political Theory and Policy Analysis at Indiana University. He currently is co-principal investigator (with Professors Elinor Ostrom and Gordon P. Whitaker) for a National Science Foundation (RANN)-funded study of the organization of police service delivery in medium-sized metropolitan areas across the United States.

David Reed is a PhD candidate and instructor in the Sociology Department at Northwestern University. His field of specialization is the sociology of law. He has done research on the implementation of change by police organizations and on non-institutional responses to crime.

Anne L. Schneider is a research scientist at the Oregon Research Institute, Eugene, Oregon. Her research interests include the application of social science theory and methods to the evaluation of the criminal justice system. She currently is conducting a study comparing victimization data with official police reports, under a grant from the National Institute of Law Enforcement and Criminal Justice.

Alfred I. Schwartz is a senior research associate at the Urban Institute. He has represented the Police Foundation as the evaluation director of a major experiment in team policing in Cincinnati, Ohio. His investigations of the effectiveness and efficiency of employing civilians in police departments, for selected tasks traditionally performed by sworn officers, produced guidelines for national use.

Frederick Shenk is a research analyst in the Office of Demographic Analysis, U.S. Bureau of the Census. He currently is engaged in the analysis of National Crime Panel victimization data. Previously he was involved in probation planning and research.

Wesley G. Skogan is an associate professor of Political Science and Urban Affairs at Northwestern University. His research focuses upon crime, the police and the operation of local criminal courts. During 1974-1976 he was a visiting fellow at the National Institute of Law Enforcement and Criminal Justice, conducting victimization research.

Richard F. Sparks has been lecturer in criminal law and criminology in the Faculty of Law at the University of Birmingham, and assistant director of research at the Institute of Criminology at the University of Cambridge, England. He now is a professor at the Graduate School of Criminal Justice, Rutgers University. His publications include *Key Issues in Criminology* (with Roger Hood), *Local Prisons: The Crisis in the English Penal System* and *Surveying Victims* (with Hazel Genn and David Dodd).

Alfred J. Tuchfarber is the director of the Behavioral Sciences Laboratory and adjunct assistant professor of Political Science at the University of Cincinnati. His interests include the improvement of survey research techniques, policy analysis and evaluation research. He currently is engaged in the collection and analysis of data on the National Team Policing Demonstration Project for the Urban Institute.